National Politics in a Global Economy

National Politics in a Global Economy:

The Domestic Sources of U.S. Trade Policy

Philip A. Mundo

Georgetown University Press

Georgetown University Press, Washington, D.C. 20007
©1999 by Georgetown University Press, All rights reserved.
Printed in the United States of America
10 9 8 7 6 5 4 3 2 1 1999
THIS VOLUME IS PRINTED ON ACID-FREE OFFSET BOOKPAPER.

Library of Congress Cataloging-in-Publication Data

Mundo, Philip A.
National Politics in a Global Economy:
The Domestic Sources of U.S. Trade Policy
p. cm.
Includes index.
ISBN 0-87840-743-X (cloth). — ISBN 0-87840-774-8 (pbk.)
1. United States—Commercial policy. 2. International trade.
3. Protectionism—United States. 4. Free trade—United States.
5. Foreign trade promotion—United States. I. Title.
HF1455.M86 1999
382'.3'0973—dc21   99-18788
CIP

Contents

To Jake

Preface

I began thinking about a book on U.S. trade policy in my courses on public policy in general, and economic policy in particular. The problem was to find a book that conveyed the importance and origins of trade policy to students who would study it only as part of a broader range of issues. As a teacher, I realized that a large text would likely provide more information than needed in a course where the goal was to compare various policies, or in a course where a core text would be supplemented by numerous other readings. At the same time, I was aware that a shorter book dealing with the main aspects of U.S. trade policy in a thematic way was hard to find. My approach in this book grows immediately from my experience teaching U.S. trade policy in these courses. I wrote it with the main goal of giving students (and other intelligent nonspecialists) a sound background on U.S. trade policy presented in light of what I think is one of its most important characteristics: its foundation in the domestic policy process.

The central theme of this book is that U.S. trade policy is the outcome of the domestic policy process. International trade involves the transfer of goods and services across national borders. Trade policy affects this activity as it encourages some types of transactions and discourages others. As trade becomes more important to the economic health of individual enterprises, trade policy becomes more critical to the economic well-being of the nation as a whole. As policy makers integrate trade policy more fully into a nation's foreign policy, it comes closer to center stage in foreign affairs. As economic barriers among nations break down, domestic economic activity, along with politics and culture, become more closely interconnected with those of other nations. International trade is at the center of the trend that is commonly called globalization, and because of that, trade policy takes on even greater importance. The point should be clear. Trade policy is a factor in a nation's economic health, plays an increasingly important role in foreign policy, and is at the heart of globalization.

Foreign affairs and economic considerations certainly influence trade policy, but for the most part, trade policy must run the gauntlet of domestic policy making. In the United States, trade policy embodies fundamental economic questions: survival of individual companies, creation and retention of jobs, general economic growth. Such matters attract the attention of numerous political interests, from corporations to labor unions, from ideological conservatives disposed to laissez faire policies to those committed to the idea that government intervention in the economy is absolutely necessary. Trade policies encompass these concerns, and they can have significant consequences—both positive and negative—for a wide range of political interests in the United States. As a result, conflict over trade policy typically involves domestic interests and politics. In addition to the domestic political aspects of trade policy, the mechanisms for producing it in the United States are rooted in the domestic policy process. Trade policy moves through the phases of domestic policy much as other policies do. Because of this, trade policy takes on some attributes of domestic policy.

The main point of the book and its accompanying themes accomplish three principal objectives. First, they provide the student with an introduction to the meaning, breadth, and importance of U.S. trade policy. Second, they place trade policy in the context of domestic policy that both illuminates its essential character and permits useful comparisons. Third, while pointing out the ways U.S. trade policy is similar to other policies, they also make clear its unique importance in an increasingly globalized world. I have chosen several aspects of U.S. trade policy that provide the groundwork for a good understanding of its content, origins, development, and significance.

The first part of the book provides a general understanding of U.S. trade policy and creates a solid base for exploring several more specific aspects of it. Any claim to understanding trade policy, or any other public policy for that matter, must be supported by familiarity with history. The historical development of trade policy tells the story of the development of the relationship between the U.S. government and the American economy, and it demonstrates from its very beginnings the domestic roots of U.S. trade policy. The contemporary trade policy debate is composed of arguments grounded in economics that shape U.S. trade policy. It is not necessary to be skilled in the intricacies of economic analysis to understand the main points of the principal contenders for the policy maker's ear. Understanding the history of trade policy and the essentials of the contemporary debate on it sets the stage for learning something about how these ideas make their way into and through the domestic policy process.

U.S. trade policy after the Second World War reflected the nation's emergence as a dominant political, economic, and military leader in the world. The international circumstances in which the United States found itself set the parameters and goals of trade policy, as domestic political influences shaped its specific content. The North American Free Trade Agreement (NAFTA) captures the domestic political nature of U.S. trade policy. Its creation was the result of hardball politics among intensely interested domestic political interests. Inasmuch as NAFTA was the centerpiece of the early Clinton administration's trade policy strategy, it also reflects the heightened attention being given trade policy by the highest policy makers. Throughout the development of the general strategy of postwar U.S. trade policy, Congress and the presidency struggled with the basic matter of determining which branch of government would have control over trade policy. In part as a result of trying to settle this persistent issue, administrative relief grew as an outlet to U.S. industry feeling the heat of foreign competition. Understanding how trade policy affects specific industries helps one to get a grasp of the reach of U.S. trade policy. The steel, automobile, and semiconductor industries illustrate the different ways government interacts with industry with respect to trade policy.

*   *   *

Writing a book takes a long time and requires the assistance and patience of a great many people. I wish to thank Barry Rabe and John Tierney for their support at various times during this project. Without their continued interest, this project would not have been possible. John Samples, the Director of Georgetown University Press, has been a constant source of good advice and patience tempered by an effective measure of prodding; he has been a true professional at all stages of the work. My colleagues in the political science department at Drew University provided a working environment that has allowed me to combine my research interests with teaching. I wish especially to thank Paul Wice and William Messmer for producing a continuous stream of encouragement. Drew University also made my life easier by releasing me from some teaching responsibilities. Several undergraduates at Drew University assisted with the research at critical times; my thanks to Lori Fritz, Derek Ziegler, and Robert Benacchio for their contributions to the project. I am also grateful to several anonymous reviewers whose comments were particularly useful in the final revisions of the manuscript. Finally, I wish to thank my wife and colleague, Janet Davis, for putting up with all this for so long.

—Philip A. Mundo
Drew University

1

Introduction

In the last twenty years, international trade has become prominent on the American public policy agenda. Growth in the U.S. trade deficit, job losses, and declining competitiveness of some U.S. industries have focused public attention on America's position in the international economy. These developments have taken place against the backdrop of globalization, a term covering an increasing number of economic and political developments. At the root of globalization is the growing integration of national economies. More trade and foreign investment, easier transportation, and remarkable advances in telecommunications have connected national economies in unprecedented ways. An optimistic view sees globalization as promising unprecedented economic growth that could potentially benefit every participating nation.[1] From a pessimistic perspective, however, globalization could mean lost national sovereignty, growing inequality, and a rising potential for labor abuses and environmental degradation.[2] A more tempered view sees the advantages in globalization, but acknowledges the problems it might create.[3]

International trade is a central issue in globalization, and as the percentage of U.S. gross domestic product (GDP) connected to exports and imports has increased from 11 percent in 1970 to 24 percent in 1998, many politicians and analysts have turned to trade policy for solutions to the country's economic problems.[4] Trade policy is in part foreign policy, embedded in broad foreign policy objectives. At the same time, trade policy is linked to domestic political forces channeled through governmental institutions. Such familiar political players as interest groups, congressional committees, bureaucrats, and top administration officials play a major role in translating domestic economic and political interests into trade policy. This book concentrates on the domestic aspect of trade policy, examining how the domestic policy process affects trade policy outcomes. A central premise of this study is that understanding U.S. trade policy requires understanding how the domestic policy process produces it.

The first part of this chapter briefly describes the growing importance of trade policy in the United States at the close of the twentieth century. I review the main issues and current debate over trade policy and pay particular attention to the nature and sources of problems and solutions. The second part of the chapter reviews competing explanations of trade policy and makes the case that American trade policy is largely the product of domestic political forces, and therefore, a domestic policy explanation is likely to be most useful.

The Trade Policy Debate

With the dramatic changes in the distribution of global military power, the United States finds itself operating with considerable uncertainty. Challenged by the growing economies of Japan and Europe, American firms have responded well. But in spite of the impressive adjustment by the American economy, lingering fears of foreign competition, job losses, restructuring, and the like create a sense of public uneasiness and inform the policy debate. Conventional classifications—like a multipolar or bipolar world—may not be very useful in contemporary global politics. Thinking of international relations as constantly in flux, with new relationships continually emerging and receding, might be more to the point. Conceptualizing foreign affairs in this way accounts for the unpredictability of political, military, and economic relations among states, and accurately, if vaguely, suggests the kind of uncertainty American policy makers face.

International trade operates within this new, extremely unpredictable world order. The Clinton administration's elevating international trade to a major foreign policy concern added to the sense of urgency that has come to surround the issue. This leads to a greater emphasis on trade policy and perhaps a tendency to give it more significance with respect to U.S. foreign policy and the American position in the world overall. In short, by the middle of the 1990s, the questions about American military power and diplomatic influence were joined to American economic strength, especially as measured by the trade deficit.

Linking Domestic Policy to Foreign Relations

In this new international environment, some U.S. domestic issues have become linked to foreign relations, and the connection is directly related to trade policy. Environmental issues are among the most important of these. Naturally transcending national borders, environmental policy has become the focus of international agreements regionally as well as on a global, multilateral scale. The creation of the North American Free Trade Agreement (NAFTA) raised these issues in relation to the economic dynamics of the United States, Mexico, and Canada. The central concern was that production would move from the United States to Mexico to take advantage of lax environmental regulation. In addition to costing American jobs, this development would increase pollution in Mexico. Environmentalists sought and won a provision in NAFTA to monitor environmental regulations in all three signatories. Opponents to the provisions argued, among other things, that this could allow a supranational body (the international commission set up to implement NAFTA's environmental provisions) to dictate domestic policy to the United States.

A second prominent domestic concern was labor. American union leaders worried that cheap labor in Mexico would cause U.S. firms to relocate there, taking jobs with them. Along with that, critics argued that Mexico might maintain poor labor standards in order to keep labor costs down and therefore attractive to American firms.

The merits of the arguments aside for now,[5] the relevant point here is that trade policy now involves other issues, in particular, issues that have been transformed from domestic to international in part because of trade policy developments. Trade policy has become considerably more complex, now coming with numerous and somewhat surprising strings attached. Analysis of trade policy and subsequent debate has become more difficult because solutions must now be found to problems that cross issue areas and national boundaries.

Politicians, journalists, pundits, and others have, correctly or incorrectly, attributed importance to international trade by linking it to major issues currently facing the United States. Set against the backdrop of the rising importance of economic strength in the post–Cold War world, these observers relate trade to jobs, economic growth, industrial competitiveness, and broader foreign policy objectives. The U.S. trade deficit, moreover, bothers many Americans; to them, it signifies economic weakness and even overall decline of the United States in international affairs. The stark trade imbalance with Japan and China magnifies these concerns still further.

President Clinton made trade a major part of the economic component of his 1992 presidential campaign, and his administration has taken measures to improve the economic relationship between the United States and its trading partners. Moreover, the Clinton administration has placed trade policy at the forefront of its foreign policy initiatives.[6] The administration has threatened withdrawal of most-favored-nation (MFN) status from China to induce Beijing to reform its human rights policy. The North American Free Trade Agreement is arguably more a matter of foreign affairs—the relationship between Mexico and the United States—than an economic issue.[7] And success in opening Japanese markets to U.S. goods and services is a major Clinton foreign policy objective.

It is clear, then, that trade issues have become a significant and increasingly visible element of the policy agenda in the United States. Although specific problems change over time, the trade policy debate consistently involves three major areas of concern: the trade deficit, jobs, and competitiveness and growth.

The Trade Deficit

Among the key problems surfacing in the public debate on trade, the trade deficit probably attracts the most attention. Journalists' accounts of the trade deficit generally accept the premise that the U.S. trade deficit is a bad thing. Reports usually indicate the rise or decline of the trade deficit along with politicians' responses to it. For example, a 19 July 1995 *New York Times* article headlined political trouble for the Clinton administration resulting from a recent increase in the trade deficit.[8] Although tracking change in the trade deficit is common, an economic debate on whether the deficit is actually a bad thing escapes most media reports. The bilateral deficit with Japan gets a great deal of press, although the trade deficit with China is now getting more notice, probably because of the linkage between China's MFN status and its human rights policy.[9]

Disputing the Trade Deficit

In very general terms, the trade deficit is the difference in value between what the United States imports and exports. Since the 1980s, the United States has been running a constant trade deficit; Americans have been buying more imports than U.S. producers have exported.[10] The overall trade deficit—between the United States and everyone else (see tables 1.1 and 1.2)—has been cause for concern, but the trade deficit the United States maintains with Japan has sharpened the debate, focusing the attention of policy makers and the public alike on America's most important Asian ally. Since the 1970s, the U.S. trade deficit with Japan has expanded in spite of government efforts on both sides of the Pacific to stunt its growth.[11] Trade relations with European nations have been somewhat more amicable, though not without occasional heated disputes.[12] But the trade relationship with the People's Republic of China has grown, nearly tripling from 1991 to 1995.[13] Even when services, in which American producers have a distinct competitive edge, are factored into the calculation, the United States still runs a noticeable trade deficit.[14]

Table 1.1
U.S. Merchandise Trade Balance with Japan, China, and the World
(census basis in millions of dollars)

	Japan	China	World
1991	−43,386	−12,691	−65,400
1992	−49,601	−18,309	−84,500
1993	−59,355	−22,777	−115,600
1994	−65,669	−29,494	−151,100
1995	−59,137	−33,790	−158,700
1996	−47,683	−39,517	−166,600

Source: United States Bureau of the Census, *Statistical Abstract of the United States: 1996,* 117th ed. (Washington, D.C.: U.S. Government Printing Office, 1996), 796, 801, 802; *Statistical Abstract of the United States: 1997,* 117th ed. (Washington, D.C.: U.S. Government Printing Office, 1997), 800, 803, 804.

Table 1.2
U.S. Trade Balance in Goods and Services: 1994 to 1996 (in millions)[15]

	Goods	Services	Total
1994	−166,123	61,742	−104,381
1995	−173,424	68,366	−105,064
1996	−187,617	73,388	−114,229

Source: United States Bureau of the Census, Statistical Abstract of the United States: 1997, 117th ed. (Washington, D.C.: U.S. Government Printing Office, 1997), 800.

The dispute about American trade deficits turns on two broad questions. First, what exactly does the trade deficit indicate about the economies involved and the relationship between them? Second, what can governments do to reduce trade deficits? The policy debate is infused with competing answers to these questions and the innumerable issues embedded in them. The central goal here is not to evaluate these contending positions to determine which is most correct. Rather, I approach these disputes with their importance for the policy process in mind. The considerable disagreement on the meaning and causes of the trade deficit open the door to vastly different interpretations of the issue.

What the Trade Deficit Means

Although the trade deficit attracts a great deal of media attention and stirs political debate, it is not clear how much of a problem it really is. In the short term, the extent to which the trade deficit warrants action is usually linked to claims about its relationship to jobs. Those who worry about the issue believe that a trade deficit indicates lost American jobs and, subsequently, displaced American workers. The logic here is that, as Americans buy goods and services produced abroad, they do not buy American-made products, thus causing a loss of jobs in the United States.[16] A contrary view suggests that jobs are not directly linked to the trade balance. Reducing or eliminating the trade deficit in itself will not create jobs in the United States in the long term; job creation depends on factors other than trade. According to this view, the short-term effects of a trade deficit should not be the cause of concern.[17]

Trade deficits may cause problems in the long term, however. The existence of a trade deficit indicates that a country is a net debtor; it buys more than it sells internationally and therefore must give foreign-based producers something to cover the costs. The United States has accomplished this by selling assets—real estate, stocks, bonds, and sometimes entire corporations. The downside of this practice is that the United States will continuously owe money to foreign real estate owners, foreign bondholders, and foreign stockholders, representing a steady drain on American resources. Although an economy the size of the United States can sustain such a drain for a long time, "the big economic risk is that as the United States becomes a massive net debtor it will be exposed to financial crises whenever the confidence of foreign investors is shaken."[18] Politically, moreover, being a net debtor at least raises the possibility of compromise to national sovereignty, giving critics ammunition to bolster their case for economic nationalism.[19]

The bulk of popular arguments on the trade deficit begin and conclude with the observation that it is decidedly bad. Perhaps connected to national pride, politicians and some economists point to trade deficits as a vague indication that the American economy is weak. For American industry, trade deficits reflect their losses to foreign competitors. The health of the American economy aside, a firm finding its own economic horizon cloudy may seize upon trade deficits as a national problem, an attractive way to call for a public solution to what some would call a private problem.

What Causes the Trade Deficit?

The trade deficit may be the result of several developments in the American economy. Some argue that American producers have declined in their ability to provide innovative products at internationally competitive prices. These shortcomings have been most evident in some heavy industries in which American manufacturers had been the leaders. The automobile industry provides a good example. After dominating the American market in addition to many foreign markets, American automobile makers encountered stiff competition from foreign manufacturers—mainly Japanese. The lethargic and ineffective response of the Big Four, and later the Big Three automobile manufacturers,[20] resulted in American car companies' losing market share to Japanese firms both in the United States and abroad. The dramatic shift in dominance of the automobile industry contributed heavily to the

American trade deficit with Japan and was symbolic of overall American economic decline.[21]

The competitiveness of American firms in other industries added to the image of general malaise in the former economic powerhouse. By the late 1980s, it was difficult to find American-made consumer electronics, and the semiconductor industry—America's high-technology wunderkind—suffered a competitive shock as foreign firms, mainly Japanese and later Korean, moved in on the lucrative dynamic random access memory (DRAM) chip market.

The presumed collective decline of American industries, according to some, is one major contributing factor to the country's trade deficits. Other circumstances contribute to the deficit as well. In general, when the dollar increases in value, Americans are able to buy more foreign products, while American producers find it more difficult to sell in foreign markets. When the dollar declines, the opposite should happen; imports should decline as exports rise.[22]

According to most mainstream economists, the most important factor is Americans' savings rate. In the private sector, consumers buy more and save less than they might, increasing imports and adding to the trade deficits. Government's contribution to the savings shortfall is captured in the so-called twin deficits position, which contends that the main source of the country's trade deficit (and other economic problems as well) is the federal budget deficit. The government's continuous need to borrow funds draws foreign investment into the United States, which appears as a deficit in the current account.[23] The fact that the trade deficit has persisted after the budget deficit began to decline in 1992 reflects the continued low savings rate in the private sector.[24]

Analysts who subscribe to the idea that Americans' savings rate and the federal budget deficit are principal causes of the trade deficit tend to be skeptical about the potential effectiveness of trade policy initiatives in reducing the trade deficit. They give little credit to managed or strategic trade, arguing that the best thing to do to reduce the trade deficit is to increase private and public savings in the United States.[25] Not all analysts agree with the twin deficit conceptualization. Such dissenters to the mainstream orthodoxy contend that the trade deficit's principal cause is not the federal budget deficit, and, therefore, the federal government can do a great many things to reduce the trade deficit.[26]

Finally, the trade deficit is blamed on the practices of foreign companies and countries. Unfair trade practices encompass a wide range of sins committed by foreign governments and foreign companies. Government activities considered to be unfair include providing subsidies to industry and protecting industries in the domestic market. Subsidies might come in the form of export promotion, tax credits, direct support of research and development, and direct support of production. Governments can protect domestic markets in a variety of ways outside of using tariffs. Discriminatory regulations—licensing, environmental, safety—can give domestic producers an unfair advantage over foreign competition. Limits on retail distribution and inadequate intellectual property protection make penetrating the market an uphill battle for foreign producers.

Companies can engage in unfair trade practices on their own or in connection with government actions. From the American perspective, one of the most irritating of such activities is selling goods in a foreign market at less than a fair price—a practice known as dumping. Other unfair trade practices include discriminatory use of suppliers and violation of intellectual property rights. The central point is that these unfair practices either increase imports into the American market or reduce American exports and, therefore, increase the trade deficit. Those who accept this analysis of the root cause of the trade deficit generally favor aggressive government intervention in the form of managed trade.[27]

What Can Government Do?

As the discussion suggests, the significance of the trade deficit and, in particular, what causes it are open to dispute. How proponents of different positions construct their arguments, use expert analyses, and package information are essentially political questions.

The debate on what is to be done about the trade deficit breaks down into two camps: those who would like to make trade policy an instrument for opening foreign markets and promoting certain strategic American industries (semiconductors, for example); and those who believe that the trade deficit is better addressed by changing some American macroeconomic conditions, mainly the public and private savings rate. Managed-trade proponents argue that a significant cause of the trade deficit is closed foreign markets. They usually have Japan in mind, where foreign producers find the domestic market difficult to enter. The way to expand U.S. exports is to negotiate with the Japanese government to open its domestic market to foreign goods and services.[28] Opponents of this view contend that macroeconomic factors cause the trade deficit, and the better way to reduce it would be to increase savings in the private sector and cut the federal budget deficit, for example.[29] Numerous variations of these positions exist of course, but the basic logic of each position remains fairly constant.

Economic Jitters

The discomfort generated by international uncertainty has been worsened by economic uncertainty at home. The job losses of the 1970s and 1980s were largely confined to blue-collar workers. This in itself created considerable consternation among policy makers, along with the personal pain among unemployed manufacturing workers. The situation has gotten worse; the beginning of the end of widespread access to the American dream has been reenforced by recent losses of professional jobs. Shrinking, newly reinvented corporations have cut thousands of white-collar workers in efforts to improve efficiency and become more competitive. A wave of mergers in banking, telecommunications, and entertainment has also resulted in lost jobs.[30] At the same time, new jobs have usually been created in low-end services—for example, fast-food counter clerks. Add to all this a growing gap between the wealthiest Americans and everyone else, and the great American middle class is feeling somewhat less buoyant than it has anytime since the end of World War II. Most mainstream economists believe that free trade is responsible for a small percentage of job losses. Such factors as technological change, they argue, are more likely to make jobs obsolete. Trade may have more to do with growing inequality, however, as the premium on education and skill goes up, leaving low-skill, poorly-educated workers in steadily deteriorating circumstances.[31]

In this nervous economic environment, developments in international trade take on greater importance than they might otherwise deserve. Fears of more job losses, increased foreign investment, and even dark rumors of foreign influence over policy development put an edge on trade issues.[32] The willingness of politicians to capitalize on these tensions for their own benefit makes the problem still worse.

Seeking to assuage this fear, President Clinton—and other policy entrepreneurs, like Secretary of Labor Robert Reich—claimed that while some low-paying, low-skill jobs would disappear, they would be replaced by better-paying, high-skill jobs. Other less optimistic observers agree with only part of this analysis—that new jobs will be created in the United States, but these jobs will be found in low-pay, low-skill service employment. By their reckoning, steelworkers will be replaced by fast-food counter clerks.

This pessimistic outlook frequently underlies protectionist impulses. Through trade policy, the government should protect traditional manufacturing jobs that once gave high school–educated people entry into the middle class. Opponents to NAFTA made precisely this point in their efforts to block congressional approval of the free-trade agreement. Supporters responded by arguing that, first, protection leads to slowed economic growth and decline, and second, that these "good" manufacturing jobs were bound to go away in any event.

Competitiveness and Growth

The disagreement over jobs is part of a related, broader debate on the importance of high-technology and service industries in America's economic future. Electronics, biotechnology, and telecommunications—prime examples of high-tech industries—replace traditional manufacturing industries, like "big" steel, in forming the country's industrial base. Similarly, banking, legal services, and software applications are the leading, knowledge-intensive service sectors. The question is, what can and should government do in trade policy to insure the health of these industries?

Free-trade purists answer with a simple, "nothing." These industries will be most healthy only when subjected to domestic and international competition. Managed-trade advocates reject this position with the strategic industries argument, contending that certain key industries—semiconductors and telecommunications, for example—warrant government assistance, mainly with gaining access to foreign markets, but also with protection against unfair trade practices by foreign-based companies and foreign governments.

Competing Explanations of Trade Policy

Throughout its history, American trade policy has consisted mainly of adjusting tariffs, a major source of revenue. Congress and the president have changed tariff levels on specific goods from the Civil War to 1930. Since the Second World War, trade policy has become more complex. Multilateral agreements, the replacement of tariffs by nontariff barriers (NTBs) as the principal issue in trade policy negotiations, and the recent rise in importance of trade in services and intellectual property protection makes the tariff adjustments of the late nineteenth and early twentieth centuries look rather simple by comparison.

Scholars have attempted to explain trade policy, paying attention to the politics of the tariff for the earlier time period, then expanding their efforts to incorporate the wide range of issues encompassed by trade policy. Analyses of trade policy can be placed into two general categories: those focusing on the international system and those concentrating on domestic factors. The essential premise of the international focus is that a nation's foreign trade policy is fundamentally a result of the nature of the international system. Nations operate more or less rationally within the constraints of the international system.

The international approach can be broken into two schools of thought: realist and liberal. The realist school is marked by a calculation of national interest. Nations do what is necessary to enhance their power and to protect their interests. Altruism and morality play no role in this model. In this view, nations use trade policy as just another means to achieve their overall foreign policy goals.[33] The liberal model allows for more complexity in motives and actions among nations. The liberal view is based on the premise that international relations is not a zero-sum game; with the proper rules, everyone is better off. This perspective grows out of classical liberalism and economic theory, in which economic growth is most important and government's role is limited to establishing rules to permit it. On the international level, this means promoting trade liberalization by means of international rules and institutions, such as the General Agreement on Tariffs and Trade (GATT), for example.[34]

Trade policy analyses that focus on domestic factors fall into two categories: state-centered and society-centered approaches. State-centered approaches to trade policy concentrate on the formal government, usually taken to mean the executive branch and, in some cases, the legislature. In the extreme, government can be viewed as a rational actor operating in a unitary and rational way. For the most part, scholars have debunked this view of national governments, acknowledging that governments are complex organizations with numerous participants and well-developed and frequently mystifying internal dynamics.[35]

The bureaucratic politics model of policy making replaced the rational actor. This approach focuses on the interactions among executive branch agencies to determine policy outcomes. Bureaucratic determinants of policy include, for example, bureaucrats' efforts to preserve jurisdiction over a policy area, officials' professional training, allocation of responsibility for and authority over particular policies, traditions, historical patterns of interaction, and rivalry and competition among agencies over policy turf. This set of factors within bureaucracy is further complicated as the president, Congress, and interest groups compete to influence bureaucrats' behavior.

The state-centered approach has led to analyses based on the capacity of government to make policies and carry them out. Governments insufficiently insulated from societal forces and too decentralized to allow policy makers to make tough decisions and implement them produce policies that tend to be inconsistent, difficult to predict, and unreliable. Political systems in which government is insulated from the immediate political concerns of societal forces and sufficiently centralized to make decisions expeditiously are more likely to produce clear policies and carry them out.[36]

A third variant on the state-centered theme is the "new institutionalism."[37] Essentially, this approach concentrates on the characteristics of government organizations and the relationships among them. The objective is to find characteristics that consistently affect policy outcomes. Although the focus need not be on the executive branch, most research conducted in this vein has done so.[38] Analyses might also focus on how institutions structure and process ideas and interests.[39] Or one could examine the relationship between Congress and the presidency with the institutional focus in mind.[40]

State-centered approaches comprise only a part of scholars' efforts to understand domestic influences over trade policy. Analyses focusing on societal forces comprise most of the rest. Such work mainly focuses on interest groups and political parties to evaluate their influence on trade policy. E. E. Schattschneider's work on the passage of the Smoot–Hawley Tariff in 1930 remains the classic of this type of research. Interest groups representing producers pressured Congress into passing the most protective tariff in recent history, greatly adding to the global economic catastrophe of the time.[41] Much of the work on interest groups has concentrated on producers that favor some kind of protection.[42] Recent studies have illuminated the fact that interest groups also represent free-trade–oriented interests, providing some check on the overall direction of interest-group influence over trade policy.[43]

Political parties constitute the other societal factor evaluated by scholars in search of domestic influences over American trade policy. Party control of the government is associated with patterns of trade policy. From the late nineteenth century through the early twentieth century, the Republican Party generally supported protection, while the Democrats favored reducing tariffs. Each party's preference was based on the economic interests of its members: Industrial interests associated themselves with the Republican Party, farmers with the Democrats. After the Second World War, party preferences had changed to some extent, and by the 1990s, parties had switched position on trade, as Democrats opposed trade liberalization, while Republicans supported it.

Society-centered approaches have been based on public choice models of politics as well. Researchers using this approach examine the determinants of policy makers' decisions, including the electorate, interest-group pressure, partisanship, and party control of government. The underlying principle is that policy makers act rationally; members of Congress, for example, cast votes that will enhance their election chances or at least not damage them. The analytic goal is to determine which conditions or factors are most likely to influence an official's choices. Public choice models focus on societal factors in an attempt to formalize the relationship between them and government decision makers.[44]

Domestic approaches to American trade policy have provided a considerable number and range of explanations of specific policy outcomes. There is more research to be done, of course, and this work serves as a sound basis on which to build.

How This Approach Compares

Although trade policy involves both domestic and international considerations, its roots lie in the domestic policy process. For example, international trade agreements, although negotiated by the executive, typically involve congressional approval of some sort—for example, congressional authority to negotiate agreements on a "fast-track" basis. Congressional involvement necessarily opens the door to domestic political pressures. Implementation of trade policies draws the federal bureaucracy into the picture. Agencies responsible for trade policy—the International Trade Commission (USITC) and the Department of Commerce, for example—are subject to the political forces normally directed at bureaucracies implementing any kind of federal program. Interest groups, moreover, pressure government officials with respect to trade policy, with protectionist groups enjoying considerable success.[45]

The central goal of this book is to understand the domestic policy aspects of U.S. trade policy. I do not claim that all trade policy can be explained by domestic politics, but it is fairly clear that a great deal of political pressure and policy development involves domestic politics and institutions. Moreover, the domestic policy process deals with political forces from both domestic and international sources. Thus, the executive responds to international political pressure on trade but still must cope with the domestic policy apparatus and participants to accomplish its objectives. The executive can lead in this regard, but it cannot act alone. The goal here, then, is to use various approaches to domestic policy development to better understand American trade policy.[46] A growing body of research has developed theoretically-grounded domestic explanations of American trade policy. This book builds on these analyses to construct a more complete picture of how the domestic policy process affects trade policy outcomes.

Attributing American trade policy to domestic causes is not new, as this brief review of some main analytic themes indicates. The fact that the Constitution gives revenue-raising authority to Congress, and thus primary authority over trade policy, sets trade policy apart from the rest of foreign policy. The initial congressional authority, then, places trade policy development in the domestic arena. Moreover, the political conflict connected to trade policy typically involves high economic stakes for the country as a whole, or short of that, major economic consequences for parties immediately affected by international trade. Political conflict in the United States has traditionally involved economic disputes, a set of issues that can directly damage or help a wide range of interests. The salience of the issue leads to its resolution in the arena closest to the interests involved—that is, domestic politics.

Analyses of domestic causes of trade policy that deal with government organizations have been especially successful in describing and explaining the relationship between Congress and the presidency. Congress's delegation of some measure of trade policy authority to the executive is well documented.[47] The key issues here are how Congress gave the executive more control over trade policy while retaining significant congressional influence in the area by procedural means.[48] The interactions among executive branch agencies in trade policy formation and implementation presents an equally important set of issues meriting serious attention. Precisely how is trade policy authority distributed among executive branch agencies? How has the role of the United States Trade Representative (USTR) changed since Congress created it? Indeed, did it ever serve its original purpose of providing Congress with a foothold in executive branch actions on trade policy? Going beyond the interactions among executive branch agencies, it would also be useful to understand how the different organizational characteristics of each major agency affect its contribution to American trade policy. Studies of the domestic roots of American trade policy, moreover, could benefit from the analysis of the entire domestic policy process—from agenda setting to implementation—understanding the roles played by various participants at different stages of policy development.

I do not want to suggest that analysts have ignored these issues; they certainly have not. But there is room for further work in at least three areas. First, and most simply, recent developments in trade policy have been major and swift. The magnitude and speed of these changes call our attention to the domestic roots of trade policy to look for explanations. Past work provides the necessary illumination to find explanations for recent developments. Second, focusing on government institutions is essentially the state-centered approach described earlier. The information produced by this type of analysis is useful, but tends to be static. Placing an analysis of government organizations, in this case the executive branch, in the context of a policy process will be useful because it will demonstrate how agencies interact at different phases in the policy process. Thus, it will be possible to consider the role of the USTR during agenda setting, program adoption, and implementation. The significance of its changing role—assuming it changes at all—adds to our understanding of the domestic roots of trade policy. Third, the political system, of course, comprises not just government organizations; interest groups, political parties, the electorate, and the news media play major roles in policy development. The state-centered approach tends to ignore inputs from these societal forces.[49] The approach I adopt here demonstrates the connection between government and these nongovernmental political forces.

Analyses of societal forces that influence trade policy tend to focus on interest groups and political parties. The assumption apparently is that these are the principal means by which public preferences are transmitted to government officials. This suggests a weakness of this approach from the outset; it does not deal very much with how the concerns of the electorate influence policy makers apart from interest groups and political parties, nor does it consider the importance of the news media in transmitting information between the people and political institutions. Aside from these shortcomings, the analyses of interest groups and political parties characteristic of these studies get mixed reviews.

Interest groups certainly influence American trade policy, just as they influence virtually all policies. The consequences of pressure applied by producer interests have been dramatic. Interest-group pressure, in combination with an accommodating congressional decision-making process, resulted in the Smoot–Hawley Tariff. Producer groups have sought and achieved special provisions in the U.S. trade law that protect them from imports, even as the bulk of the law liberalizes trade in most other areas. Thus, sugar cane growers continue to win protection from foreign imports.[50] The same could be said for American automobile and semiconductor manufacturers.[51] Recent efforts to assess the influence of interest groups favoring free trade on American trade policy have added balance to the body of analysis in this area.

There is more to the story of interest-group influence than these examples suggest, however. Following the precedent set by Raymond A. Bauer, Ithiel de Sola Pool, and Lewis Anthony Dexter[52] and in a sense updating their work, analyses of interest-group influence over trade policy could go further to assess the degree of dissent within interest groups, disagreements among interest groups representing firms in the same sector, and the political miscues of some sectors (though by no means all) of corporate America. Moreover, evaluations of interest groups could be more exacting in their assessments of precisely how interest groups exert influence over trade policy.

Analyses of political parties have successfully demonstrated the salience of partisan differences on trade policy since the late nineteenth century. Party positions are not always reflected in congressional party activity. Partisanship in Congress is translated through party leaders and other factors that structure the legislator's voting choice. Whether party considerations always supersede other factors is an open question that merits some consideration. Moreover, seemingly dramatic change in the party system in the 1990s may lead to a new partisanship on trade policy. Although drawing final conclusions now would be premature, some assessment of such developments as the apparent rise of the Republican Party and decline of the Democratic Party, along with indications that more people consider themselves Independents, suggest possible consequences for American trade policy.

The news media play an important role in politics, of course; communication of ideas, problems, solutions, and government actions is central to how the public perceives policies and the extent to which it supports or opposes them. Analysts have spent little time on the importance of the news media and trade policy. How the news media influence problem definition, selection of solutions, and public perceptions can be crucial, especially at the agenda-setting stage of trade policy development.

Overall, analyses of the domestic roots of American trade policy have gone far in some areas, but they have come up short in others. I have suggested some of the holes in the research that can be addressed by designing studies to deal with specific problems—for example, disagreement among interest groups representing firms in the same sector. But more can be gained by, first, eliminating the clear distinction between statist and societal factors in trade policy development, and second, considering the entire package in terms of a dynamic policy process model.

The Domestic Policy Process

Three basic components of politics underlie the process by which policy is made and implemented: interests, ideas, and institutions. Scholars have constructed theories with one or more of these components at the center. I use all three in this study: Economic interests are clearly involved in determining trade policy; the trade policy debate is about ideas; and both interests and ideas are mediated by political institutions. A major part of the analysis presented here involves determining the relative importance of each of these components and the nature of their interaction as both relate to trade policy outcomes.

Focusing on interests, ideas, and institutions results in a static analysis unless some notion of process is included. To address this problem, I use a straightforward approach to the domestic policy process that incorporates the standard features of most analyses.[53] The process consists of three stages: agenda setting, program adoption (or formulation), and implementation. The process may be described in a linear way as steps in a logical, rational progression. But the world is rarely that simple. A policy may move back and forth in the process, and two or even all three stages may be in operation at once.

Agenda Setting

Noting that policy analyses tend to focus on program adoption and implementation, social scientists have begun to give serious attention to the question of precisely how issues get to the policy agenda.[54] The central question is this: Under what conditions do social and economic problems become public policy issues?

The answer to this question involves two distinct activities: (1) the development of solutions and (2) the creation of political conditions that allow solutions to be attached to problems on the policy agenda. As discussed earlier, there is no shortage of potential policy solutions as policy entrepreneurs of all sorts routinely create ideas and push them into political discourse. Any number of factors may stimulate ideas; they may be generated from long-term ideological commitments, years of study and expertise, or political experience, for example. The policy entrepreneur's task is to attach her ideas to recognized problems so that other players in the policy process recognize it to be a credible solution.

Policy makers' recognition that a problem exists creates the opportunity to turn an idea into a credible solution. Critical events, shifts in public opinion, and crises force attention on a policy problem. The public's concern for adequate health care caused various participants in the policy process to recognize flaws in the current system and allowed proponents of such concepts as health care purchasing cooperatives to introduce their ideas into the debate as viable solutions. The collapse of the savings and loan industry forced policy makers to examine the regulatory and economic problems associated with it and gave those who believe economic regulation is a good idea an opportunity to suggest it as a solution to the problem.

Once the problems and solutions have entered the debate, the political conditions must be right to allow the issue to reach the policy agenda. Some combination of political elites and public opinion disposed toward considering an issue a legitimate public policy question must exist. A shift in public opinion may give political elites who favor putting an issue on the agenda the political opportunity to do so. A vague public discomfort may be crystallized by political elites, as they articulate and give shape to the unformed public opinion.

Program Adoption

Program adoption is what is usually meant by policy making. Typically, the legislature carries out program adoption, although the executive can do so as well—for example, through a presidential executive order. The structure of the legislature and the way members are elected are central to how it makes public policy. Constituent and interest-group pressure on legislators affects their votes, of course, and to the extent a legislator worries about getting reelected, these pressures are likely to get more intense. Procedure and internal structure are also pivotal in policy making. The ability to form clear goals and coherent policy, build consensus, and maintain continuity in policy making over time shapes policy outcomes.

Implementation

Officials throughout the executive branch make implementation decisions. Political pressure, limited information, uncertainty, time limits, institutional norms, as well as the formal scope of authority constrain their decisions. Their implementation decisions frequently alter programs considerably as they deal with technical and political contingencies unaccounted for in the legislation passed by Congress.

A concern for how institutions affect the policy process runs throughout the analysis. Organizational characteristics shape and limit policy makers' actions. Moreover, the relationships among institutions—Congress and the president, for example—can affect policy outcomes. The various approaches encompassed by the "new institutionalism" illuminate the importance of institutions in policy development.[55] I apply these concepts to trade policy in subsequent chapters.

Summary

These three stages of the domestic policy process may deal with entire issues or parts of them, serially or simultaneously. Program adoption and implementation involve a constant flow of information from legislature to executive. Outcomes may lead to new or modified issues reaching the policy agenda. Crises that focus the public's attention on a particular problem can open the door to an army of policy entrepreneurs hoping to get their ideas accepted as credible solutions. Applying this approach to the domestic policy process will illuminate the domestic roots of the components of trade policy.

Major Elements of U.S. Trade Policy

U.S. trade policy consists of government activities concerning numerous issues, all somehow related to international trade. These issues range in scope, public salience, and relationship to broad foreign policy goals, and they include U.S. trade laws (including tariffs and forms of administrative relief), the General Agreement on Tariffs and Trade, free-trade areas in general and the North American Free Trade Agreement in particular, bilateral sectoral agreements, and the use of trade sanctions to achieve foreign policy objectives. Taken together, these issues do not constitute a simple, coherent policy area. They may be more accurately characterized as a collection of related issues that bear distinctive political characteristics. Thus, the political dynamics of the passage of NAFTA differ considerably from those underlying sector-specific agreements between the United States and Japan. These distinctions constitute the basis of the analysis I will present in the book and are summarized in the following sections.

U.S. Trade Law

U.S. trade law sets tariff schedules, provides administrative remedies to companies adversely affected by imports or experiencing difficulty entering foreign markets, delegates negotiating authority to the president, prescribes terms of congressional approval of agreements negotiated by the executive, and distributes trade policy authority among executive branch agencies. Congress amends trade law periodically, altering it as a result of experience and adding provisions as new issues reach the trade policy agenda. For example, the concern for the international competitiveness of U.S. industry in the early to mid 1980s resulted in the incorporation into law of explicit provisions to enhance American competitiveness.

The program adoption stage of U.S. trade law bears the typical characteristics of any major legislation: lengthy committee hearings, intense interest-group activity, some measure of partisanship, protection of vital constituent interests, and ideological clashes. One would expect Congress to respond to domestic political forces in a predictable way. For example, responding to pleading from industries under pressure from foreign competition, Congress would likely strengthen import relief provisions of the law or make it easier to qualify for them. As I. M. Destler and others argue, Congress has also responded to growing consensus that protectionist measures are bad for the economy as a whole and that the U.S. interest lies in moving in the direction of free trade by insulating itself from industry requests for protection through delegation of the authority to grant import relief to the executive.[56]

Import relief is an administrative matter with heavy participation by the USITC, the Department of Commerce, the USTR, and the president. Import relief decisions made in the executive branch are essentially implementation decisions. As such, they involve officials from the president down to career bureaucrats. Congress has given the president and these agencies considerable leeway in determining when an industry merits import relief, and the decisions these officials make comprise a major component of U.S. trade policy. Factors such as limited information, time constraints, and institutional traditions also determine to some degree these decisions.

The GATT

The General Agreement on Tariffs and Trade and the World Trade Organization (WTO) are the principal vehicles through which nations conduct multilateral trade negotiations. Created after the Second

World War, the GATT led to dramatic tariff reductions and a global cooperative effort to achieve free trade. The United States played a major role in the creation of the GATT. In its new role as the single global economic power following the Second World War, the United States sought to liberalize trade throughout the world as part of its overall foreign policy. Subsequent U.S. support for the GATT reflects its long-term support for global trade liberalization as well as its general commitment to multilateral negotiations. The United States has been a major (if not *the* major) participant in GATT negotiations over the last forty-five years.

The president leads the United States into GATT negotiations. Congress gives the president authority to negotiate and approves the final agreement. GATT negotiations and congressional involvement normally do not attract a great deal of public attention. Such issues as intellectual property protection, rules for trade in services, and a schedule for the reduction of agriculture subsidies do not make for news stories interesting to the entire public. On the other hand, business interest groups and labor unions are extremely interested in GATT negotiations. Indeed, at the conclusion of the Uruguay Round in Geneva, representatives from a wide range of internationally-traded industries lobbied American negotiators for provisions favorable to their industries.

In sum, presidential leadership, tempered by congressional approval, is the defining characteristic of the politics of this component of U.S. trade policy. Nevertheless, interest-group activity is intense. The private sector brings political pressure to bear on U.S. negotiators through industrial lobbyists. The political dynamic is considerably different than it is in the case of the adoption and implementation of the basic U.S. trade law, or in the case of bilateral sectoral agreements. Thus, the scope of U.S. interests in the GATT and the level of domestic political involvement set it apart from other components of U.S. trade policy.

Free-trade Agreements

Ideally, free-trade agreements allow for unimpaired passage of goods and services between countries. The United States entered into free-trade agreements with Israel and Canada in the 1980s, and NAFTA (which essentially expanded the agreement with Canada to include Mexico) in 1993.

As is the case with respect to the GATT, the president takes the lead in negotiating free-trade agreements, but as the NAFTA episode clearly illustrates, the entire complement of political participants can get involved. In the NAFTA story, congressional debate over approval of the agreement was a high-profile affair with all the drama of a major political showdown. Interest-group activity was heated and frenetic, and President Clinton worked Congress over in the spirit of Lyndon Johnson working to get a chunk of the Great Society passed into law. The NAFTA fight in Congress bore all the characteristics of a domestic political battle. Indeed, the struggle for congressional approval of NAFTA was much more about domestic economic relationships and political upheaval than trade.

NAFTA, then, provides an example of trade policy that grew out of a domestic political struggle among economic interests. The political dynamic of its adoption stage in Congress is a good example of an old-fashioned American-style political brawl. In this respect, to analyze NAFTA accurately, one must consider it in terms of the domestic policy process.

Bilateral Sectoral Agreements

Threats of trade sanctions resulting either from a country's unwillingness to open its domestic market to American products as stipulated by U.S. trade law or from a foreign country's or company's unfair trade practices have led to bilateral sectoral agreements. In lieu of having its exports to the United States limited by import relief regulations, foreign countries—mainly Japan—have agreed to sectoral agreements on trade in the threatened industry. The USTR negotiates these agreements to avoid engaging sanctions, and the result is typically some sort of self-imposed constraint on the part of the exporting country—for example, Japan's voluntary export agreement with the United States with respect to Japanese export of automobiles to the American market.

Bilateral sectoral agreements, then, result from the executive's threats to implement trade sanctions. These agreements are in essence new programs that were created as a result of an effort to implement sections of U.S. trade law. The relationship between implementation and program adoption demonstrates an earlier point: that the domestic policy process is anything but linear, allowing ample opportunity for feedback and for the executive, not just the legislature, to engage in program adoption. At the same time, intense interest-group pressure accompanies the initiation, negotiation, and conclusion of these agreements. Although the public has little concern or knowledge of these matters, they are of utmost importance to the industries affected by them.

Trade as a Foreign Policy Instrument

In some instances, the president uses trade nearly exclusively as a foreign policy instrument. The General System of Preferences (GSP), for example, is intended to make it easier for less-developed nations to export their products to the United States. The rationale for this policy is that allowing imports into the United States from these countries at a reduced tariff is a cheaper way to aid their economic development than direct aid. Trade can also be used as a stick. Threatening withdrawal of MFN status from China is perhaps the clearest example of this use of trade policy. And several administrations have limited trade to outlaw countries like South Africa and Cuba in an effort to force their governments to make policy changes.

These actions are initiated by the president in cooperation with Congress. Although clearly in the realm of foreign policy, they involve domestic political actors, such as interest groups and Congress. Thus, these actions can be analyzed in terms of the domestic policy process.

The preceding description accounts for the main components of U.S. trade policy. In most cases, trade policy is produced through the domestic policy process. The politics and relevance of various aspects of the domestic policy process differ for each type of policy, making analytic distinctions possible. Thus, to understand trade policy thoroughly, it is necessary to examine it as a domestic policy. Doing so will provide insights into its causes and character, allow for comparisons with other domestic policies, and provide the basis on which to anticipate how different trade policies will develop.

Plan of the Book

The analysis begins with a historical overview of U.S. trade policy concentrating on policy themes and development throughout American history. Chapter 3 reviews the contemporary debate over trade policy and connects this to the domestic policy process. The following three chapters consider the main components of U.S. trade policy in terms of domestic policy and politics: U.S. leadership in the development of the GATT; the struggle over NAFTA; and the significance of administrative trade relief. Chapter 7 examines how these policies affected the American steel, automobile, and semiconductor industries. The conclusion summarizes the central theme of the book and suggests the future direction of U.S. trade policy, given the realities of domestic political constraints.

Conclusion

As trade policy continues to become more prominent in terms of international relations and American foreign policy, the importance of understanding its domestic roots is clear. Presidents cannot manipulate trade policy in the same way they handle traditional foreign policy matters. The constitutional authority over trade policy claimed by Congress automatically draws the legislature into the middle of trade policy development and requires that it be handled through the domestic policy process.

A major objective of the book is to guide the reader to an understanding of the fundamental questions that lie at the root of U.S. trade policy. One set of questions considers what is at stake in trade policy. Three principal concerns come to mind: individual economic well-being; the nation's economic well-being; and the national interest. In the debate over trade policy, one frequently hears policies justified in terms of economic efficiency and growth. Economic efficiency, which leads to maximum growth, benefits everyone as the wealth increases. Some may benefit more than others, but that is not a central concern. From a national economic perspective, this goal is worth pursuing, and free-trade advocates argue precisely that. How this is to be accomplished is debatable, however.

Critics point out that, even under conditions of maximum growth, some individuals lose; it is not necessarily the case that everyone is automatically better off. Accepting this proposition leads to policies that call for government intervention to help those who do not benefit from trade liberalization. The magnitude of government intervention varies, but the justification is essentially the same. In this instance, the principal concern is for individual economic well-being.

But what of the national interest, an extraordinarily difficult concept to define? Is economic growth in the national interest, particularly if it is at the expense of other goals, like equity, for example? Clearly, critics of free trade answer that it is not. Some measure of economic growth may be sacrificed in order to insure equity, social justice, and the like. A laissez-faire perspective disputes the point; the national interest is the same as national economic well-being, so policy should maximize economic growth through trade liberalization.

Aside from the disputes over meaning of these terms and which should be the general goal of trade policy, one must also consider what, if anything, can be done. For free traders, government that does least does best. The less government intervention the better, and market forces govern the allocation of resources leading to greater efficiency and growth. Some economists, however, believe that government intervention can do better than pure free trade in maximizing a nation's economic growth. The problem for this position is that, even if government ought to do something, in practice American government cannot. For critics of free trade who see the downside in unfettered economic growth, government is the only resort, and they favor policies shaped to address specific problems caused by freer trade worldwide.

Endnotes

1. See, for example, Gary Burtless, Robert Z. Lawrence, Robert E. Litan, and Robert J. Shapiro, *Globaphobia: Confronting Fears about Open Trade* (Washington, D.C.: Brookings Institution, 1998).
2. See, for example, Robert Kuttner, "Managed Trade and Economic Sovereignty," in Robert A. Blecker, ed., *U.S. Trade Policy and Global Growth* (Armonk, N.Y.: M. E. Sharpe, 1996), 3–36; and William Greider, *One World, Ready or Not* (New York: Simon & Schuster, 1997).
3. Dani Rodrik, *Has Globalization Gone Too Far?* (Washington, D.C.: Institute for International Economics, 1997).
4. Geza Feketekuty, "An American Trade Strategy for the 21st Century," in Geza Feketekuty and Bruce Stokes, eds., *Trade Strategies for a New Era:*

Ensuring U.S. Leadership in a Global Economy (New York: Council on Foreign Relations, 1998), 4.

5. See chapter 5.

6. Indeed, trade policy may be the only foreign policy area where the Clinton administration has enjoyed some success. In June 1995, the administration concluded an agreement with Japan to open its markets to American-made automobiles and auto parts. The following month, Japan and the United States agreed to allow Federal Express Corporation greater access to the Japanese market, mainly from the carrier's new Asian base at Subic Bay in the Philippines. See Bob Davis and Emory Thomas, Jr., "Push in Asia Set by Federal Express Corp.," *Wall Street Journal,* 24 July 1995, A2, A14.

7. Paul Krugman, "The Uncomfortable Truth about NAFTA: It's Foreign Policy, Stupid," *Foreign Affairs* 72 (November/December 1993): 13–19.

8. David E. Sanger, "A Deepening Political Issue in Trade Deficit for May," *New York Times,* 19 July 1995, D1, D5.

9. In 1995, the Clinton administration chose to decouple China's MFN status and its human rights policy. Although some in Congress complained about this move, neither the House nor the Senate has taken action to reverse it. In mid-July 1995, the House had the opportunity to make a strong statement in a vote on the U.S. economic relationship with China, but after some fierce speeches, the House voted overwhelmingly to maintain the *status quo.* See Michael Wines, "In House, Tirade on China, but a Vote to Keep Trade as It Is," *New York Times,* 21 July 1995, A3.

10. The U.S. balance in merchandise trade with the world has been negative since the mid 1970s. The balance on current account and the balance on goods and services were both positive in the early 1980s before becoming deficits by 1982 and 1983 respectively. United States Bureau of the Census, *Statistical Abstract of the United States: 1995,* 115th ed. (Washington, D.C.: U.S. Government Printing Office, 1995), 798.

11. United States Bureau of the Census, *Statistical Abstract of the United States: 1996,* 116th ed. (Washington, D.C.: U.S. Government Printing Office, 1996), 802.

12. Note, for example, the 1985 dispute between the United States and the European Community over Mediterranean citrus exports. In response to the failure to resolve this dispute, the United States increased tariffs on EC pasta exports, and the EC retaliated with higher tariffs on American walnuts and lemons. The episode was quickly dubbed the "pasta wars." See Steve Dryden, *Trade Warriors: USTR and the American Crusade for Free Trade* (New York: Oxford Univ. Press, 1995), 312. In 1998, the EU squabbled with the United States over the effects of U.S. trade sanctions, a loophole in U.S. tax law permitting around 3,000 American companies to avoid paying taxes on

export earnings, and several issues connected to the export of certain American products to Europe. See Paul Magnusson, "Rougher Sailing Across the Atlantic," *Business Week,* 27 July 1998, 29.

13. United States Bureau of the Census, *Statistical Abstract of the United States: 1996,* 116th ed., 801.

14. United States Bureau of the Census, *Statistical Abstract of the United States 1997,* 117th ed. (Washington, D.C.: U.S. Government Printing Office, 1997), 800.

15. The data in table 1.1 do not match those of table 1.2 because of different methodologies used to calculate the numbers. The trend remains the same, however. See United States Bureau of the Census, *Statistical Abstract of the United States: 1997,* 117th ed., 800.

16. A number of factors may be involved in the composition and level of employment, including trade. See William T. Dickens, "The Effects of Trade on Employment: Techniques and Evidence," in Laura D'Andrea Tyson, William T. Dickens, and John Zysman, eds., *The Dynamics of Trade and Employment* (Cambridge, Mass.: Ballinger, 1988), 41–85.

17. Gary Burtless, Robert Z. Lawrence, Robert E. Litan, and Robert J. Shapiro, *Globaphobia: Confronting Fears about Open Trade* (Washington, D.C.: Brookings Institution and Progressive Policy Institute; New York: The Twentieth Century Fund, 1998), chap. 3; Paul Krugman, *The Age of Diminished Expectations: U.S. Economic Policy in the 1990s* (Cambridge, Mass.: MIT Press, 1992), 36–39; and Krugman, "Domestic Distortions and the Deindustrialization Hypothesis," in Robert C. Feenstra, Gene M. Grossman, and Douglas A. Irwin, eds., *Papers in Honor of Jagdish Bhagwati* (Cambridge, Mass.: MIT Press, 1996), 33–49.

18. Krugman, *The Age of Diminished Expectations,* 41.

19. Ibid., 41–42.

20. The original Big Four included Ford Motor Company, General Motors Corporation, Chrysler Corporation, and American Motors Corporation. Chrysler subsequently swallowed American Motors, to leave the Big Three American automobile companies.

21. For a detailed account of Ford and Nissan—two car companies going in decidedly different directions—see David Halberstam, *The Reckoning* (New York: Avon, 1986). See also Michael L. Dertouzos, Richard K. Lester, and Robert M. Solow, *Made in America: Regaining the Productive Edge* (Cambridge, Mass.: MIT Press, 1989), 171–87.

22. Although the general relationship between the value of the dollar and trade holds, the predicted effect of fluctuations in the dollar is not necessarily immediate. For example, the decline in value of the dollar in 1995 did not result in an immediate decrease in imports. The reason for this is that the short-term consequence of the falling dollar was to raise the prices of imports.

Until the volume of imports adjusted to the new prices, the temporary effect was to increase the dollar amount of imports. See "Down, Down, Down," *The Economist,* 16–22 September 1995, 30.

23. Krugman, *The Age of Diminished Expectations,* 42–47.

24. Burtless, et al., *Globaphobia,* 107.

25. For a pointed argument in support of free trade, see Anne O. Krueger, "Free Trade is the Best Policy," in Robert Z. Lawrence and Charles L. Schultze, eds., *An American Trade Strategy: Options for the 1990s* (Washington, D.C.: Brookings Institution, 1990), 68–96. For a closely argued defense of trade liberalization by means of multilateral negotiations, see Jagdish Bhagwati, *The World Trading System at Risk* (Princeton, N.J.: Princeton Univ. Press, 1991).

26. Robert A. Blecker, *Beyond the Twin Deficits: A Trade Strategy for the 1990s* (Armonk, N.Y.: M. E. Sharpe, 1992).

27. See, for example, Greg Mastel, *American Trade Laws after the Uruguay Round* (Armonk, N.Y.: M. E. Sharpe, 1996).

28. Laura D'Andrea Tyson, *Who's Bashing Whom? Trade Conflict in High-Technology Industries* (Washington, D.C.: Institute for International Economics, 1992); and Clyde V. Prestowitz, Jr., "Beyond Laissez Faire," in Jeffrey A. Frieden and David A. Lake, eds., *International Political Economy: Perspectives on Global Power and Wealth,* 3rd ed. (New York: St. Martin's, 1995), 506–18.

29. Krugman, *The Age of Diminished Expectations,* 48–50.

30. It is interesting to note that although mergers are credited with creating more efficiency and blamed for cutting jobs in doing so, the self-induced breakup of AT&T into three companies also cost jobs. See Mark Landler, "AT&T, Reversing Strategy, Announces a Plan to Split into Three Separate Companies," *New York Times,* 21 September 1995, A1, D8.

31. See Burtless, et al., *Globaphobia,* chap. 4.

32. Pat Choate, *Agents of Influence,* 1st Touchstone ed. (New York: Simon and Schuster, 1991). The United Automobile Workers strike at GM in the summer of 1998 focused on job security in light of the possibility of union members losing their jobs as plants moved abroad. See Aaron Bernstein, "Up in Arms, but Not in Clout," *Business Week,* 3 August 1998, 36–37.

33. Jeffrey A. Frieden and David A. Lake, "Introduction: International Politics and International Economics," in Jeffrey A. Frieden and David A. Lake, eds., *International Political Economy,* 3rd ed., 12–13. For examples of this approach, see Stephen D. Krasner, "State Power and the Structure of International Trade," in Frieden and Lake, eds., *International Political Economy,* 3rd ed., 19–36; and David A. Lake, "International Economic Structures and American Foreign Economic Policy, 1887–1934," in Jeffrey A. Frieden and David A. Lake, eds., *International Political Economy: Per-*

spectives on Global Power and Wealth, 2nd ed. (New York: St. Martin's, 1991), 120–38.

34. Frieden and Lake, "Introduction," 10–11.

35. In spite of this, scholars, journalists, and various political actors tend to refer to government actions as though they were the products of a single actor.

36. See Theodore J. Lowi, *The End of Liberalism: The Second Republic of the United States,* 2nd ed. (New York: W. W. Norton, 1979), 67–126.

37. See chapter 3.

38. See, for example, R. Kent Weaver and Bert A. Rockman, eds., *Do Institutions Matter? Government Capabilities in the United States and Abroad* (Washington, D.C.: Brookings Institution, 1993); and Sharyn O'Halloran, *Politics, Process, and American Trade Policy* (Ann Arbor, Mich.: Univ. of Michigan Press, 1994).

39. An excellent example is Judith Goldstein, *Ideas, Interests, and American Trade Policy* (Ithaca, N.Y.: Cornell Univ. Press, 1993).

40. For an analysis of Congress, the executive branch, and the relationship between them with respect to trade policy development, see I. M. Destler, *American Trade Politics,* 3rd ed. (Washington, D.C.: Institute for International Economics; and New York: The Twentieth Century Fund, 1995); Helen Milner, "Maintaining International Commitments in Trade Policy," in Weaver and Rockman, eds., *Do Institutions Matter?,* 345–69; Sharyn O'Halloran, *Politics, Process, and American Trade Policy;* and Susanne Lohmann and Sharyn O'Halloran, "Divided Government and U.S. Trade Policy: Theory and Evidence," *International Organization* 48 (Autumn 1994): 595–632.

41. E. E. Schattschneider, *Politics, Pressures and the Tariff* (New York: Prentice Hall, 1935).

42. See Peter Alexis Gourevitch, "International Trade, Domestic Coalitions, and Liberty: Comparative Responses to the Crisis of 1873–1896," in Frieden and Lake, *International Political Economy,* 3rd ed., 90–109; and Jeff Frieden, "Sectoral Conflict and U.S. Foreign Economic Policy, 1914–1940," in G. John Ikenberry, David A. Lake, and Michael Mastanduno, eds., *The State and American Foreign Economic Policy* (Ithaca, N.Y.: Cornell Univ. Press, 1988), 59–90.

43. I. M. Destler and John S. Odell, *Anti-Protection: Changing Forces in United States Trade Politics* (Washington, D.C.: Institute for International Economics, 1987); and Helen Milner, "Resisting the Protectionist Temptation: Industry and the Making of Trade Policy in France and the United States during the 1970s," in Frieden and Lake, eds., *International Political Economy,* 3rd ed., 368–86.

44. See Robert E. Baldwin, *Trade Policy in a Changing World Economy* (Chicago, Ill.: Univ. of Chicago Press, 1988), 42–72; and Stephen P. Magee,

William A. Brock, and Leslie Young, *Black Hole Tariffs and Endogenous Policy Theory* (New York: Cambridge Univ. Press, 1989).

45. Schattschneider, *Politics, Pressures and the Tariff.*

46. This approach follows that suggested by G. John Ikenberry, who urged analysts to get inside the "black box" of policy development in the United States. See G. John Ikenberry, "Conclusion: An Institutional Approach to American Foreign Economic Policy," in Ikenberry, Lake, and Mastanduno, eds., *The State and American Foreign Economic Policy,* 219–43.

47. Destler, *American Trade Politics,* 11–38, 65–104; Stephan Haggard, "The Institutional Foundations of Hegemony: Explaining the Reciprocal Trade Agreements Act of 1934," in Ikenberry, Lake, and Mastanduno, eds., *The State and American Foreign Economic Policy,* 91–119; and Susanne Lohmann and Sharyn O'Halloran, "Divided Government and U.S. Trade Policy: Theory and Evidence," *International Organization* 43 (Autumn 1994): 595–632.

48. James M. Lindsay, "Congress, Foreign Policy, and the New Institutionalism," *International Studies Quarterly* (1994) 38: 291–92; and Sharyn O'Halloran, "Congress and Foreign Trade Policy," in Randall B. Ripley and James M. Lindsay, eds., *Congress Resurgent: Foreign and Defense Policy on Capitol Hill* (Ann Arbor, Mich.: Univ. of Michigan Press, 1993), 283–303.

49. Destler is among the exceptions. See his discussion of congressional response to societal-based political pressure in *American Trade Politics,* 11–38, 65–104.

50. This continues to be true, even as tough-minded House Republicans seek ways to cut "corporate welfare" and unleash the free market. See Mireya Navarro, "Congressional Proposal Adds Element of Risk to Sugar-Growing Business," *New York Times,* 28 June 1995, A10.

51. Voluntary Export Restraints (VERs) have reduced the number of Japanese-made automobiles entering the American market. The American semiconductor industry benefited from antidumping provisions of the Semiconductor Trade Arrangement of 1986 between the United States and Japan.

52. Raymond A. Bauer, Ithiel de Sola Pool, and Lewis Anthony Dexter, *American Business and Public Policy: The Politics of Foreign Trade* (New York: Atherton, 1963), 321–99.

53. For a good review, see Michael T. Hayes, *Incrementalism and Public Policy* (New York: Longman, 1992).

54. See John W. Kingdon, *Agendas, Alternatives, and Public Policies,* 2nd ed. (New York: HarperCollins, 1995); Deborah A. Stone, *Policy Paradox: The Art of Political Decision Making* (New York: W. W. Norton, 1997); and Frank R. Baumgartner and Bryan D. Jones, *Agendas and Instability in American Politics* (Chicago, Ill.: Univ. of Chicago Press, 1993).

55. See Bert A. Rockman, "The New Institutionalism and the Old Institutions," in Lawrence C. Dodd and Calvin Jillson, eds., *New Perspectives on American Politics* (Washington, D.C.: CQ Press, 1994), 143–61; Karen Orren and Stephen Skowronek, "Beyond the Iconography of Order: Notes for a 'New Institutionalism,'" in Lawrence C. Dodd and Calvin Jillson, eds., *The Dynamics of American Politics: Approaches and Interpretations* (Boulder, Colo.: Westview, 1994), 311–30; Hugh Heclo, "Ideas, Interests, and Institutions," in Dodd and Jillson, eds., *The Dynamics of American Politics*, 366–92; and O'Halloran, *Politics, Process, and American Trade Policy.*
56. Destler, *American Trade Politics*, 11–38.

2

Historical Overview of Trade Policy

The national government has played a role in foreign trade since the founding of the republic. At stake from the very beginning was the fundamental question of the proper role of government in the economy, of which trade policy was a part. Issues connected to this question included the nature of the economy—whether agrarian, commercial, or industrial; the distribution of the population—concentrated in centers of commerce and industry or dispersed throughout the land on small farms; and the basic nature of government—limited or interventionist. The role the national government eventually played in trade policy reflects the ways national leaders ultimately resolved these questions.

A second major aspect of trade policy in the United States is that it has always involved domestic political and economic considerations. From the 1780s through the early twentieth century, government officials raised and lowered tariffs mainly on the basis of domestic politics and economics. Through the middle and end of the twentieth century, other foreign policy considerations emerged, particularly as government officials recognized the effects trade policies had on international affairs. The foreign policy component became more important in trade policy development, but domestic issues remained at its foundation.

This chapter begins with the ideological split between Alexander Hamilton and Thomas Jefferson. Hamilton's and Jefferson's perspectives on the role of government in the economy established the parameters of the debate and the policy that followed. Much of the current debate on trade policy and on economic policy in general can still be understood in terms of the positions taken by Hamilton and Jefferson. After establishing these broad ideological categories, the remainder of the chapter deals with trade policy in three time periods: 1880–1860, late nineteenth century through 1930, and 1934 to the present.

The Logic Behind the Tariff

Hamilton and Jefferson presented strikingly different views of the proper role of government in the economy, and the differences between the two perspectives have served as a dividing line in the debate on government and the economy throughout American history and into the 1990s.[1] In the spirit of keeping government limited, Jefferson preferred a small role for government in the economy. A limited government fit well with an agrarian economy based on a widely-dispersed rural population, few, if any, urban centers, and little commercialization or industrialization. Jefferson did not envision government as a promoter of American economic interests; economic activity was properly a private matter, not within the purview of government. There is no room within Jefferson's view for a strategic trade policy—one, for example, that was designed to enhance the development of certain American industries.

In contrast to Jefferson's view of America, Hamilton believed that the American economy could not be limited to agriculture; the country's vast resources underlay unheard-of commercial and manufacturing promise. But industrial success, from Hamilton's perspective, required an active government that would create the financial institutions and developmental policies necessary to insure economic growth. The government could accelerate economic growth through such activities as creating infrastructure—building roads, bridges, canals—and by creating financial institutions, like the Bank of the United States. To finance this activity, the government needed a steady source of revenue. Because the Constitution did not provide for an income tax, the government had to resort to other means to finance itself, the main one among these being the tariff.

Hamilton wished to accomplish two goals with the tariff. The first was to raise money for the national government, a purpose the tariff served throughout the nineteenth century. The second was to protect domestic industries against imports until those industries became more competitive. In this, Hamilton articulated the infant industry argument, where a national government protects new domestic industries with high tariffs until those industries can compete with imports on their own.[2]

Jefferson and Hamilton initiated an enduring debate on the relationship between government and the economy in the United States. Although the degree of government involvement in the economy has continued to be a matter of political conflict, from the outset some significant government interference in the economy seemed inescapable. Following the British legacy of mercantilism,[3] the new government sought to create an environment that would foster economic growth. Toward this end it defined and protected property rights, recognized corporations as legal entities, and enforced contracts, all three of which proved central to America's economic development.[4]

1780s to 1860

Following Hamilton's logic, the primary purpose of the tariff at the end of the eighteenth century and through much of the nineteenth century was to raise funds to run the government. Congress passed the Tariff Act of 1789 (only the second law it passed) explicitly to provide revenue for this purpose.[5] The tariff also served the purpose of protecting domestic industries from imports. Grounded in a mercantilist justification, government officials continued to use the tariff throughout the nineteenth century for the secondary purpose of achieving economic goals. In general, government leaders increased the tariff during hard economic times and to pay for wars, and reduced tariffs during periods of relative economic well-being.[6]

After raising tariffs to finance the War of 1812, the national government enacted in 1816 the first tariff clearly intended to protect domestic industry. This law increased tariffs some 42 percent over their prewar levels and led to still more tariff increases. In legislation passed in 1824, 1828, and 1832, the United States established a high tariff wall to protect several of its key industries (cotton, wool, and iron) in the hope that this would allow them to develop and become established competitors in the market.[7] The Tariff Act of 1828 (the Tariff of Abominations) was a particularly odious tariff hike; it precipitated a constitutional crisis based on a geographic split, with the agrarian South opposing tariffs and the industrialized North supporting them. Shortly after 1832, protectionist measures began to draw less enthusiastic support.[8] Congress passed the Tariff Act of 1833 (the Compromise Tariff) to quell the crisis, which ushered in a ten-year process of lower tariffs;[9] thus, by 1842, duties were lower than what they had been in 1816.[10] Tariffs continued to fluctuate until the Civil War; a high tariff enacted in 1842 was lowered in legislation passed in 1846 and reduced still further by the Tariff Act of 1857.[11]

Throughout this period, economic interests underlay positions on tariffs. Southern and western agrarian interests opposed the tariff; northern industrialists supported it largely to protect themselves from British producers, and northern commercial interests split on the issue, but tended to side with the South.[12]

The Civil War to Smoot–Hawley: Protection and Internationalization

During the second half of the nineteenth century, American trade policy was largely protectionist. Although Congress generally kept tariffs high, by the turn of the century the executive led an effort to expand foreign markets for U.S. products, largely through the use of a form of reciprocity. Strong partisan division along with interest-group pressure characterized the domestic politics of the time, cast against the backdrop of a growing American presence in an international system still dominated by Britain.

The cost of prosecuting the Civil War forced the federal government to seek revenue from a variety of sources, including dramatically increased tariffs. These tariffs were intended to be temporary; the money they raised would be used to pay for the war effort and would no longer be necessary once the war debt had been paid off. But they were not eliminated or reduced. Instead, they "were retained, increased, and systematized, so developing gradually into a system of extreme protection."[13]

The last quarter of the nineteenth century enjoyed a measure of economic prosperity, periodically interrupted by economic recessions and depressions. The American economy industrialized during this period and became a powerhouse. Dramatic advances in the railroad, oil, steel, and financial industries produced tremendous economic growth and a new wealthy class. At the same time, however, agriculture lagged behind. Increasing numbers of farmers left rural America and headed for the cities and factory jobs.[14] These economic developments reshaped American politics.

The late nineteenth century experienced long-term currency deflation. While the financiers and industrialists of the East were not harmed by it, southern and western farmers were. Out of this economic pain grew political discontent, given voice mainly by the populist movement. Behind the leadership of William Jennings Bryan, the Populist Party sought government action that would address the plight of the farmer. Principal among these policies was movement to a silver standard for currency, which would have the effect of inflation, benefiting the farmers. Agriculture interests also opposed tariffs, reenforcing a geographically based political divide on the issue.[15]

In this late nineteenth-century context, the tariff persisted as a major political issue frequently used by politicians to enhance their positions and as leverage to obtain objectives on other issues.[16] The political battle over tariffs during this period, then, broke down along clear partisan lines, as party politics determined tariffs in large measure.[17] Throughout these years, Democrats and Republicans squabbled over tariff policy, spending a great deal of legislative energy on the issue. Party preferences reflected the economic interests of these geographic bases: Democrats in the South, Republicans mainly in the East, but also with some agriculture support in the West. Democrats opposed tariffs by arguing that they exploited farmers and workers. Republicans were largely pro-tariff, protecting the industrial and commercial interests that made up its constituency. In addition to partisan differences, economic interests played a role in setting American tariff levels. A burgeoning manufacturing sector and an established agricultural sector sought to influence Congress throughout the tariff squabbles. At the same time, the executive took a leading role in seeking foreign markets for American products. Behind the leadership of both Democratic and Republican presidents, the United States sought to open foreign markets while protecting U.S. producers with high tariff walls.[18]

Enter Reciprocity

In 1879 and 1880, fifty tariff bills were introduced in Congress dealing mostly with specific commodities.[19] Whereas Democrats led the efforts to reduce tariffs, Republican President Chester Arthur and his Secretary of State Frederick T. Frelinghuysen continued along a new path initiated by their predecessors (Republican President James A. Garfield and Secretary of State James G. Blaine) to expand American commerce in foreign markets.[20] Although adjusting tariff rates was still the main component of American trade policy, expanding foreign markets for U.S.-manufactured products was added to the mix.[21] American policy makers had a restrictive notion of the meaning of reciprocity. According to their view, the United States would threaten to raise tariffs if another country did not open its markets to American-manufactured products. Policy makers did not consider the possibility of lowering American tariffs either as an incentive or reward to other countries for allowing access to their markets. Thus, reciprocity at this time involved only the stick, leaving the carrot out of the equation.[22]

Continuing the pattern in the 1890s, the two major pieces of tariff legislation passed during this decade sought to protect American producers at home, while finding markets abroad mainly through reciprocity.[23] With a slim Electoral College victory (though losing the popular vote), Republican Benjamin Harrison became president in 1888. He brought to the White House his party's preference for high tariffs, but at the same time looked for new markets abroad. The McKinley Tariff of 1890 was a product of Harrison's political handiwork, raising the average tariff rate to 49 percent. It also contained reciprocity provisions aimed at Latin American countries "in which the (United States) would admit sugar, coffee, tea, and raw hides free of duty while (Latin American nations) would grant, in return, preferential duties on a specified list of American agricultural and manufactured items."[24]

By 1894, the Democrats, having recaptured the presidency with Grover Cleveland's second term, negotiated a modest reduction in tariffs with the Wilson–Gorman Tariff, but eliminated the reciprocity provisions of the McKinley Tariff. The Wilson–Gorman Tariff removed the duty on raw wool, produced mostly in Latin America's southern cone. The intent behind eliminating this duty was to expand American exports to this region of the world.[25] The 1894 tariff reduction was short-lived, however, because the Republican Party, in power after the election of William McKinley in 1896, pushed tariff levels back up. The ebb and flow in tariffs reflected the fluctuating political fortunes of the Democratic and Republican parties.[26] Whatever the exact positions of Republicans and Democrats during the last part of the nineteenth century, the tariff was the subject of partisan rancor.[27]

The Dingley Tariff Act of 1897 returned to the pattern established by the McKinley Tariff. It raised tariffs to unprecedented levels and delegated to the president authority "to enter into commercial agreements on specified articles to secure reciprocal and equivalent concessions."[28] The act also limited tariff cuts to 20 percent and established for the first time countervailing duties. "The secretary of the treasury could offset any export bounty imposed by another country by levying countervailing duties equal to the net amount of the subsidy."[29]

The Payne–Aldrich Tariff Act of 1909 introduced a system of maximum and minimum tariffs into American trade law. Following Republican guidelines, the law allowed the president to add 25 percent to any tariff if the source country of the import was not engaging in "reciprocal and equivalent" treatment with respect to exports from the United States. If the country did adhere to that standard, the minimum tariff would apply. The law also created the Tariff Board—the predecessor to the Tariff Commission, which eventually became the United States International Trade Commission—which evaluated domestic and foreign costs of production.[30]

The partisan pendulum swung back to the Democrats with the election of Woodrow Wilson to the presidency in 1912. Consistent with its historic position, the Democratic Party pushed through the Underwood Tariff Act of 1913, which lowered tariff rates, eliminated the maximum and minimum tariff, and established the competitive tariff, intended to set rates high enough to allow domestic producers to compete with imports, but no higher. Congress delegated to the president the authority to negotiate tariffs, but retained veto power over it. Finally, the Underwood Tariff eliminated the Tariff Board.[31]

Sharyn O'Halloran sums up trade policy during this period well:

In the period from 1890 to 1913 . . . Congress set tariff schedules according to partisan preferences: Republicans enacted high tariffs, Democrats reduced tariffs. At the same time, however, both parties established the precedent of delegating authority to the president to negotiate reciprocal concessions or to adjust tariff levels along the lines of an "objective" criterion. This trend continued even after the tariff no longer served as the federal government's primary source of income.[32]

Partisan politics is one explanation of American trade policy in the last quarter of the nineteenth century. Peter Gourevitch provides another, explaining trade policy during this period in terms of economic interests. Comparing the American experience with those of western European countries, Gourevitch argues that producer interests, represented by interest groups, determined trade policy. In the American case, powerful economic sectors supported government action to find new markets for American products.[33] Gourevitch's argument provides an interest-group–based explanation of American trade policy for a time period well before Congress passed the Smoot–Hawley Tariff, the classic example of interest-group influence over trade policy. Parties and interest groups, then, have been major participants in the domestic policy process related to American trade policy.

This domestic political activity took place in an international economic system dominated by Britain. The unchallenged global economic leader of the time, Britain led other countries in reducing tariffs. Britain's willingness to do so can be explained in terms of the nature of the international system and Britain's position in it. As the dominant force—the hegemonic power—in global affairs, Britain had an interest in reducing tariffs and the economic and political power to do it. The United States, a lesser but growing power at the time, had little interest in reducing tariffs unilaterally. To the extent the United States did chip away at its tariff wall, it did so to gain reciprocal agreement from foreign countries. The goal, of course, was to open those markets to American products.[34] Thus, domestic political forces in the United States influenced American trade policy in the context of the realities of the international setting.

Reciprocity provisions built into tariff acts in the last years of the nineteenth century and the first part of the twentieth century were intended to protect American producers at home and to gain access to foreign markets. The concept of free trade did not enter into the rationale behind these provisions. Thus, the United States further sought to find foreign markets while protecting U.S. industries through the early part of the twentieth century, mainly through bilateral agreements with European countries.[35] Both Republican and Democratic presidents continued the trend toward reciprocity, reflecting the importance of the executive in leading the nation in the direction of trade liberalization. The executive understood and sought policies to fulfill the nation's international economic interests.[36]

Post–World War I: Rising Protectionist Tide

After the First World War, a new wave of isolationism influenced American foreign policy, evident in the nation's unwillingness to embrace the League of Nations and its rejection of the Treaty of Versailles. The free-trade component of Woodrow Wilson's Fourteen Points was rejected as well.[37] Reflecting the isolationist mood, the Fordney–McCumber Tariff Act of 1922 raised the average tariff to a level 50 percent higher than the Underwood Tariff of 1913. In addition to raising tariffs, the 1922 legislation added measures to American trade law that continue to be important seventy years later. For example, the law gave the U.S. Tariff Commission, which had been resurrected a few years earlier with more investigative powers, added authority to investigate unfair trade practices undertaken by foreign-based companies. It also strengthened antidumping provisions established by the Antidumping Act of 1921 and broadened the definition of unfair trade practices.[38] Thus, in the immediate postwar period, Congress enacted trade laws that continued the policy of protecting American producers from import competition and strengthening provisions of the trade law intended to thwart additional trade practices that might damage them.

With the Republican Party controlling both Congress and the presidency in 1930, policy makers embarked on a plan to give limited protection to the withered American agriculture sector and added protection to industries that had been hard hit by the economic troubles that began with the 1929 stock market crash. To accomplish these objectives, President Herbert Hoover called a special session of the 71st Congress to enact the appropriate legislation. The extension beyond the original moderate goals began in the House Ways and Means Committee, whose members gave a large number of industrial products additional protection; more were added on the House floor. The same thing happened in the Senate Finance Committee. By the time the legislation had reached the Senate floor, the process was beyond the control of party leaders. The resulting Smoot–Hawley Tariff adjusted tariffs on over 20,000 items, with an average overall tariff of 53 percent.[39]

In addition to raising tariff levels with Smoot–Hawley, Congress delegated authority to the U.S. Tariff Commission to adjust tariffs. The result of the dispute over how much authority to give the Tariff Commission and how much discretion to give to the president in dealing with the commission's recommendations was an arrangement by which the Tariff Commission investigated the differences in the production costs on all items specified in the tariff, leaving to the president the option of declaring a new duty based on these findings.[40]

E. E. Schattschneider attributed this surprising outcome to the excessive influence of interest groups representing producer interests. Through a process of "reciprocal noninterference," or logrolling, members of both congressional chambers sought protection for industries they favored; policy was the outcome of competition among organized interests with government as a passive broker. Congressional structure and procedures permitted interest groups to shape the Smoot–Hawley Tariff. Logrolling, which is a function of the individual member's needs to satisfy his or her constituents, allowed legislators to add one tariff after another to the legislation as each legislator sought to shore up his or her popularity. Motivated by self-interest—mainly, getting reelected—members of Congress were open to interest-group pressure as they wrote legislation in a congressional structure designed to accommodate this behavior. Interest, political pressure, and institutional structure combined to produce a policy decidely not in the public interest. Schattschneider's work set the tone for subsequent analyses of interest groups, focusing on their strategies, internal operations, and representative quality.[41]

Schattschneider ended his analysis with the discomforting conclusion that narrow economic interests are more powerful than the general interest. The law Congress eventually passed and Hoover signed had little to do with a particular view of the national economic interest and more to do with the particular concerns of business interest groups and an all-too-responsive Congress.[42] Business groups have a large hand in creating policies whose connection to the greater interest is not readily apparent, and business groups certainly outweigh the influence exerted by the general public.[43] Schattschneider summarizes his conclusion starkly:

Capitalism is a power relation including dominant and subordinate elements in which some interests are the vassals of others. Pressure politics expresses economic authority as well as interest. In the business world opinions are communicated from the higher levels to the lower, but rarely in the other direction. Influence is the possession of those who have established their supremacy in the invisible empires outside of what is ordinarily known as government. From this point of view the function of pressure politics is to reconcile formal political democracy and economic autocracy. If the overlords of business are not masters of the state, they seem at least to negotiate with it as equals.[44]

The Smoot–Hawley Tariff did not cause the Great Depression, but it did add to the already downward spiral of the global economy. Between 1929 and 1933, world trade declined approximately 70 percent in volume and 35 percent in dollars, while American exports declined from $5.2 billion to $1.4 billion, and imports dropped from $4.4 billion to $1.4 billion.[45]

Reciprocal Trade: 1934–1962

The Reciprocal Trade Agreements Act of 1934

The economic collapse with which the Smoot–Hawley Tariff had become identified precipitated a dramatic change in American trade policy. Faced with a shrinking global economy and buoyed by the leadership of Secretary of State Cordell Hull, Congress sought to change the fundamental thrust of American trade policy. A remarkably short document (a three-page amendment to the 1930 law, in fact), the Reciprocal Trade Agreements Act of 1934 (RTAA) turned over major responsibility for making trade policy from Congress to the president. The RTAA, passed by a new Democratic congressional majority over Republican opposition, also shifted the authority to modify duties and import restrictions from the Tariff Commission to the president. This move allowed the president to sidestep the slow-moving Tariff Commission and enter into reciprocal trade agreements with other nations by executive proclamation. Additionally, Congress gave the president discretion to enter into commercial agreements and change tariff rates without congressional approval, tasks that had been under congressional prerogative.[46]

Although Congress gave the president unprecedented authority over trade policy with the RTAA, it did not relinguish trade policy-making responsibility completely. The president could reduce tariffs by as much as 50 percent, but the executive's authority to do so had to be renewed every three years. Moreover, Congress did not leave the president free of the influence of various interested parties. It built in procedures that required public hearings and disclosure before rate changes and new agreements, and it required the president to consult the Tariff Commission and other federal agencies before acting.[47] Finally, the RTAA left intact antidumping, countervailing duties, and unfair trade practices provisions.[48]

The RTAA reflects the consistent partisan division that had characterized trade policy since the immediate post–Civil War period.[49] It also demonstrates the conflict among domestic economic interests within the United States. Internationalists—for example, American banks that wanted to engage in business abroad—eventually won the day only after the Great Depression discredited sectors more inclined toward economic nationalism.[50] The reluctance to take the nation into an unfettered internationalist direction is reflected in the institutional relationship between Congress and the presidency established by the RTAA. Whereas the executive pressed for trade liberalization with the partial approval of Congress, there was less than widespread agreement among economic sectors within the United States on its advantages. It also ushered in the congressional practice of delegating trade policy authority to the executive based on the rationale that the executive was in a better position to resist protectionist pressures than members of Congress were. This became a central theme in the institutional relationship in trade policy making for the next fifty years.

The institutional realignment gave the executive considerably more control over trade policy than it had previously, but protectionist interests still had ample access to the process through, for example, the required-hearings process mentioned above. The trade liberalization resulting from the RTAA was also tempered by the Agriculture Adjustment Act (AAA), which gave farmers relief from the consequences of low-priced imports. Thus, while the shift of trade policy authority to the executive corresponded to achieving the goal of trade liberalization so tirelessly pursued by Cordell Hull, the institutional rearrangement was not a wholesale transformation of American trade policy machinery. Congress set limits on the executive, and interests that would be hurt by trade liberalization successfully won compensation.[51]

Effects of the RTAA: 1934–1945

The RTAA required Congress to renew the president's trade policy negotiating authority every three years, which Congress did four times until the end of World War II. Congress granted similar authority seven more times after the war, until the early 1960s. Following the guidelines set down by the RTAA, the president negotiated twenty reciprocal agreements by the beginning of World War II, reducing the average tariff to 35 percent, down from the 52 percent set by the Smoot–Hawley Tariff.[52]

The eleven-year period following enactment of the RTAA established the institutional pattern initiated by the law. Congress continued to delegate authority to the executive to negotiate trade agreements, reflecting congressional fears that the characteristics of Congress and the constant electoral pressure to respond to constituent and interest-group demands would not permit members of Congress to resist protectionism.[53] Cognizant of the hazards of unfettered protectionism as exemplified in the Smoot–Hawley Tariff, Democrats in Congress wanted to turn over trade policy authority to the executive, which, they believed, could resist protectionist pressure and negotiate lower tariffs with foreign countries. It is important to note that, as in 1934, Congress did not totally delegate authority to the executive on trade policy. Congress attached strings to the president, not the least of which were limiting how much tariffs could be lowered and requiring renewal of executive trade negotiating authority every three years. The lessons learned during this period led to a more ambitious, internationalist American trade policy immediately following World War II.

Postwar Trade and the General Agreement on Tariffs and Trade

The United States assumed a new global leadership role in the aftermath of the Second World War. With Europe and Japan decimated, the U.S. economy was easily the world's economic powerhouse. In addition to vast economic advantage, the United States enjoyed military superiority (by virtue of a monopoly on nuclear weapons) and a position of political leadership. Guided by an internationalist executive with the acquiescence of a reluctant Congress, the United States led the world in developing the modern trade system with its continuing efforts to liberalize trade. The American experience with the reciprocal trade agreements led some policy makers to believe that similar positive results could be achieved in a multilateral framework. In addition to a domestic political mood that would accommodate a more internationalist approach to trade policy, the United States and Britain found the possibility of a multilateral trade organization desirable for the purpose of avoiding the economic chaos of the 1930s. This is not to say, however, that supporters of economic nationalism in the United States were not strong or influential; the American internationalist push for a multilateral agreement on trade was limited by suspicion of international organization, on one hand, and a desire to protect American industries on the other.[54]

In the spirit of the Bretton Woods talks, which initiated the formation of the International Monetary Fund (IMF) and the World Bank, the United States and other nations tried several times in 1947 and 1948 to establish an international organization for trade. The United States led the way in writing the charter of the proposed international organization,[55] but the proposed International Trade Organization (ITO) never became a reality largely because of American unwillingness to endorse it.[56] The General Agreement on Tariffs and Trade (GATT), a less ambitious form of international cooperation, grew out of the talks over the establishment of the ITO.

The impetus to establish an organization like the ITO came from the executive, not the Congress. Republican congressional majorities were disinclined to approve of American commitment to the ITO with its built-in supranational authority. Although the Republican legislators had moved some considerable distance from their historic isolationist position,[57] they were not yet full-fledged internationalists in the Wilsonian mold. With the Republican Party firmly in opposition, congressional resistance was sufficient to block American entrance into the ITO. The executive branch submitted the ITO charter to Congress in April 1949 for approval. A year later, the House Foreign Affairs Committee held hearings on the proposal. That was as far as it got in the legislative labyrinth; the committee chose not to report it to the full House. The executive branch gave up on the issue, choosing not to resubmit the charter to Congress at a later date.[58] Without American support, which was critical in the effort to establish the ITO, the proposed international organization was doomed.

At the 1947 Geneva meeting on the formation of the ITO, a parallel meeting took place among twenty-three countries, at the behest of the United States, to reduce tariffs in the short term. The tariff-cutting exercise's results were embodied in the GATT, which was intended to be incorporated in the trade chapter of the ITO. These negotiations were completed in August of 1947, and the GATT went into effect on 1 January 1948. Thus, the founders of the GATT did not intend it to be a permanent, independent international mechanism through which trade agreements could be devised. When, in effect, it became just that, its limited original purpose left certain gaps in the GATT's structure.[59]

The failure of the ITO to obtain ratification from the United States and its subsequent demise left the GATT standing alone as an international vehicle through which trade policy could be negotiated. Even this more modest multilateral effort met with resistance in Congress. Although Congress had given the president authority to negotiate trade agreements, it had not given the executive the authority to join an international organization, like the GATT originally was. So the GATT charter was rewritten so that it was not formally a supranational organization with autonomy extending beyond its member countries. The "contracting parties" to the revised GATT—that is, the countries that wished to enter into it—became the supreme authority, thus removing official authority from the supranational organization.[60] Moreover, Congress never formally approved American participation in the GATT. Congress had delegated authority to the president to negotiate bilateral reciprocal trade agreements, but owing to lingering protectionist views, it was unwilling to ratify the GATT as a formal treaty; indeed, cognizant of the congressional mood, President Truman did not even submit the GATT for ratification. This left the GATT inferior to U.S. domestic laws, which in practice has meant essentially that the United States could disregard GATT rules without violating domestic laws.[61]

In the story of the ITO and the GATT, partisan differences remained significant, though not nearly as clearly defined as they had prior to the Second World War. A Republican-controlled Congress forced modification of the GATT because it had not and would not delegate to the president the authority to commit the United State to an international organization with supranational authority, but a Democratic-controlled Congress also refused even to give serious consideration to the ITO. Thus, the historic partisan split did not play a role in the congressional refusal to join the ITO. Internationalism had not fully captured Americans of any political stripe, as economic nationalism and suspicion of international organizations prevented the United States from joining the new trade entity.

The ITO and GATT episodes suggest the limits of congressional willingness to delegate trade policy authority to the executive. Although accepting the principle of trade liberalization as generally beneficial, and facing an inevitable leading role for the United States in global affairs, Congress was unwilling to relinquish too much of its constitutional authority over trade policy. The pattern of congressional delegation to the executive begun with the RTAA had not been derailed, certainly, but it had clearly found limits.

Finally, perhaps hearing from producer interest groups and worrying about electoral repercussions for joining the ITO, members of Congress hesitated. It was possible to take a half step by joining the GATT and by diminishing its authority, at least formally. But the American public, in the view of legislators, was not ready for this next step into the international community.

The 1950s: More of the Same

Throughout the 1950s, Congress continued to delegate authority to the president to negotiate tariffs. Although tariff reduction remained the central goal of this delegation, Congress also authorized the president to raise tariffs by as much as 50 percent, this in partial response to protectionist pressures. Additionally, Congress guarded its constitutional prerogative over trade policy, setting limits on the president with each renewal of tariff adjustment authority. Thus, the institutional pattern between Congress and the president established by the RTAA continued through the 1950s; although Congress continued to delegate authority to the executive, it did so only with strings attached. Finally the partisan division on trade policy was showing signs of breaking down. Democrats, responding to the protectionist demands of some large, newly import-affected industries, sided with Republicans in Congress to set limits on trade liberalization.[62]

Trade Expansion: 1962–1988

From the end of the Second World War through the 1950s, the American economy had been the strongest in the world by a wide margin. However, by the time John F. Kennedy moved into the White House, the reemerging economies of Japan and Europe began to challenge the dominance of American firms in the international market. The economic challenges presented by Japan and Europe did not subside over the next three decades; indeed, as Japanese and European firms became more competitive globally, including the American market, U.S. firms began to request assistance from the national government, mainly in the form of protection. Beginning with heavy industries in the 1960s and 1970s, joined by industrial labor unions in the 1970s, and high-technology electronics in the 1980s, Congress and the president have been the target of a constant stream of requests for help in dealing with foreign competition. This renewed protectionist pressure, of course, has had a profound effect on the development of American trade policy during this period.

In addition to resurgent protectionist pressure, the substance of trade policy was changing in another significant way. With U.S. tariffs reduced significantly as a result of the process begun by the RTAA of 1934, lowering American tariffs as a means of reducing other countries' tariffs (the basic logic of reciprocity) had become less pressing. In effect, tariffs were comparatively low by the 1960s, and there was not much dramatic cutting left to be done. In connection with this, and perhaps as a result of it, trade policy turned to other issues.

The new focus of American trade policy included foreign countries' trade practices, the competitiveness of foreign-based firms in the American market, compliance with international trade laws (mainly the provisions of the GATT), and perhaps most important, the identification and reduction of nontariff barriers (NTBs) to trade. The policy response to these issues resulted in a dramatic leap in the complexity of American trade policy. Instead of dealing with tariff reductions, the U.S. trade policy apparatus now had to deal with such matters as government subsidies of foreign-based firms, predatory pricing in the American market (dumping), deliberate exclusion of American-made goods and services from foreign markets, injury incurred by American firms and workers as a result of fairly traded foreign-made products sold in the United States, and more.

The policy response to this range of novel and complex trade problems has been equally novel and complex. For example, since permanent increases in tariffs are unacceptable both on domestic political grounds and according to international law, the United States has resorted to other measures to assist workers adversely affected by foreign competition—so-called trade adjustment assistance (TAA). Other new additions to the American trade policy arsenal since the 1960s include, for example, bilateral sector-specific trade agreements, a maze of provisions in the basic U.S. trade law intended to provide administrative remedies made necessary by both fair and unfair trade practices, and the linking of American trade policy to human rights.

The added complexity of American trade policy has required additional institutional capability. The trade policy apparatus has grown, as has its requirement for technical expertise. As the problems become more complex and impenetrable to nonspecialists, the nature of the debate and the locus of decisions change as well.

The partisan division on trade policy began cracking after the Second World War and had broken down more clearly by the 1960s. No longer was there a clear division between free-trade Democrats and protectionist-leaning Republicans. Major parts of the Democratic constituency had been hurt by imports. Heavy industry and labor unions began to call for protectionist measures. Their Democratic legislators responded, completing the shift from the Democratic Party's historic commitment to tariff reduction and toward government intervention in trade that proved injurious to party constituents. At the same time, mainstream Republicans took up the ideological mantle of laissez-faire, eschewing government involvement in the economy, including bald protectionism. But even with the apparent shift in positions, partisan conflict did not resume on a clear divide, with Democrats and Republicans trading places. Instead, trade policy since the 1960s has increasingly cut across party lines.[63] For example, congressional Democrats have advocated protection of some manufacturing industries. Meanwhile, the isolationist wing of the Republican Party has found a leader in Patrick Buchanan, who advocates an America-first approach to trade policy, which in practice means opposition to trade liberalization. Finally, the 1994 congressional vote to approve the North American Free Trade Agreement (NAFTA) saw Democrats voting with Republicans to support the agreement.

Transition and Complexity: Trade Policy from 1962 to 1988

Congress has enacted only five major pieces of trade legislation over the recent three decades: one each in 1962, 1974, 1979, 1984, and 1988. These laws, particularly since 1974, deal primarily with nontariff issues; permanent adjustment of tariffs as trade policy basically ended with the 1962 Trade Expansion Act. The central thrust of these non-tariff measures was to make it easier for American producers to get relief from injurious import competition. These measures addressed such issues as unfair trade practices (for example, dumping and subsidies), access to foreign markets (mainly Japan's), and fairly traded imports that damaged American producers (for example, textiles).

The Trade Expansion Act of 1962

The 1962 act marked a departure from the legislative pattern established by the RTAA of 1934. John Kennedy, in requesting unprecedented negotiating authority from Congress, intended to make dramatic tariff cuts in all tariffs and even to eliminate some with the European Economic Community (EEC) altogether. A Democratic-controlled Congress handed this authority over to the president.[64] The new law went beyond congressional delegation of authority to the president to negotiate reciprocal trade agreements. It was the first law that authorized the president to engage in multilateral trade negotiations—namely, through the GATT. Congressional approval did not come without a concession by the administration to the textile industry; Kennedy "negotiated a five-year agreement to limit textile imports to about six percent of the domestic market."[65]

In addition, the 1962 act modified several key provisions of the basic U.S. trade law. Section 252 of the Trade Expansion Act gave the president the authority to retaliate against nations engaging in unfair trade practices in agriculture. This provision of the law was the predecessor to Section 301, enacted in the 1974 legislation, that gave the executive similar authority over a wider range of goods.

To give itself a formal voice in trade policy decisions in the executive branch, Congress also created the Office of the Special Trade Representative (STR) in this law. A creature of Congress, the STR would become a conduit of congressional and interest-group pressure on the executive, beginning a process of drawing trade policy authority away from the State Department, which was considered by many legislators as making trade issues too easily a distant second to broader foreign policy objectives.[66]

Finally, the 1962 act marked a change from earlier legislation in that it was a departure from the premise that the only way to assist domestic industries damaged by imports was to grant some sort of relief. The 1962 law replaced this with the understanding that some industries will inevitably be hurt by changes in trade patterns and the appropriate way to assist them was to provide trade adjustment assistance.[67]

The 1970s–1990s: Response to Global Economic Pressure

Beginning in the 1970s, the United States began to feel the heat of increased competition from foreign producers. Auto and steel manufacturers in Japan and Europe primarily gained a growing presence in the American domestic market, following the successful footsteps of foreign consumer electronics producers. The American economy was experiencing significant problems that were proving immune to traditional macroeconomic solutions. Paying for the Vietnam War and Great Society programs had put the federal budget in the red, and dramatic increases in oil prices caused by the successful cartelization of the industry by the Organization of Petroleum Exporting Countries (OPEC) helped push the U.S. economy into recession. At the same time, inflation was running rampant and was accompanied by high unemployment. In the end, tough economic measures—such as a tight money policy instituted by the Federal Reserve—wrung inflation out of the economy, but there was considerable government activity prior to that intended to address various economic problems.

Policy makers sought to use trade policy to respond to some of these economic woes. These efforts reflected the growing complexity and scope of trade policy. Where tariffs once were the main concern of trade negotiations, a wide array of NTBs took center stage. Reducing tariffs is a fairly straightforward exercise; reducing NTBs, like domestic regulations, turned out to be far more difficult. Where the United States had enjoyed hegemonic status since the end of the Second World War, it now faced economic challenges from countries that had recovered from the devastation of war, in no small part, of course, as a result of U.S. policies like the Marshall Plan and enduring support of trade liberalization through the GATT.[68] The United States addressed these developments with different policy instruments, not necessarily consistent with one another.

Multilateral Negotiations

The United States participated in several rounds of GATT talks in the 1970s and 1980s. These negotiations led the GATT into more complex trade issues, like NTBs, intellectual property protection, services, and foreign investment. The expanded agenda reflects the widening concerns connected to international trade, and it is reasonable to expect further expansion into such areas as the linkage between international trade and the environment. In these talks, the United States sought to incorporate into multilateral accords matters that were increasingly important to the American economy. Protecting intellectual property, for instance, is crucial to the success of industries like software and entertainment in foreign markets. Service industries have become more important in the American economy, and American producers wish to expand to foreign markets. Doing so would be easier, of course, with multilateral agreement on how to manage trade in an area where the old rules established for manufacturing may not apply.

Major Trade Legislation

Congress and the president enacted several major trade bills in the 1970s and 1980s. These bills attempted to draw together a growing list of trade-related issues, instituted congressional–presidential interaction on trade policy, and put teeth into American efforts to eliminate unfair trade practices. U.S. trade law incorporated measures to deal with NTBs and strengthened trade law provisions that aimed at foreign private and public activities deemed to be unfair—to name a couple of especially controversial ones, dumping and maintenance of closed markets. The 1974 trade bill instituted a fast-track procedure as the norm for congressional–presidential interaction on trade. This measure allows Congress its constitutional prerogative over foreign commerce, but with congressional approval it gives the president sweeping negotiating authority. Taking all of this into consideration, what is most striking about the trend in major trade legislation is the sheer volume of issues now considered connected to trade policy. This may be the product of the legislative process, or it may be more a consequence of the increasing complexity of foreign commercial policy. As such, these bills tell the story of how the American political system has responded to the onslaught of globalization.

Free-trade Agreements

Free-trade agreements involving several countries fall short of the global multilateral idea of trade liberalization, but they do establish freer trade within a limited region. Ideally, free-trade agreements allow for the unfettered trade of goods and services across national borders. Citing immediate economic and political benefits, and perhaps long-term ones as well,[69] the United States has entered three such agreements: with Israel, with Canada, and extending that agreement, with Canada and Mexico to form the North American Free Trade Agreement. Aside from the immediate economic benefits free-trade agreements produce, the United States has also garnered political benefits in terms of foreign policy gains.[70] Although initiated by the executive, Congress retains final approval authority over such agreements; for example, in the case of NAFTA, Congress approved the agreement on a fast-track basis. The agreements involved intense political haggling, pitting economic interests against one another and frequently crossing party lines. The nonpartisan nature of the political battles suggests the declining or, at least, changing significance of party with respect to trade policy.

Since congressional approval of NAFTA in 1993, the United States has not taken the initiative with respect to similar accords with other countries or with respect to the expansion of NAFTA to Chile, the nation most likely to be the next member. Domestic political changes—namely, the Clinton administration's preoccupation with other matters and a Republican-controlled Congress's unwillingness to hand the Democratic chief executive a political victory—have thwarted any effective efforts to expand the idea of regional free-trade agreements. And an economic crisis in Asia squelched any ideas the Clinton administration might have had about developing further the nascent

Asia-Pacific Economic Cooperation (APEC) forum. Nonetheless, the idea remains in play among policy makers and may reemerge when the international and domestic political conditions are right.

Administrative Relief and Bilateral Agreements

In recent years, the United States has increasingly turned to bilateral and sometimes unilateral trade strategies to address the problems created for American industries by competitive imports and to expand foreign markets for American-made goods and services. While encompassing a considerable range of activities, these strategies share one thing in common: They do not involve multilateral negotiations under GATT auspices. Responding to protectionist pressures, but unable to engage in outright protectionism (for example, raising tariffs), American officials use these policies to placate producer interests. This category of trade strategies, defined more in terms of what they are not than what they are, includes use of sections of the U.S. trade law intended to assist import-damaged industries, bilateral trade regulating agreements, sectoral agreements, and the creation of free-trade zones.

The use of these instruments is controversial and complex. Because they circumvent or ignore altogether a multilateral forum for trade negotiations, foreign government officials may view them as antithetical to the spirit of global trade liberalization. Each strategy involves a narrowly focused, complex set of political dynamics, quite different from each other and from the politics associated with creating and revising the basic U.S. trade law. The interaction between Congress and the president is more intricate in dealing with these matters than in negotiating the basic U.S. trade law. The goals of each use of these strategies need to be sharply defined, and success is uncertain. Moreover, they have become connected to foreign policy in subtle and not-so-subtle ways. Thus, the uncertainty of these strategies is matched by the stakes they raise. Finally, the ability of the United States to engage in these kinds of strategies, outside the established multilateral GATT framework, reflects the power of producer interests domestically and the political power of the United States internationally.

These bilateral trade strategies are relatively recent developments in American trade policy history. They suggest a two-front approach to trade by American policy makers. On one hand, the United States

continues to pursue multilateral agreements and the institutionaliza-
tion of a multilateral forum through which global trade can be regu-
lated. Note, for example, the recent American support for the GATT
successor, the World Trade Organization (WTO). On the other hand,
American policy makers accommodate producer demands for import
relief through various bilateral agreements.

Congress has incorporated a number of procedures through which
import-affected industries can seek administrative relief. These remedies involve varying degrees of administrative discretion, and the
extent to which the executive branch has been willing to grant relief
has been at the root of conflict over the use of these provisions of the
U.S. trade law. In general, seeking administrative relief from imports
has become popular among American producers since the 1950s, the
point at which some U.S. industries began to feel the pinch from
foreign competition.[71]

Sections 201 and 301 of the U.S. trade law empower the federal
government to take measures to relieve import-induced damaged to
American industry. Section 201, which descended from the peril point
provisions in earlier versions of the trade law, allows American firms
to ask for import relief if they are injured by imports. Section 201 does
not require the import to be unfairly traded; it merely states that if it
damages U.S.-produced goods, then the U.S. producer can petition for
relief.[72] Section 201 relief has never been easy to get. Most claims pass
the first step of the process, a United States International Trade
Commission (USITC) analysis showing that the industry has in fact
been damaged by imports, but fail the second step, the granting of
some kind of relief. Section 201 has been used less and less in recent
years because American firms seeking import relief find the hurdles
difficult to clear and choose instead to get relief using the more
controversial Section 301.[73]

Section 301 has been used to address activities of foreign governments and corporations that damage American exports. Such practices
include, for example, violation of trade agreements and unreasonable
or discriminatory practices that limit commerce. These general restrictions allow for broad interpretations of "unreasonable" and "discriminatory." Complaints brought under Section 301 can be initiated by
American firms or the U.S. government itself. Section 301 is considerably more flexible than other administrative remedies, allowing the
president and the United States Trade Representative (USTR) to ad-

dress the issue of opening foreign markets to American products by means of reciprocity.[74]

In addition to these provisions, Congress has created a number of means by which industries may address unfair trade practices on the part of foreign companies and countries. Antidumping provisions, countervailing duties, and Section 337 provisions, which usually deal with infringement of intellectual property rights, allow individual companies to seek government remedies for these unfair practices.[75] In addition to escape clause relief provided by these measures, trade adjustment assistance can be used to ameliorate some of the damage done by an influx of imports. (TAA is essentially a transfer payment given to workers who lose their jobs because of foreign competition.[76]) The politics of resorting to these provisions of the U.S. trade law to address trade problems are complex and subtle, domestically initiated but involving foreign policy considerations as well.[77]

Bilateral negotiations, moreover, are frequently related to the use of or the threat of using, administrative trade remedies—such as Section 301 and Special 301.[78] Foreign governments find negotiations more attractive than trade sanctions. The United States has negotiated numerous trade deals like this with different countries for a considerable range of products. These efforts are intended to address specific trade problems, which usually involve opening foreign markets to American exports primarily, along with intellectual property protection and dumping of foreign products in the American market.

Bilateral negotiations can be limited to a single sector, or they can cover more generic problems. In both cases, they usually address some alleged unfair trade practice engaged in by foreign governments or companies. Such activities can be relevant to any number of industries. For example, inadequate intellectual property protection affects many industries. Other objectional behavior may deal only with one industry—automobiles, insurance, air travel, and so on.

Most international trade analysts agree that a multilateral approach is the shortest path to global free trade.[79] Using the negotiating mechanism embodied in the GATT and now the WTO has resulted in reduced tariffs and the lowering of NTBs. The WTO adds a new dimension to this international trade regime by providing a dispute resolution mechanism.

Bilateral agreements, on the other hand, are limited to two countries and do little good for trade beyond them. This is especially true with respect to sectoral agreements. While it could be argued that bilateral free-trade agreements—for example, establishing a free-trade zone between two countries, as in the U.S.–Canada Free Trade Agreement (FTA)—can lead to trade liberalization, the same argument is more difficult to make for sector-specific pacts. General free-trade agreements between two countries affect most, if not all, of each economy.[80] The benefits are not limited to a specific sector. Moreover, a bilateral free-trade agreement can be expanded to include more countries; the U.S.–Canada FTA set the stage for the creation of NAFTA, which included Mexico and had been intended to include Chile as well. More countries benefit as larger chunks of the global economy are brought under a free-trade umbrella.

Sectoral agreements do not promise such expansion. Proponents, however, argue that such agreements are desirable for two reasons. First, they may in fact lead to trade expansion, though by a completely different route than the one taken by bilateral free-trade agreements. Sectoral agreements frequently include market-opening provisions as a primary goal or at least a secondary one, as the 1986 Semiconductor Trade Arrangement (STA) did. If the agreement successfully causes a country to make its domestic market more open to foreign producers, then it is arguably furthering the cause of trade liberalization, albeit one country at a time. Indeed, this logic seems to underlie one of the major objectives of the Clinton administration's trade policy. The United States is engaged in numerous bilateral negotiations, both generic and sector-specific, which are aimed at opening foreign markets to American exports, thereby increasing international trade. USTR Charlene Barshefsky has emphasized the importance of bilateral negotiations in the Clinton trade policy, as has the president himself.[81]

Second, in the case of high-technology industries, the classical rules of comparative advantage may not apply. Proponents of sectoral agreements in high-technology industries argue that managed trade is the better choice over pure free trade. The logic is that governments can create comparative advantage in high-technology industries; a nation's natural attributes determine comparative advantage in such industries as agriculture and manufacturing, but high-technology industries can be located anywhere. If this is the case, then it follows that there is a legitimate, even required, role for government, assuming that government exists to benefit the public. Thus, public policy can help to create comparative advantage for high-technology industries.[82] This rationale for bilateral, sectoral agreements does not attempt to fit this strategy into trade liberalization. It argues instead that the logic of multilateral free trade based on the classical concept of comparative advantage simply does not apply to high-technology industries.

Trade agreements can be based on rules or results. The GATT, for example, is a multilateral pact based on rules; adherence to the pre-scribed rules for engaging in international commerce is the test of whether or not a country is in compliance with the international accord. Similarly, NAFTA is rule-based; the signatories agreed to trade with one another according to a set of rules and procedures. In neither case is the success of the agreement or the compliance of the signatories determined by the volume of trade or by the share a country's firms have of any country's domestic market. The goal here is to establish equitable rules by which everyone must live. In the ideal case, with the (more-or-less) level playing field established, firms win and lose de-pending on their competitiveness. Governments establish an appropri-ate environment in which markets can work.

Results-oriented agreements follow a different logic. Such a deal's success and the signatories' compliance is determined by the extent to which producers from one country make inroads into the domestic markets of the other. If the targeted market share is not reached, then the agreement is a failure. If the government of the country whose domestic market is under scrutiny does not take actions sufficient to reach the target, then the country has violated the accord. Sometimes viewed as having the subtlety of a crowbar, results-oriented agreements seek a specific market outcome. The STA is precisely such an agree-ment, with its unofficial target of 20 percent of the Japanese semicon-ductor market going to foreign producers, mainly from the United States. In its reverse form, the automobile Voluntary Export Restraint (VER) had a target as well; the Japanese could export a certain number of cars to the United States. In both cases, market share was the measure of success and compliance.

Free-trade proponents usually fly into fury in opposition to results-oriented deals. They argue that the proper role of government is to establish fair rules and procedures to which all participants must adhere. The market should then be able to decide who wins and who loses. Results-oriented trade agreements let governments make that determination, in effect choosing winners and losers. Analogous to domestic industrial policy, such an approach to economic well-being is bound to fail according to those who place their faith in market forces, both domestically and internationally.

Proponents of results-oriented agreements counter this claim by arguing that the GATT has not removed obstacles to entering the Japanese market. As a result, American firms are at a disadvantage in Japan, where they must negotiate numerous roadblocks to market entry. This, according to defenders of results-oriented agreements, is inconsistent with the spirit of trade liberalization. Opening the Japanese market, even when using a clumsy method, means that the flow of goods and services across national borders increases, which is precisely the goal of trade liberalization. In any event, once markets are opened by government intervention, the awkward use of targets can be put aside.

Proponents of bilateral, sectoral, results-oriented agreements state their claims in terms of fair trade, a necessary corollary of free trade in the context of high-technology industries and the peculiar role of government in them. Defending these deals for traditional manufacturing industries is another story. It is difficult to claim, for example, that manufacturing automobiles is a cutting-edge enterprise in which the classical notion of comparative advantage does not apply. Those who think the Japanese automobile VER was a good idea make a simpler argument. The American automobile industry was suffering from the effects of Japanese competition. Regardless of how the Big Three ended up in this unfortunate position, the fact of the matter was that they needed help if they were to survive. The VER, then, was straightforward, unapologetic protectionism. It was accompanied by little pretense about industrial recovery, fair trade, or a multilateral international trade regime.

In sum, bilateral, sectoral, results-oriented trade agreements are suspect among international trade analysts. Setting aside protectionist motives and outcomes, the claim that these agreements lead to trade liberalization is open to heated debate.

Politics

Changes in international and domestic politics had clear effects on U.S. trade policy from the 1970s to the 1990s. By the 1970s, the United States was no longer the clearly dominant nation on the globe; other countries' economies had developed quickly and had closed the gap with the American economy. Foreign-made products challenged American manufacturers in the domestic markets; imported cars, stereos, steel, and semiconductors had dented American producers' dominance of their home market. The economic turbulence set policy makers on edge as they groped for ways to deal with unprecedented problems.

In spite of these challenges, the United States maintained its leadership role with respect to trade liberalization, but it opened up avenues to American producers to some form of protection. By the 1990s, U.S. commitment to multilateralism, while still strong, was not without serious detractors. The Clinton administration fought hard for free-trade victories: NAFTA in 1993 and acceptance of the results of the Uruguay Round of GATT negotiations in 1994. Challenges to free trade came from both the left and the right. Managed trade—the use of government to address trade problems and enhance the national interest by giving American producers a level playing field—gained advocates from among moderate liberals. While supporting free trade as an end, managed traders argue that simple notions of free trade make little sense in a world of complex government intervention in the international and national economies. A little farther to the political left, unions call for protection of some industries; loss of American jobs, from their perspective, is too high a price to pay for the ostensible advantages that come with free trade. Interestingly enough, American business joined these positions, advocating some form of government intervention to assist them in foreign markets as well as the domestic one. From the political right, populist orators like Patrick Buchanan have tried to arouse nationalist passion, contending that free trade by means of multilateral negotiations sacrificed American jobs and, worse, national sovereignty.

In this political context, it is hardly surprising that the traditionally free-trade executive is having trouble advancing the cause. This was most starkly demonstrated in Congress's unwillingness in 1997 to grant President Clinton fast-track negotiating authority. Although this did not stop administration efforts entirely, it certainly applied the brakes to U.S. efforts to pursue free trade. Whether Congress's collective cold feet on trade liberalization is more a matter of short-term political maneuvering or a signal that the United States is less willing to pursue free trade remains to be seen.

Conclusion

Contemporary American trade policy is immeasurably more complex than it was throughout the nineteenth century and into the twentieth. Early trade policy involved setting tariff levels primarily to raise revenue to operate the government and to protect domestic producers from foreign competition. As the American economy developed and as the United States became more integrated into global affairs, political leaders found reciprocity to be a good instrument for opening foreign markets to American products. The content of trade policy changed dramatically in the post–World War II era. As the unquestionable world economic leader, the United States took the lead in creating international organizations for regulating and promoting international trade. Comfortable in its dominant position, the United States continued to advocate reduction of tariffs and trade liberalization. By the 1970s, challenges to American economic dominance initiated a process of rethinking American trade policy that continues through the 1990s. While still advocating trade liberalization in principle, the United States has taken action to protect its industries against fierce foreign competition and to open foreign markets to American-made goods and services.

In the next five chapters, I examine these key issues in relation to the major components of U.S. trade policy. This discussion begins with a review of the current trade policy debate. In many ways, this is a contemporary version of the original disagreement between Jefferson and Hamilton on the proper role of the national government in the economy. The next chapter reconsiders this central question in light of three approaches to trade policy: free trade, managed trade, and protectionism.

Endnotes

1. See John H. Makin and Norman J. Ornstein, *Debt and Taxes: How America Got into Its Budget Mess and What to Do about It* (New York: Times Books, 1994), 35–39.
2. For the general argument, see Alexander Hamilton, *Report on the Subject of Manufactures,* vol. 10 of *The Papers of Alexander Hamilton* (New York: Columbia Univ. Press, 1966), 230–340. See also Douglas A. Irwin, *Against*

the Tide: An Intellectual History of Free Trade (Princeton, N.J.: Princeton Univ. Press, 1996), chap. 8.

3. Irwin, *Against the Tide,* chap. 2.

4. Richard Lehne, *Industry and Politics: United States in Comparative Perspective* (Englewood Cliffs, N.J.: Prentice Hall, 1993), 9–10.

5. Susan C. Schwab, *Trade-Offs: Negotiating the Omnibus Trade and Competitiveness Act* (Boston, Mass.: Harvard Business School Press, 1994), 13.

6. Ibid., 16.

7. F. W. Taussig, *The Tariff History of the United States,* 8th ed. (New York: Putnam, 1931), 1–7, 25–59, 63, 68.

8. Ibid., 63–64.

9. Schwab, *Trade-Offs,* 16–17.

10. Taussig, *The Tariff History of the United States,* 63–64.

11. Ibid., 109. Interestingly, after 1840, the young or "infant" industries justification for tariffs was replaced by the argument "that American labor should be protected from competition of less highly paid foreign labor." Ibid., 65.

12. Judith Goldstein, *Ideas, Interests, and American Trade Policy* (Ithaca, N.Y.: Cornell Univ. Press, 1993), 78–79.

13. Taussig, *The Tariff History of the United States,* 155.

14. James W. Lindeen, *Governing America's Economy* (Englewood Cliffs, N.J.: Prentice Hall, 1994), 43–44.

15. Ibid., 45–46.

16. Tom E. Terrill, *The Tariff, Politics, and American Foreign Policy: 1874–1901* (Westport, Conn.: Greenwood, 1973), 7, 32.

17. Sharyn O'Halloran, *Politics, Process, and American Trade Policy* (Ann Arbor, Mich.: Univ. of Michigan Press, 1994), 51–52.

18. David A. Lake, "The State and American Trade Strategy in the Pre-hegemonic Era," in G. John Ikenberry, David A. Lake, and Michael Mastanduno, eds., *The State and American Foreign Economic Policy* (Ithaca, N.Y.: Cornell Univ. Press, 1988), 40–56.

19. Ibid., 30, 33–58.

20. Ibid., 68–89.

21. David A. Lake, *Power, Protection, and Free Trade: International Sources of U.S. Commercial Strategy, 1887–1939* (Ithaca, N.Y.: Cornell Univ. Press, 1988), 91–118.

22. Goldstein, *Ideas,* 93–94.

23. Lake, "The State and American Trade Strategy in the Pre-hegemonic Era," 42.

24. Ibid.

25. Ibid.

26. Schwab, *Trade-Offs,* 17–18.

27. Terrill, *The Tariff, Politics, and American Foreign Policy,* 210–17.

28. O'Halloran, *Politics, Process, and American Trade Policy,* 79.

29. Ibid.
30. Ibid., 80.
31. Ibid., 81.
32. Ibid.
33. Peter Alexis Gourevitch, "International Trade, Domestic Coalitions, and Liberty: Comparative Responses to the Crisis of 1873–1896," in Jeffrey A. Frieden and David A. Lake, eds., *International Political Economy: Perspectives on Global Power and Wealth,* 3rd ed. (New York: St. Martin's, 1995), 90–109.
34. Stephen D. Krasner, "State Power and the Structure of International Trade," in Frieden and Lake, eds., *International Political Economy,* 3rd ed., 19–31; and David A. Lake, "International Economic Structures and American Foreign Economic Policy, 1887–1934," in Jeffrey Frieden and David A. Lake, eds., *International Political Economy: Perspectives on Global Power and Wealth,* 2nd ed. (New York: St. Martin's, 1991), 120–30.
35. Lake, *Power, Protection, and Free Trade,* 6.
36. Lake, "The State and American Trade Strategy in the Pre-hegemonic Era," 33–58.
37. Schwab, *Trade-Offs,* 19. For a discussion of Wilson's failure to turn America outward as a global leader, see David Fromkin, *In the Time of the Americans: The Generation That Changed America's Role in the World* (New York: Knopf, 1995), 57–292.
38. Schwab, *Trade-Offs,* 19–21; and O'Halloran, *Politics, Process, and American Trade Policy,* 82.
39. Schwab, *Trade-Offs,* 21–22.
40. O'Halloran, *Politics, Process, and American Trade Policy,* 84.
41. E. E. Schattschneider, *Politics, Pressure, and the Tariff* (New York: Prentice Hall, 1935), chaps. 3, 4, and 5.
42. Ibid., 145.
43. Ibid., 283–87.
44. Ibid., 286–87.
45. Schwab, *Trade-Offs,* 23.
46. O'Halloran, *Politics, Process, and American Trade Policy,* 85–86.
47. O'Halloran, *Politics, Process, and American Trade Policy,* 86; and Schwab, *Trade-Offs,* 35.
48. Schwab, *Trade-Offs,* 35.
49. The Democrats were hardly united on the issue, however. Split into four factions, the congressional Democrats eventually followed the lead of Secretary of State Cordell Hull, a Wilsonian internationalist. See Stephan Haggard, "The Institutional Foundations of Hegemony: Explaining the Reciprocal Trade Agreements Act of 1934," *International Organization* 42 (Winter 1988): 96–99.

50. Jeff Frieden, "Sectoral Conflict and U.S. Foreign Economic Policy, 1914–1940," in Ikenberry, Lake, and Mastanduno, eds., *The State and American Foreign Economic Policy, 59–90.*

51. Haggard, "The Institutional Foundations of Hegemony," 100–10, and passim.

52. Patrick Low, *Trading Free: The GATT and U.S. Trade Policy* (New York: The Twentieth Century Fund, 1993), 37.

53. I. M. Destler, *American Trade Politics,* 3rd ed. (Washington, D.C.: Institute for International Economics; and New York: The Twentieth Century Fund, 1995), 11–38.

54. Low, *Trading Free,* 38.

55. Two U.S. government documents—*Proposals for Expansion of World Trade and Employment* (1945), and *Suggested Charter for an International Trade Organization of the United Nations* (1946)—served as the basis for the proposed ITO and GATT. See Goldstein, *Ideas,* 158.

56. For a discussion of specific objections, see Goldstein, *Ideas,* 161.

57. Even Republican Senator Arthur Vandenberg of Michigan, a principal spokesman for isolationalism and against an internationalist foreign policy in the 1930s, acknowledged that the United States had no choice but to take a leading role in the post-World War II world. See Fromkin, *In the Time of the Americans,* 473–74.

58. Low, *Trading Free,* 41.

59. Ibid., 39–40.

60. Ibid., 40.

61. Ibid., 42–50; O'Halloran, *Politics, Process, and American Trade Policy,* 88.

62. O'Halloran, *Politics, Process, and American Trade Policy,* 89–92; and Robert E. Baldwin, *Trade Policy in a Changing World Economy* (Chicago, Ill.: Univ. of Chicago Press, 1988), 26–29.

63. Robert E. Baldwin, *Trade Policy in a Changing World Economy* (Chicago, Ill: Univ. of Chicago Press, 1988), 26–29.

64. O'Halloran, *Politics, Process, and American Trade Policy,* 92–93.

65. Ibid., 94.

66. Low, *Trading Free,* 54–55.

67. O'Halloran, *Politics, Process, and American Trade Policy,* 93.

68. Robert Kuttner, "Managed Trade and Economic Sovereignty," in Robert A. Blecker, ed., *U.S. Trade Policy and Global Growth: New Directions in the International Economy* (Armonk, N.Y.: M. E. Sharpe, 1996), 3–36.

69. There is considerable debate among trade experts whether such trade areas or trade blocs enhance the prospects for global trade liberalization or reduce them. See, for example, Rudiger W. Dornbusch, "Policy Options for Freer Trade: The Case for Bilateralism," in Robert Z. Lawrence and Charles L. Schultze, eds., *An American Trade Strategy: Options for the 1990s* (Washing-

ton, D.C.: Brookings Institution, 1990), 125–28; and Robert Z. Lawrence, "Discussion," in Lawrence and Schultze, eds., *An American Trade Strategy,* 136.

70. Paul Krugman, "The Uncomfortable Truth about NAFTA: It's Foreign Policy, Stupid," *Foreign Affairs* 72 (November/December 1993): 13–19.
71. Destler, *American Trade Politics,* 139–73.
72. Goldstein, *Ideas,* 187–90.
73. Low, *Trading Free,* 78–80.
74. Goldstein, *Ideas,* 195–96; and Low, *Trading Free,* 87.
75. Goldstein, *Ideas,* 197–208.
76. Ibid., 190–94.
77. Chapter 6 analyzes the use of Sections 201, 301, and 337, TAA, antidumping, and countervailing duties.
78. See chapter 6.
79. See, for example, Anne O. Krueger, "Free Trade Is the Best Policy," in Lawrence and Schultze, eds., *An American Trade Strategy,* 68–96; and Jagdish N. Bhagwati, *Protectionism* (Cambridge, Mass.: MIT Press, 1988); and *The World Trading System at Risk* (Princeton, N.J.: Princeton Univ. Press, 1991).
80. Some industries may be excluded from the pact or given exemptions. For example, agriculture remained a special case in the U.S.–Canada Free Trade Agreement.
81. William Jefferson Clinton, letter of transmittal, United States Trade Representative, *Study on the Operation and Effects of the North American Free Trade Agreement* (Washington, D.C.: Office of the United States Trade Representative, 1997).
82. Laura D'Andrea Tyson makes this point in *Who's Bashing Whom? Trade Conflict in High-Technology Industries* (Washington, D.C.: Institute for International Economics, 1992), chap. 2.

3

The Trade Debate and the Domestic
Policy Process

For years, scholars have studied trade in terms of domestic policy and
politics. Their analyses can be roughly grouped into two categories:
state-centered and society-centered explanations. State-centered explanations focus on the executive mostly and on the legislature to a
lesser extent. Presidential decision making, the location of decision-
making responsibility in the bureaucracy, the shift of authority among
agencies, and the properties of the institutions in which officials make
decisions are typical targets of state-centered analyses.[1] In addition,
some analyses take account of the internal dynamics of Congress
and its relationship to the presidency.[2] Society-centered explanations
focus on political actors outside formal government, usually interest
groups and political parties. For example, in his classic work,
E. E. Schattschneider explained the Smoot–Hawley Tariff of 1930 as
the result of interest-group pressure. Other analysts explain trade
policy preferences and outcomes from the post–Civil War period to
the 1930s in terms of partisan differences.[3]

The analysis I present here examines trade policy as a product of
the domestic policy process, which consists of three phases: agenda
setting, program adoption, and program implementation. Participants in the policy process can play a single role on any given issue,
or they may play several roles at different points in the process. For
example, the United State Trade Representative (USTR) is certainly
pivotal in program implementation, but the USTR can also initiate
policy (agenda setting) and influence the creation of new policies
(program adoption). Interest groups are likely to be involved in every

phase in the process, while on some trade issues, political parties may play no role at all.

Political organizations, either within government or outside it, participate in this process. An analysis of their institutional characteristics should reveal a great deal about their role and importance in the policy process. Officials of these organizations operate in part on the basis of their interests. A key to our understanding is knowing how the organization with which an official is associated constrains and shapes those interests.

Along with examining the process and participants involved in trade policy in the United States, this analysis pays special attention to the importance of ideas in policy development. The substance of trade policy disputes is typically complex, technical economic analysis. The way participants package this information can have significant consequences for policy choices. This analysis examines the use of information throughout the policy process, especially in the agenda-setting phase. At this point, how participants define a problem seriously limits the choices available to policy makers in the program adoption phase.

Finally, like all public policy, trade policy is rooted in basic American values. This might seem a bit unusual, but it is worth remembering that public policy is not created in a vacuum; it is rooted in political culture, of which values are the basic components. Considerations like fairness, for example, underlie the goals of public policy. Understanding the conflict among basic values and how this conflict appears in trade policy illuminates the debate in general and connects it to more fundamental concerns about the good society and the proper role of government in it.

The central concern here is how the domestic policy process deals with the competing approaches to trade policy. How do they make their way into the policy process? What happens to them as they encounter the realities of American politics? To answer this question, I begin with an account of the trade policy debate.

The Trade Policy Debate

The main approaches to American trade policy fall into three main categories: protectionism, free trade, and managed trade. Although coming in a variety of forms, the essential purpose of protection is to shield American producers from foreign competition. Free-trade proponents recommend reduction of tariffs and nontariff barriers (NTBs) to stimulate international trade and enhance economic growth. Managed trade encompasses a range of policy options premised on the idea that, while free trade is preferable, the realities of government policies throughout the world make it unattainable without inducing foreign governments to behave in a manner more consistent with free trade. When that is impossible, the U.S. government should shield American producers from the effects of unfair trade.

Protection

In its simplest form, protection is government intervention to shield an industry from foreign competition. Hardly controversial in the nineteenth century, protection in the form of tariffs was routinely used to protect domestic industries from foreign competition and to raise revenue to fund the national government. At the end of the nineteenth century and into the beginning of the twentieth century, U.S. officials reduced tariffs usually in exchange for better access to foreign markets. The Smoot–Hawley Tariff signaled a dramatic shift in American policy because it unilaterally increased tariffs to protect its shattered domestic producers. Since the Second World War, the United States has consistently reduced tariffs, but continues to protect domestic producers from foreign competition. With tariffs reduced to unprecedented levels as a result of postwar international trade agreements, the United States and other countries have turned to NTBs to provide protection. Nontariff barriers to trade include anything that interrupts the free flow of goods and services across national borders. Licensing requirements and procedures, regulations, content specifications, and distribution systems are all examples of NTBs.

The justifications for protection vary considerably. The purest version contends that whenever foreign competition threatens an industry, government should protect it. In the nineteenth century, the infant industry argument provided the underlying rationale for this form of protection. Following the logic of Hamilton's *Report on Manufactures*,[4] U.S. officials sought to protect upstart domestic producers from foreign competition that would certainly damage them and even put them out of business. As clear a statement of industrial policy as there ever has been, the infant industry argument called for government intervention in the economy to promote economic development. This mercantilist position faded by the end of the nineteenth century, replaced by a simple, unfettered justification for protection: It is in American interests to prevent domestic producers from going out of business. Underlying this position was the logic that the American economy could do well on its own; the productive potential seemed unlimited, as did the domestic market. The United States did not need the ostensible benefits of trade liberalization and an increasingly integrated global economy.

This general policy continues today, although the requirements to obtain protection have changed and tightened somewhat. Until the mid-twentieth century, this type of protection meant tariffs. In the last forty-five years, import quotas have joined tariffs as a means to check foreign competition. In this simplest of scenarios, the affected domestic industry need not demonstrate anything other than that it has been damaged by foreign competition. Protection can also be justified by unfair trade practices by a foreign government or company. Such activities as government subsidies and dumping discriminate against American producers. Aggressive government action is the only way to end these practices or to neutralize their effects.

A positive view of government's role in the economy supports unbridled protection. Government, as the representative of the general interest, ought to intervene in the economy to achieve economic outcomes that benefit either segments of society or the population as a whole. Moreover, distribution of wealth cannot be left to the market. Although international market mechanisms might allocate resources most efficiently, efficiency should not be the primary objective. Job losses and better consumer prices may make economic sense, but they do not achieve equity, according to this view. It is more fair to preserve some jobs, even at the expense of optimal efficiency. The health of a society cannot be defined exclusively in economic terms; an equitable distribution of resources must also figure into the equation.

Protection has also been justified as a means to enhance economic well-being and national power. An economic nationalist perspective suggests that the country is better off if the government intervenes to enhance economic growth. The infant industry justification for protection is consistent with this view of the proper role of government in the economy, as is its modern high-technology counterpart. National security is connected to this theoretical basis for protection. The United States uses export controls to monitor and restrict transfers of technology that could be used for military purposes. The government has limited the export of computers for years for this purpose, and only recently has any administration considered relaxing those controls.[5] As is the case for economic nationalism, national power is the central concern, but here, national power is defined in terms of military security.

Protection can serve the purpose of preserving elements of a nation's culture. Canada insisted on including provisions in the North American Free Trade Agreement (NAFTA) that protected elements of the country's culture important to its citizens. Similarly, France protects its movie industry as a cultural artifact, seeking to keep it from being overwhelmed by foreign (mainly American) movie makers. Many countries justify protection of their agriculture sectors in terms of preserving a way of life. Note the benefits attached to the rural lifestyle, the yeoman farmer, and the family farm in American political rhetoric, for example.

Whether protection is justified in terms of equity or national power, the assumption that government can accomplish these objectives underlies both. Engaging in protection for these purposes means that several conditions must be met. First, policy makers must have access to adequate economic information. Second, officials must understand accurately the relationship between cause and effect. Third, government must be able to adjust protectionist policies to meet the challenges of unexpected contingencies. Fourth, government must be able to act in a sufficiently decisive way to avoid muddling of objectives and strategies. Taken together, this is a tall order. Those who contend that protection is worthwhile accept to varying degrees the premise that these conditions are met.

Protectionist ideas and justifications come from a variety of sources, many of whom would find little else on which to agree. An alliance of manufacturers and unions generated the initial push for protection in recent years. Strained by foreign competition, mainly from Japan, the automobile industry and the United Automobile Workers (UAW), for example, pressured U.S. officials for protection, which came in the form of import quotas.[6]

In recent years, the Economic Policy Institute (EPI) has expressed the economic interests of large manufacturing industries. A labor-supported think tank with a liberal orientation, EPI uses economic analyses of issues to present the case for protection. Its role in the policy process represents the relatively recent proliferation of think tanks that advocate an explicit point of view. Although the effect of such organizations on policy is uncertain, it seems that the use of academic or expert analyses is intended to give credibility to its positions.

Business and labor operate primarily on the basis of their own interests. The prospect of lower profits and lost jobs resulting from foreign competition causes these policy participants to push for some form of protection. With this in mind, business and labor define problems in ways that serve their interests. Thus, cheap labor builds popularly priced foreign cars. Japanese auto firms benefit from membership in *keiretsu*, government subsidies, and government protection of their domestic market. Japanese semiconductor manufacturers dump chips into the American market, taking a loss in order to gain market share and drive out American firms. Problems defined in these ways lead to solutions created by EPI and other such organizations. In this case, ideology is moot; interest is everything. Efficiency, in the sense that trade liberalization can create it, means little to supporters of this position. Security, on the other hand, is extremely important, as business and labor struggle to preserve their profits and jobs. Whereas their arguments may draw upon rhetorical allusions to equity, the bottom line remains business's and labor's security.

In addition to business and labor, politicians have articulated various forms of the protectionist argument. Most recently, the shrillest call for protections has come from the populist right. Contending that high tariffs are a good thing for American workers, Patrick Buchanan strikes a populist chord in his America-first policies. Buchanan also rejects U.S. membership in multinational organizations like the World Trade Organization (WTO) because such membership requires, according to Buchanan, the relinquishment of a measure of sovereignty.[7] Thus, free trade by means of multilateral negotiations sponsored by the WTO ultimately damages American power and security. Ross Perot joined Buchanan in the populist camp when he vigorously opposed NAFTA. Like Buchanan, Perot argued that NAFTA would cause American jobs to go south.[8]

The populist impulse to protect American producers grows out of a fierce commitment to security defined both in terms of the individual and the nation as a whole. Buchanan's America-first campaign places national interests above international ones; in trade policy, this translates into rejection of NAFTA and the WTO. For Buchanan, opening American borders to foreign goods undermines American economic power, and membership in international organizations compromises American sovereignty. Thus, concern for individual security is linked to national security. The main issue for populists is saving jobs, not insuring profits. Buchanan's plan to raise tariffs to save jobs is aimed directly at the angry white males of the 1990s, who perceive their livelihoods to be under attack. Perot's warning about the "great sucking sound" of American jobs going to Mexico taps this vein of insecurity among workers as well. Less prominent, though connected nonetheless to individual security, is a concern for equity. Implied in Buchanan's and Perot's positions on trade policy is the point that lost jobs caused by trade liberalization is fundamentally unfair to workers. Wall Street benefits at the expense of ordinary Americans.

Liberal politicians, such as Representative David Bonior (D-MI) and Representative Richard Gephardt (D-MO), also express a concern for security and equity, but mostly at the individual level; they do not seem as fearful of international organization and loss of national sovereignty. Their concern for the individual is based on a notion of equity; ordinary Americans should not shoulder the burden of economic growth.

Although similar in views on at least some trade policies, Perot and Buchanan have carried their message into the policy development process somewhat differently from the way liberal Democrats have. The populists have relied mainly on defining problems in simple terms—job losses result from free trade with Mexico. American sovereignty is threatened by some nebulous force lurking behind international organization. Buchanan has used celebrity and presidential candidacy to deliver the message, relying very little on analysis. Perot has tapped his vast personal wealth to buy television time to convey his populist views on trade policy.

In sum, protection has attracted the support of populists and some liberals. Ranging from simple tariff hikes to complex managed-trade formulas, policy participants from divergent political camps have advocated protecting American firms in some fashion. The basis of protectionist claims draws on the values that underlie American policy goals. Equity and security are at the root of protectionist arguments, expressed through traditional political means, advocacy think tanks, and direct communication through the news media.

Free Trade

The basic goal of free trade is simple: elimination of all barriers to trade. The classical argument for free trade rests on the theory of comparative advantage, which states that countries enjoy an advantage in the production of certain goods owing to the existence of certain key factors. Each country ought to produce the goods it is best suited to make, trading freely across national borders. This arrangement maximizes efficiency, and under pure free-trade conditions, everyone is better off. The theory distinguishes between absolute advantage and comparative advantage.

> A nation has an absolute advantage over another nation in the production of a good when it can produce that good using fewer inputs per unit of output. The classical economists focused on labor cost, so absolute advantage meant lower unit labor requirements (or higher labor productivity). By contrast, comparative advantage referred to differences between nations in the relation between labor productivity in the production of different goods. A country has a comparative advantage, say, in the production of cheese, when the ratio between its labor productivities in cheese and wine exceeds that ratio in another country. The country specializing in cheese is proportionally rather than absolutely more productive in that good.[9]

Contemporary arguments for free trade are based on the advantages trade liberalization creates for the global economy, national economies, and individuals. The greater efficiencies achieved by means of freer trade yield economic growth and an increase in the general welfare. This is not to say that there are no costs to free trade. Some individuals will pay for the greater good with loss of their jobs as firms collapse under the weight of foreign competition. But, the pain caused to some people because of lost jobs will be more than compensated for by the gain to others in the form of new jobs, more and better products, and lower prices.[10]

Several assumptions support free trade's central premise. First, free trade limits government's role in the economy. The market is the best means by which to allocate resources. Government decisions are likely to distort this process and result in less-than-optimal economic growth and well-being. Even assuming that governments intend to make policies that achieve economic prosperity, free trade assumes that governments cannot do so. Free-trade advocates are highly skeptical of government's ability to allocate resources efficiently.

In addition to problems with efficiency, the classical economics on which free trade is based assumes economic wealth is central to human happiness. Out of this central premise grow corollaries that are consistent with the idea of free trade. A market economy encourages entrepreneurship and risk taking, which lead to further economic growth. While risk exists and may be high at times, the payoffs make the risk worth taking. At the root of this logic is a version of individualism that suggests that individuals can gain through their own efforts, but they may also lose. In either case, the individual is responsible for her actions, and there is little reason for government to insure somehow her well-being. Extending this logic a bit, it is not hard to come to the conclusion that the proper role of government is limited. Applied to trade policy, government should not upset the natural selection of the market with barriers to trade.

So far, skepticism about government effectiveness, assigning material wealth an important place in overall human happiness, and reliance on the individual to succeed or fail underlie the logic of free trade. Not surprisingly, free trade does little to address equality. As is true for market-based theories on any level, free trade does not strive for equal outcomes; indeed, competition will produce anything but equality. But, for free-trade advocates, equity is served by the absence of barriers to trade. In the ideal case, more people are better off under conditions of free trade than not. Although not ending up equal in any sense, being better off is viewed as fair or equitable. This notion of equity is not what protectionists have in mind. Free trade comprehends equity in the aggregate, but the adjustments necessary to achieve economic growth go unattended. Thus, the worker who loses his job or the town that loses the factory around which its economy is based may suffer to advance the cause of free trade. While society is better off, and although one may even believe that individuals can adjust by finding new jobs, the shock to individuals' lives and to the social structure of communities falls outside of free-trade logic. Thus, free trade ignores equity issues that arise as a result of economic adjustments necessitated by trade liberalization.

In sum, the ideological basis of free trade lies in classical liberalism stressing material wealth, individualism, and restrained government. In its contemporary form, skepticism of government capabilities reenforces these basic tenets, as faith in the market obscures concerns for equity. Confidence in the market, disaffection with government, and the concern for economic growth have become major themes in contemporary political discourse. The question is, how did they get there?

Economic ideas have played a crucial role in pushing American policy makers toward free-trade policies since the 1930s. Greatly influenced by Wilsonian internationalism, Secretary of State Cordell Hull tirelessly moved the Roosevelt administration in the direction of freer trade. Since the Second World War, academic economists have carried these ideas into the policy development process. Leading free traders like Jagdish Bhagwati and Anne O. Krueger expose and criticize various forms of protection and press for trade liberalization.[11] Economic ideas, finally, emanate from think tanks, such as the moderate-to-liberal Brookings Institution, the conservative American Enterprise Institute, the extremely conservative Heritage Foundation, and the libertarian Cato Institute.[12]

Policy entrepreneurs of various types carried these ideas into the debate. Mainstream economists have been reliable proponents of faith in the market; the invisible, but cold hand of the market best selects winners and losers and therefore promotes economic growth. This central tenet leads to advocacy of free trade in the international context. Although mainstream economists may allow for some legitimate role for government in the international marketplace—for example, enforcing intellectual property protection—they nonetheless opt for free trade.

Free-trade proponents vary in their views on how to get from the current state of affairs to a true global free market. Taken to the extreme, free traders would argue that the United States ought to drop trade barriers unilaterally—that Americans benefit even if other countries do not act in the same way. A less zealous view of the benefits that accrue to free trade strongly supports the use of multilateral institutions to obtain trade liberalization. The General Agreement on Tariffs and Trade (GATT), of course, has filled this role since the end of the Second World War, and, presumably, the World Trade Organization will do so now. Short of this, some analysts believe that the creation of trade blocs may be the way to global trade liberalization. Politically more feasible, trade blocs create free trade among a finite number of countries. Optimists suggest that this can be expanded to include more nations, but pessimists take a dim view of trade blocs, maintaining that a multilateral approach is the only dependable path to global trade liberalization.[13]

Although free-trade advocates may prefer multilateral agreements, practical considerations may force them to settle for bilateral negotiations. Beginning in the 1930s, Congress authorized the president to negotiate reciprocal trade agreements with foreign governments. The goal was to use the lowering of U.S. tariffs as an incentive to other countries to lower theirs. To the extent that these bilateral agreements worked in this way, the cause of free trade was advanced.

In sum, free-trade supporters base their positions on the premise that free trade makes every nation better off. The best way to attain trade liberalization remains open to question, although a multilateral approach draws more support than either unilateral dismantling of trade barriers or the creation of trade blocs.

Supporters of free trade acknowledge its potential negative consequences and propose ways to address them. Free trade will displace some workers and contribute to social inequity to some extent. Whether the number of workers is small, as most free-trade advocates believe, or unexpectedly large, government has an important role in preparing jobless workers for new jobs. Free trade will also worsen the widening gap between the top and bottom of the economic scale, a matter of social inequity or injustice that requires appropriate public policy.[14]

The New Protectionism: Managed Trade

Managed trade generally refers to a collection of policies that fall somewhere between pure free trade and unapologetic protectionism. Managed-trade approaches are frequently *ad hoc,* created by policy makers to meet the demands of a rapidly changing, uncertain economic environment. Thus, as a sanctuary for a variety of approaches and rationales, managed trade is the most complicated category of trade strategies. As such, it is reasonable to expect a lack of the theoretical coherence and development evident in both free-trade and protectionist approaches.

The premise of managed trade is that contemporary economic and political conditions have altered the factors that underlie the logic of free trade. According to managed-trade proponents, the classical notion of comparative advantage no longer applies in the context of widespread government intervention in national economies and the development of high-technology industries.¹⁵ Each of these factors is crucial to the rationale supporting managed trade and deserves some elaboration.

From the perspective of managed-trade proponents, the inescapable fact is that governments throughout the world are deeply involved in their nations' economies. Such involvement results in advantages accruing to industries located in countries that enjoy particularly effective government intervention in the economy. Practices such as subsidies for new industries that promise long-term payoffs for the economy as a whole, regulatory systems that discriminate against imports, and uneven enforcement of intellectual property protection laws benefit domestic producers at the expense of their foreign competitors. Whereas it would be desirable to eliminate these government activities by means of multilateral negotiations through international organizations, doing so is a painfully slow process beset by setbacks and disappointment. Some government officials might view the glacial pace of international trade negotiations as acceptable, but domestic producers might find it to be their death knell.¹⁶

While free trade grows out of a traditional liberal view of government, the economy, and society, and protection is grounded in both practical mercantilist considerations and twentieth-century liberalism, managed trade draws on a new ideological variant in American politics. Rejecting the idea that government ought to solve all social and economic ills, but lacking confidence in market choices in the contemporary international economic environment, managed-trade advocates take a moderate approach that includes government action, but only if it is clearly warranted and only if it is effective. Managed traders wish to limit legitimate government activity with respect to international trade, but to encourage activity within those limits. Embedded in managed trade is the belief that government can and should pick economic winners and losers. If properly designed and implemented, trade policy can be effective. In a sense, the ideology out of which managed trade grows is linked to the neoliberalism of the 1970s, which called for government action, but only with a hard-nosed evaluation of its effectiveness.

Managed-trade proponents frequently weigh in on the side of producers, contending that foreign government practices must be addressed immediately. If multilateral negotiations prove ineffective, then the time pressures of the market require the U.S. government to act, alone if necessary, to compensate for the unfair competition American producers face at home and in foreign markets as well.

Managed-trade advocates also contend that the peculiar charac-teristics of high-technology industries call for government intervention in trade—that comparative advantage does not necessarily apply to high-technology industries. Factors that give a country an advantage in producing a certain good can be created by government intervention. For example, the basic knowledge and technical expertise required to make semiconductors is a result of how well a nation's educational system produces people with these skills. A country's climate, geo-graphic location, and topography have little to do with its ability to make high-technology products.[17] Moreover, high-technology indus-tries can have so-called spillover effects; development of technology in one sector encourages and aids innovation in another. The process of technological innovation produces new knowledge that can be applied in related high-technology industries. Thus, to allow producers in a certain high-technology industry to fail because of foreign competition could mean even further losses in the potential for future technological innovation and subsequent economic growth.[18]

Moreover, managed-trade strategies that in essence pick economic winners and losers should, assuming they work effectively, benefit industries that produce "good," high-skill, well-paying jobs. Low-pay-ing jobs will go abroad as the U.S. economy becomes increasingly based on high-technology manufacturing and services. In this sense, managed trade parses the concept of security quite delicately; it is necessary to lose some jobs, causing considerable pain to those who held them, in exchange for creating better jobs in more desirable industries. The lucky individuals who obtain these positions benefit; their economic security depends in part on the extreme insecurity of less-skilled workers in low-technology industries. For those who suffer from these economic changes, government should make sure that workers can acquire the skills necessary for well-paid jobs.[19]

Managed-trade advocates have created a fairly coherent argument for their position—though by no means undisputed—at least with respect to high-technology industries. The case for managed trade extends to other more traditional industries as well, but the rationale is different. Managed-trade advocates wish to address unfair trade prac-tices of foreign governments and foreign-based companies with trade policy—mainly, the threat or implementation of sanctions. Such an approach to trade policy is justified on the basis of providing fair treatment to American producers and opening foreign markets. In the latter case, fair-trade proponents argue that managed trade is far from protectionist; indeed, its leading to opening of foreign markets is very much a part of trade liberalization.[20]

Other policies that are consistent with the logic underlying managed trade may be categorized as industrial policy. Managed-trade proponents argue that the U.S. government can and should engage in a considerable range of activities intended to benefit American producers, especially those in high-technology industries. The impressive array of policies includes, for example, research and development tax credits, export promotion, and government-sponsored research consortia (e.g., SEMATECH). Targeting public policies on certain industries gives them the opportunity to succeed in the global market. Since foreign-based firms benefit from such government largesse, it is only reasonable that the U.S. government do the same, if for no other reason than to "level the playing field."

Managed trade can be linked to several basic goals underlying American public policy. One of managed trade's articulated purposes is to achieve fairness in international trade; establishing a level playing field is the preferred metaphor of most managed-trade tracts. Insofar as managed trade is concerned with unfair trade practices, its proponents argue that they simply want American producers to have the opportunity to compete with foreign firms. Whether American companies win or lose, say the managed traders, is not relevant to their argument.

Managed trade is grounded in a notion of efficiency. As high-technology industries create spillover effects, the economy will enjoy a measure of technological innovation and, therefore, increased economic growth. Technological innovation encourages productivity and efficiency, resulting in better conditions for the economy as a whole.

Finally, more than free trade or protection, managed trade relies on effectiveness. Managed-trade strategies call on government to make policies that are narrowly targeted and finely tuned. Securing the health of certain high-technology industries to insure technological innovation requires something more than a blunt, across-the-board tax cut. While free trade asks government to do less, and protection requires only relatively simple policies—mainly tariffs—managed trade requires constant adjustment, analysis, and precision. Out of necessity, therefore, managed-trade strategy places faith in the capacity of government to set policy objectives and to accomplish them.

Managed trade is the newest of the three basic approaches to trade policy. Unlike protection, the justification for which was clearly articulated before the practice, and free trade, which is supported by volumes of economic theory and analysis, the notion of managed trade has been created in part after the fact. As the United States struggled to deal with increasingly intense foreign competition, Congress and the president invented ways to deal with specific problems. These techniques evolved into a pattern of government intervention to aid domestic producers.

The three approaches to trade policy constitute the ideas that play a role in agenda setting. Each can frame the identification of goals, problems, and solutions differently than the others. This is the central element of agenda setting. I turn now to the question of how and in what form trade gets on the agenda.

Agenda Setting

Agenda setting is perhaps the least studied phase of the policy process. Determining who creates proposals and how they become matters of public policy is difficult to do empirically. I present here an approach to agenda setting that is based on the works of John W. Kingdon and Deborah A. Stone.[21] I begin with a discussion of goals, problems, and solutions, which are the main elements of public policy. This is followed by a description of how issues get onto the policy agenda.

Ideas, the Media, and the Use and Misuse of Information

Defining problems and solutions in trade policy involves a great deal of highly complex information that the news media interpret. What information the media convey is particularly important inasmuch as public opinion has some influence over what policy makers do. With respect to international trade, reporters frequently focus on trade deficits as the most important aspect of the topic, but media coverage of the trade deficit infrequently captures the complexity of the issue. Instead of dealing with the trade deficit in light of other economic conditions—for example, the federal budget deficit or levels of foreign investment—journalistic accounts typically focus on the most recent numbers reflecting the trade deficit the United States carries with the rest of the world, or more specifically, with a nation currently embroiled in a foreign policy controversy.[22]

The media follow the trade deficit because of its political visibility and significance, which President Bill Clinton enhanced with his emphasis on the international competitiveness of American industries during his 1992 bid for the presidency. In doing so, he helped to increase the public's perception that foreign imports displaced American-manufactured products and foreign competition caused the loss of American jobs. Against this background, reports of higher trade deficits make the news; the American public is aware of some relationship between trade deficits and domestic economic prosperity, and politicians are obliged to do something—or, at least, appear to do something—about them.

It is not difficult to find examples of this sort of development. The Clinton administration has made opening Japanese markets to American-made products one of its main economic goals.[23] Increasing exports helps the American economy and reduces the trade deficit with Japan. On the political extremes, fear of trade deficits accompanied by simplified understandings of international trade have led politicians to advocate stark measures. The Democratic leadership in the House of Representatives, for example, opposed the passage of NAFTA for fear of job losses to Mexico, and conservative commentator and occasional presidential candidate Patrick Buchanan advocates closing economic borders, ultimately using tariffs as the main source of funding for the federal government. Thus, fear of trade deficits and foreign competition has ignited populist responses on both the political left and right.

Goals and Problems

Goals underlie every policy. Determining them leads to the definition of problems and the choice of solutions. While specific objectives differ by issue area, of course, they nevertheless reflect basic principles, or goals, that provide the fundamental direction to government in general. Basic goals include security, efficiency, effectiveness, equality, equity, and liberty.[24] Two points need to be made about these goals. First, all are not necessarily involved in every policy question. Second, they can be ambiguous; indeed, there is likely to be considerable conflict over the precise meaning of any basic goal.

The importance of these goals is clear in trade policy. For example, free-trade advocates base their argument on efficiency grounds; trade liberalization leads to more efficient production, which means everyone is better off. Protectionists are more concerned with security and equity. Preserving jobs helps to secure the economic well-being of workers. The benefits of freer trade are frequently distributed unevenly across society; it is thus inequitable for workers to bear the consequences of trade liberalization in the form of reduced wages and lost jobs. Free traders might claim that liberty is served with trade liberalization, because consumers have greater choices of products, whereas protectionists might contend that lost wages resulting from reduced protection limit a worker's liberty to consume. The central point is that the choice to pursue a particular objective is explicitly or implicitly informed by these fundamental goals.

The choice of goals influences the identification and definition of problems. Problems do not exist in an absolute sense; conditions become problems when someone defines them as such. Thus, a Japanese market closed to imports from the United States was not a problem in the 1950s and 1960s because the American economy was growing rapidly and American producers did not need another market in which to sell their products. When that situation changed, the condition of a closed Japanese market became a problem.

Information and Numbers

Since trade policy is typically difficult to understand and frequently accessible only to experts, participants in the policy process can manipulate information to suit their political and policy objectives. Use of numbers in characterizing problems and solutions is central to the presentation of information to satisfy these objectives.[25]

Players in the policy process try to present problems in ways that will accomplish their objectives: demonstrating the seriousness of the problem, defining it, determining its cause to lead to a preferred solution, justifying added public expenditures, and the like. To exaggerate the importance of a particular problem, a government official might be selective in presenting data to support her case. Take a recent trade example. As the United States and Japan were involved in negotiations over access to the Japanese automobile market, the

U.S. government released the latest trade data showing the U.S. trade deficit with Japan to be at a near record high. This fact helped to underscore the significance of the ongoing effort to allow American car and car parts manufacturers to sell more of their products in Japan. The major news media picked up the announcement, making it a top story on the television network news programs and in the major print media.[26] Although the effect of this story is hard to measure, it is likely that it at least reenforced the U.S. position in the negotiations. What was left out of the flow of information was any attempt to explain the causes of trade deficits beyond trade in certain goods and services. Thus, no story contained an analysis of the potential importance of the federal budget deficit in keeping America's trade deficit high.[27] A consideration of other causes of the trade deficit would have demonstrated the complexity of economic exchange among nations and indicated the ambiguity of the issue. It might also have undermined the tough American stance with respect to opening the Japanese car market to American firms.

In sum, participants in the policy process manipulate information to present their positions in the best possible light. This practice is not necessarily unethical; barring outright distortion of the truth, selection of facts favorable to one's argument is generally accepted and expected. Because of its technical complexity, however, international trade is quite amenable to such manipulation, as this examination of various aspects of American trade policies will show.

Policy participants concerned with international trade need not focus exclusively on the trade deficit. For example, some analysts consider the trade deficit to be a minor concern; more products for less for the consumer is the central goal. To the extent trade policy undermines this central goal, it is a problem. Such analysts can live with a trade deficit if the consumer benefits. Others view international trade in the context of international relations in general. Foreign trade is less important than diplomatic and military issues that make up much of traditional foreign policy. Thus, the trade deficit is a reasonable price to pay to maintain good diplomatic and military relations with Japan. Still other analysts, also not much concerned with the trade deficit, consider job losses and economic insecurity to be problems. If government intervention to save jobs and to improve economic security also reduces the trade deficit, that is merely a coincidental benefit.

Solutions

Solutions come from a variety of sources—academicians, journalists, legislators, legislative staff members, bureaucrats, think tanks. The solutions one prefers are determined in large part by how the problems and its causes are defined.[28] Consider the following examples of trade policy and the relationship between solutions and problems.

Trade sanctions are designed to open foreign markets to imports, mainly from the United States. Sanctions are a specific kind of solution to a trade problem; in this case, the background problem is the trade deficit. One of the problem's causes is the inability of American firms to sell their products in foreign markets. The logic of using trade sanctions as a solution to this problem assumes that foreign markets are artificially closed, or closed somehow as the result of government policy. Change the policy, and the markets open up.

The relationship between solutions and problems is observable here at several levels. First, there is the broad matter of the trade deficit; closed markets are considered a cause and therefore they should be opened by means of U.S. government action. At the second level, closed markets are the problem, and the cause is government policy. This definition of the problem also warrants U.S. government action, this time in the form of trade sanctions. The true nature of the problems and their causes can be debated at both levels. It is common to argue that the trade deficit has nothing whatever to do with the openness of foreign markets; other factors are more important. And even if one accepts that closed markets are the problem, it is still another step to accept the proposition that government policy is the culprit. It is quite arguable that such factors as culture, economic structure, and the distribution of retail outlets have more to do with the openness of a market than government regulations.

Suppose policy participants define the trade problem as suboptimal economic growth resulting from insufficient trade liberalization. Everyone is better off with freer trade, so limits on it are the problem. One way to address this problem is through multilateral negotiations under the auspices of international organizations. The WTO is one such organization. The definition of the problem in this case could easily be attacked, mainly by those who doubt that free trade is achievable, believe that the United States frequently gives up too much in such negotiations, and suspect international organizations of any type.

One more example should finish the case. Suppose that the main trade problem is declining American industries and associated job losses. The blame goes to foreign competition underselling American firms at home. The solution is to protect these industries with higher tariffs. The logic is simple; higher tariffs make it harder for foreign producers to compete in the American market. Other problems—economic growth, efficiency, even the trade deficit—are not as important as sustaining certain American industries.

In all these cases, how one defines the problem and attributes cause leads to certain solutions. This is not a deterministic relationship; problem definitions and causes do not necessarily lead to one and only one solution. But they certainly narrow the choice.

Summary

Goals, problems, and solutions are interrelated. Policy is not made in a vacuum. Participants in policy development are constrained by the fundamental goals of society, which underlie all public policy, the definition of problems and causes, and the availability of solutions.

The roles of goals, problems, and solutions in policy development should be understood in light of the importance of ideas and information. Defining problems and causes involves packaging and distribution of information. Solutions grow out of ideas. The complex interplay of these factors characterizes the policy development process.

Goals, problems, and solutions, then, are connected. Goals fundamental to American society set the boundaries for specific policy goals and are reflected in them. Conditions become problems when, for whatever reason, the condition is no longer acceptable to society. Solutions begin as unattached alternatives and only become solutions when they are attached to a problem.

Alternatives, Solutions, and Problems

The question here is how alternatives become solutions to problems.[29] The necessary prerequisite to this transformation is the identification of a problem. This can occur in several ways, including the onset of a crisis, a shift in public opinion, or crossing some threshold.

A crisis, or some precipitating event, draws the attention of the public and government officials to a policy problem. A dramatic increase in the trade deficit occurring at a time when trade negotiations are in progress can be enough of an irritant to draw attention to possible new solutions—for example, new sanctions against countries with which the United States is running an especially high deficit.

Conditions can cross a threshold beyond which policy makers, the public, and other participants determine that a problem exists. China's increased stature in international trade, along with the ballooning U.S. trade deficit with China, cause American news media to take notice, drawing calls for some sort of government intervention from politicians.

Solutions to Proposals

At this point in the agenda-setting process, problems have been identified, and alternatives have been transformed into competing solutions by being connected to the problems. Solutions do not automatically become part of the policy process, however. A particular solution must attract sufficient political support for it to be considered a serious proposal. Thus, solutions such as limited driving hours to reduce air pollution or the elimination of Medicare to bring the federal budget under control have not become viable proposals. They may be analytically coherent, but they lack political support.

The policy entrepreneur is pivotal in turning a solution into a viable proposal. Policy entrepreneurs—legislators, bureaucrats, academicians, interest group officials, and the like—favor a particular solution and work to get it accepted by other participants in the policy process. If successful—that is, typically getting a proposal turned into legislation with considerable support in Congress—then the solution is ready to progress to the next stage of the policy process.

Program Adoption

Owing to the initial revenue-raising function of tariffs, Congress has had historical jurisdiction over trade policy long after tariffs were no longer trade policy's core. Thus, we turn to Congress as the source of trade policy creation. Doing so does not require ignoring other locations where trade policy is created, such as the bureaucracy, through its interpretation and implementation of U.S. trade law. (The importance of implementation in policy making is taken up later in the chapter.) Our approach views government institutions as the transformers of political preferences, however they are communicated to policy makers. Whether governmental or nongovernmental, established rules and patterns of behavior limit the possible policies an organization can produce. Congress is central to this process, and its institutional properties determine in large part policy outcomes. Thus, to understand Congress's role in the development of trade policy, its decision-making process and structure must be understood.

Congressional decision-making structure and procedure are at first blush straightforward, but in actual practice, they are convoluted and indecipherable to the uninitiated. Congress's relationship to the executive is at times subtle, escaping the normal reach of empirical political analysis. Studies focusing on the domestic aspects of American trade policy frequently could go further in taking account of Congress's institutional richness. This analysis relies on the considerable work of students of American politics, and Congress in particular, to paint a more complete picture of the institution and, therefore, to understand better its role in trade policy. Thus, for example, it is certainly the case that Congress has delegated a measure of trade policy authority to the executive to escape its own susceptibility to protectionist pressures. It is also clear that Congress has attempted to recover some of that authority from the executive in the 1980s.[30] Equally important are the internal dynamics of Congress on these decisions—committee behavior, party leadership influence, electoral pressures, and the differences in the approaches of the House and Senate.

Congressional Decision Making

Although the volume of analysis of congressional decision making is overwhelming, we can begin to understand the process through which Congress produces public policy by examining the roles played by congressional committees and parties.

Analysts of American trade policy have given considerable attention to political parties. According to most, trade policy in the late nineteenth and early twentieth centuries is a result of party control of

Congress and the presidency.[31] Congressional votes, however, are rarely cast on pure party lines (all Democrats versus all Republicans). Indeed, for a vote to be considered a party unity vote, only a majority of each party must vote together, allowing for a significant number of party members to vote with the other party.[32] Thus, it is hardly surprising that all Republicans did not vote against all Democrats on the Smoot–Hawley Tariff. Some defection is normal and can be explained usually by constituent concerns, or by interest-group pressure and ideology.[33]

Political parties no longer clearly align on trade issues. Party voting is most contentious when the legislation under consideration is controversial and means major changes. With respect to trade policy, contentious legislation includes votes to approve major trade agreements such as the GATT and NAFTA. The vote on NAFTA split the parties, with Republicans joining a minority of Democrats in support of Democratic President Bill Clinton to win approval of the trade agreement. This, combined with the lack of overwhelming discipline in congressional parties, suggests an important role for congressional party leaders in bringing their members into the fold on trade legislation. The power of congressional party leaders is limited, however; party votes can be attributed only in part to their efforts.[34]

Some of the most important action on legislation takes place in congressional committees. Perhaps even more than in the case of congressional parties, scholars have pored over the record of committee activity to determine how Congress produces policy. Committee influence over congressional voting patterns, control of legislative hearings and mark-ups, and the ability to determine when legislation will be considered by the entire chamber give committees enormous power over public policy. The key committees with respect to trade policy are the House Ways and Means Committee and the Senate Finance Committee. But trade policy is not limited to them. The actions taken by committee chairmen, the relationship between them and party leaders, and the relationships among the committees (assuming that there is more than one dealing with the issue) all play a part in shaping the policy outcome. Committee activity is less important when it comes to implementing various provisions of U.S. trade law, but they can play an oversight role in those matters. Finally, the relationships among key committees in the House and Senate have some bearing on the final shape of legislation. Strong and strong-willed committee chairs from each chamber negotiate, bargain, and generally haggle with each other over legislation.[35] There is no reason to believe that such interaction does not take place on major trade legislation.

The House and the Senate are likely to take different views on trade policy owing to their differing size, structure, and reelection concerns. Given the need to run for reelection every two years, representatives can be expected to be more concerned with protecting their constituents than senators, who enjoy a six-year term and with it the luxury of being able to vote against the immediate concerns of their constituents, at least early in their terms. Add to this the Senate's constitutional responsibilities in the area of foreign policy. Again, these differences are likely to be most consequential when dealing with major trade legislation.

Members of Congress ultimately must vote on legislation. Their voting decisions can be simple, the result of a single cause, but taken as a whole, an individual member of Congress will cast votes for a variety of reasons over her career. The determinants of congressional voting include constituents, other members of Congress, interest groups, committees, parties, and ideology. Of these, the most important are fellow members and a member's constituents.[36]

Interest groups certainly play a major role in public policy formation in the United States,[37] but they are not a monolithic political force that policy makers cannot resist. Interest groups seek to influence policy outcomes at various points in the process, not the least of which is at the program adoption phase in Congress. Their efforts certainly have been rewarded with legislation favorable to the interests they represent. Several reservations should be kept in mind, however, when assessing the importance of interest groups with respect to American trade policy. Foremost, interest groups ostensibly representing the same interests do not always agree. Business groups, frequently viewed as being of one mind on virtually every public policy question, disagree all the time. The classic study by Raymond A. Bauer, Ithiel de Sola Pool, and Lewis Anthony Dexter illustrates this point, as business groups involved in trade policy in the 1950s frequently had difficulty developing a single, unified position.[38] Even groups representing contemporary high-technology industries in the same sector cannot agree. Note, for example, the dispute between interest groups for the American computer industry and the Semiconductor Industry Association (SIA), the principal group representing U.S. semiconductor manufacturers.

While the SIA strongly favored limiting American market access to Japanese-made chips, American computer companies wanted precisely the opposite—a reliable supply of cheap chips.[39] Absent political unity, it is difficult to conclude that these producer interest groups exert overwhelming influence over public policy. The simple fact of the matter is that, because they disagree, they cannot all win.

Bauer, Pool, and Dexter also provide evidence for why it is difficult to assign to interest groups Goliath-like political power: Because interest groups frequently have difficulty achieving consensus among their members on a policy issue, they have little recourse but to take a bland position. The lack of a clear interest for all, or even a large majority of an interest group's members, undermines the impression that they wield insurmountable political clout.[40]

Another problem with concluding that interest groups dominate public policy is a methodological one. It is extremely difficult to show conclusively that members of Congress voted on the basis of interest-group influence. Other factors, such as constituent interests, may have weighed in as well. Moreover, it may very well be the case that the legislator would have voted a certain way in any event, and because of this vote, won the support—say, in the form of campaign contributions—of some interest groups.

Finally, members of Congress vote on the basis of a number of considerations, not solely interest-group pressure. Party and committee membership certainly influence members' votes to some degree, but members of Congress are most concerned with their constituents. Using constituent concerns to determine legislative votes is not in itself a simple, straightforward exercise; it necessarily involves a conceptualization of representation, a calculation of the effects on the legislator's reelection chances, and an analysis of what is in the constituents' interest.

A member of Congress may view her job as somehow to represent her constituents. That may mean following their stated preferences, made known through public opinion polls, meetings, or constituent communications to the member's office, or it may mean doing what is best for the people one represents even if that goes against their stated preferences.[41] Assuming the member of Congress wants to stay in Congress, she must also estimate the effects of her legislative activity on her ability to get reelected.[42] If her constituents have suffered from job losses and general economic decline as a result of foreign competition, it is likely that she will vote against trade liberalization measures and for protectionist ones. If her constituents benefit from greater foreign trade—a major exporter might be located in her district, for example—then she will vote for freer trade. No concern for trade policy among her constituents liberates her from immediate electoral considerations.

What happens when other influences on a legislator's vote conflict with his constituents' preferences? Although constituent preferences will ultimately supersede almost all other considerations, members of Congress can feel strongly enough about an issue to find other ways to achieve their objectives. They are likely to try to achieve their goals—that is, a policy that goes against the stated preferences of their constituents—without taking blame for it.[43] One way to do this is to establish an institutional arrangement such that someone else makes the tough decisions, preferably someone located in an institution less vulnerable to the wrath of an irate electorate. This is a plausible explanation for why Congress delegated so much trade policy authority to the executive beginning in the 1930s. Recognizing the long-term benefits of lower tariffs, but also being aware of the short-term pain and subsequent damage to reelection chances that trade-liberalizing measures can cause, Congress shifted the authority to cut tariffs to the president, who was in better position to resist protectionist political pressure.[44]

At the same time, however, Congress did not abdicate its responsibility over trade policy altogether. Congress continues to develop major legislation governing U.S. trade policy, and it sets limits on the president's ability to negotiate trade agreements by requiring that the chief executive first seek fast-track authority from Congress.[45] A provision included in the Trade Act of 1974, moreover, provides a mechanism through which five members each of the Senate Finance Committee and the House Ways and Means Committee are named as congressional advisers to U.S. trade negotiations. The committees' staff members may monitor and attend negotiating sessions, and the executive is required to keep the two committees informed of important developments.[46]

The Presidency

As it does with respect to any other domestic policy, the president, cabinet members, and other top administration officials routinely work with Congress in the development of major trade legislation. Unlike other foreign policy issues, the president does not have constitutional authority to negotiate trade agreements. He is compelled, therefore, to work with Congress to develop the basic U.S. trade law and to obtain authority to negotiate with foreign governments. One would expect to see the executive branch interacting with members of Congress on trade legislation in much the same way that it does on other domestic policies. The process involves constant interaction between bureaucrats and congressional staff, top administration officials and members of Congress, and, though less frequent, direct intervention by the president to express his preferences on a particular piece of legislation. These altogether routine activities are present in the negotiations of the basic U.S. trade law.

In general, the president has been the source of trade liberalization initiatives. Beginning with the efforts of President Cleveland in the late nineteenth century through the New Deal and to the present, the executive has been in the best position to articulate an argument for freer trade.[47] In addition to this general objective, the president has tried to get fast-track negotiating authority from Congress, which requires Congress to approve or disapprove an agreement negotiated by the president in a single up-or-down vote. Limiting Congress to this kind of vote expedites the approval process, dramatically decreases the number of opportunities members of Congress have for modifying the agreement, and therefore gives the executive more credibility in its negotiations with foreign governments. To date, Congress has consistently granted fast-track authority to the president until 1997, when a Republican-controlled Congress balked at giving any political advantage that may have accompanied renewal of this authority.

Program Implementation

Administrative decisions are hardly straightforward. They involve varying degrees of discretion depending on the complexity of the program and the amount of leeway Congress gives the executive. Given this discretion, a number of considerations may enter the executive's administrative decisions: namely, professional training and bias, ideology, political pressure, and benefit–cost assessments.

In trade policy, Congress has set limits, sometimes quite broad, on the executive's implementation decisions. At the most general level, when Congress delegates trade policy authority to the president, it is in effect broadening limits on the chief executive's administrative decisions. In other words, when acting on congressional authority, the president is in fact engaged in program implementation. Congress has at times sought to rein in the executive on trade policy. For example, in the 1980s, Congress set stricter conditions under which the executive had to enforce trade sanctions against foreign countries. By limiting the executive's discretion, Congress was attempting to control the implementation of a set of programs specified under trade sanction provisions of the basic U.S. trade law.

Several executive branch components implement trade policy programs. The president, of course, is involved in all major trade policy activities, including enforcement of trade sanctions and negotiation of various types of trade agreements. A surprising number of executive branch agencies are also involved in administrative decisions. The United States Trade Representative has become the lead agency for trade policy; indeed, Congress placed the agency in the Executive Office of the President to coordinate trade policy and to provide a congressional outpost near the president.[48] In spite of the congressional intent, the USTR has become an instrument of the president. To create a more accommodating environment for injured industries, Congress shifted considerable authority to the business-friendly Commerce Department, much of which had been the Treasury Department's responsibility. The Department of Agriculture plays a key role in international trade in agriculture, and the Department of Defense guards against the free flow of technology that either compromises U.S. national security or allows foreign countries to build new, potentially threatening weapons. Although not formally part of the executive branch, the United States International Trade Commission (USITC) analyzes claims by injured industries and provides recommendations to the president.[49]

Implementation, Program Adoption, and Agenda Setting

Although the implementation phase of the policy process necessarily follows agenda setting and program adoption, its connection to them is not linear. The administrative experience leads to additions to the agenda and to the adoption of new programs. If a program is not accomplishing what it was intended to, or if it produces outcomes not at all intended or anticipated, Congress can change it. A policy may inadvertently expose previously undetected problems, or it may even create them. This turn of events could start the process of agenda setting, this time in direct response to a problem caused by government action.

Ideally, the administrative experience leading to the recognition of problems, program modification, and consideration of altogether new programs would occur in a rational way. Government would engage in a logical exercise of error correction. But government is rarely rational, at least from an outsider's perspective. Thus, the interaction between program implementation, agenda setting, and program adoption is likely to be messy and difficult to sort out analytically.

Like every other policy area, trade policy repeatedly illustrates the nonlinear nature of the policy process. Congress has numerous means by which it can monitor the executive's implementation of programs. Unlike traditional foreign policy, where Congress's role is severely limited to giving advice, limiting funds, and voicing opposition through resolutions, trade policy permits Congress to engage in activities normally associated with domestic policy. Thus, Congress can engage in traditional oversight activities—hearings, studies and analyses, appropriations—when it comes to the executive's implementation of trade policy. Congress may choose to act based on the results of these activities. As noted earlier, for example, Congress shifted some decision-making authority from the Treasury Department to the Commerce Department in the belief that Commerce would be more receptive to the claims of injured industries than Treasury.

The central point is that much of what is considered trade policy—trade sanctions, bilateral agreements, GATT negotiations—is conducted by authority of Congress. The U.S. trade law includes programs that give the executive varying degrees of administrative discretion to engage in these sorts of activities. From the perspective of domestic policy analysis, then, in conducting trade policy, the executive is in fact engaged in program implementation. Viewing the executive's activity in this way opens the door to a careful analysis of implementation, traditionally the purview of analysts of domestic policy. Doing so will provide a more accurate characterization of the dynamic between Congress and the executive, particularly the president, on these issues.

More ambitiously, taking this approach could provide new insights into and explanations of the domestic roots of American trade policy.

Trade Policy and the New Institutionalism

In recent years, students of government, politics, and public policy have refocused their attention on government organizations. The central question guiding their analyses has been how the institutional characteristics of these organizations affect what they do.[50]

Certainly the call to pay attention to institutions has had a large role in shaping political science research in recent years. However, there is nothing particularly new about analyzing institutions. ("Institution" usually means a pattern of rules and norms of behavior over time.) The practical reality of conducting research based on this nebulous concept is to examine political organizations—both governmental (executive branch agencies, for example) and nongovernmental (primarily political parties and interest groups). Political scientists have been analyzing organizations since the emergence of the discipline.[51] Despite the occasional overstatement, the new institutionalism is in fact a *re*newed interest in political organization. Perhaps in response to behavioralism and rational choice models of politics, analysts have returned to organizational characteristics on which to concentrate their research. This does not mean organization theory as developed in sociology necessarily; an institutional perspective can grow out of different methodological traditions. Current developments aside, it is important to bear in mind that political science was concerned with organization from the beginning, and while this concern may have receded in the advances of other, nonorganizational perspectives, it has never disappeared.

The policy process model proposed here incorporates the approaches of the new institutionalism. This analysis considers both the relationships among government actors in the development of trade policy and the organizational, or institutional, characteristics of each of the major participants. How does the relationship between Congress and the executive, for example, affect policy outcomes? How do the institutional characteristics of the Commerce Department affect its role in developing trade policy? Explicit, or even implicit, application of some variant of the new institutionalism sheds some light on the trade policy process.

Several institutional approaches have emerged from studies of this type in recent years. Bert A. Rockman classifies them as historic-comparative, bounded rationality, and rational choice. The historic-comparative approach examines government organizations in terms of their institutional history. The practices of past government officials establish the parameters for current government officials' actions. By examining the institutional development of government organizations, it is possible to anticipate responses to new situations. As Rockman puts it, "[p]olicy-making patterns over time suggest to us the range of feasible options for the future."[52] Using this approach to institutions, the analyst looks for historic patterns, traditions, norms of behavior, long-term connections to other political participants, and the like to identify the limits of new activities. This historical approach does not assume that a clear pattern of political change exists. Rather, it suggests that organizations proceed through time at their own pace; changes in one period do not necessarily correspond to changes in another. Thus, there is no reason to look for periods of order in events, occasionally "punctuated" by dramatic change.[53] This type of analysis places political organizations in historical context or situations allowing for analysis of them in terms of political time.[54]

The bounded-rationality approach to institutions is derived from Herbert Simon's conceptualization of organizational behavior. The central point in this approach to government organizations is that officials are limited in their ability to acquire information about a problem. Finding that obtaining all information is too costly or perhaps impossible, officials take a course of action that is satisfactory, but falls short of optimal. The rational search for solutions to a problem, then, is bounded. The boundaries to the willingness of officials to seek information are set by the organization's functions or jurisdiction. This "satisficing" behavior characterizes the routine activities of government agencies.[55]

The rational-choice approach to institutions incorporates the concept of individual rationality borrowed from microeconomics into an analysis of how individuals behave within organizations. Individuals act on the basis of their self-interest. Members of Congress, it could be argued, want most to get reelected. They will seek to structure Congress in such a way that allows them to serve their constituents and powerful interest groups, thereby enhancing their reelection chances.[56] Congress goes further by writing laws that allow it to control implementation. The president, technically responsible for implementation, responds by doing as much as possible to control the bureaucracy.

> The logic of institutional conflict is overpowering and is inherent in the separation of legislative and presidential power. Presidents politicize the bureaucracy in their own self-defense—an entirely rational response, just as it is rational for Congress to do what is expedient for the interest groups that can help them.[57]

The rational-choice variant of the new institutionalism melds a more traditional concern for organizational properties with the comparatively new rational-choice approach to analyzing public policy.

The Policy Process and Institutions

I have devoted the bulk of this chapter to laying out a policy process model that can be used to analyze trade policy. How does institutional analysis fit? Hugh Heclo provides the beginning of the answer. In a recent summation of new approaches to American politics, Heclo advises political scientists to reconsider the three main components of politics: ideas, interests, and institutions. Heclo argues that these components have always been at the root of political analysis, though one might be more popular at any point in time.[58] Thus, early students of politics concentrated their efforts on institutions. Interests have occupied center stage in recent years, as rational-choice theories focus on individuals trying to achieve goals consistent with their interests, as the principal unit of political analysis. Ideas have found their way into political analysis in studies of ideology, culture, and policy innovation.

In the spirit of parsimony, political scientists have constructed explanations of politics based on one of these factors. Everything can be explained by rational individuals acting according to their interests. Institutional structure determines policy outcomes. Political culture makes America "exceptional." Heclo suggests that efforts to boil politics down to one category of explanations—frequently trumpeted as not a good way, but the *only* way to understand politics—are unnecessary. Political science can benefit from theories that combine in some measure ideas, interests, and institutions. Implicitly, Heclo's argument, perhaps unintendedly, suggests that at this stage of the development of the discipline, such parsimony is not yet ready for prime time. There is much to be learned with richer, more comprehensive analyses, even if their predictive capacity and elegance do not measure up.

The policy process model I have described here incorporates ideas, interests, and institutions. The interaction of the three components at different points in the policy process can go a long way toward explaining American trade policy. Ideas and interests are critical during the agenda-setting phase. Alternatives consist of ideas. Policy entrepreneurs, operating on the basis of their interest in seeing a particular policy outcome become reality, turn alternatives into solutions to problems. Ideas and interests come together in agenda setting. The manner in which they combine is determined in large part by institutions. To take a simple, stark example, a solution may be attached to a problem in the form of a court case, an administrative rule, or a piece of legislation.

Institutions are central to program adoption and program implementation. Clearly, congressional structure and procedure affect policy outcomes. Whether a bill is assigned to a favorable or unfavorable committee can determine its fate. Unified House Republicans can accomplish a great deal more than fractious House Democrats. A USTR who has the ear of the president and is responsive to the chief executive's policies can be effective in administering trade sanctions, while a secretary of state, more concerned with traditional diplomacy, will likely give trade policy second-class status. A politicized USITC will bow to the prevailing political wind, while a neutral one will resist.

Conclusion

Although the trade policy debate can be complex, technical, and esoteric, the arguments frequently boil down to one of the three main positions. Free trade is rooted in the classical economics of the early nineteenth century, eschewing government intervention and celebrating the power of the market, both domestically and internationally. Protectionism grew out of the nineteenth-century American practice of shielding American producers from foreign competition both to allow them to develop and to provide revenue to the U.S. government.

Managed or strategic trade is a contemporary phenomenon, cobbled together from U.S. trade polices intended to meet the demands of economic change.

The three approaches are related to basic values that inform all public policy in the United States. At stake is the time-honored relationship between economic growth and the distribution of wealth. Policies intended to promote growth usually call for reduced government intervention and increased reliance on the market. The free-trade position, which fits here, emphasizes opportunity, individual responsibility, high rewards for success, and heavy costs for failure. Even the term "protection" captures the essence of the approach: Government has a responsibility to care for citizens—in this case, protecting them from economic hardship. An equitable distribution of wealth underlies the crass self-interest that is typically more evident in protectionist policies. Managed trade tries to find a balance between the two.[59] It promises economic growth by claiming that government intervention is necessary to extend free trade. At the same time, it offers help to displaced workers and firms resulting from otherwise desirable economic change.

The competition among trade policy positions illustrates the relationship between economics and policy. Government officials must rely on the uncertain tenets of the economics and the expertise of its practitioners to make decisions that affect the most fundamental concerns in American society. As trade issues pass through agenda setting, program adoption, and implementation, it becomes clear that trade policy is an uncertain business, laden with ideology, policy entrepreneurship, and the politics of winners and losers.

Endnotes

1. I. M. Destler, *American Trade Politics,* 3rd ed. (Washington, D.C.: Institute for International Economics; and New York: The Twentieth Century Fund, 1995), 105–37.
2. Destler, *American Trade Politics,* 11–38, 65–104; Robert A. Pastor, *Congress and the Politics of U.S. Foreign Economic Policy, 1929–1976* (Berkeley, Calif.: Univ. of California Press, 1980); Stephen D. Cohen, *The Making of United States International Economic Policy,* 3rd ed. (New York: Praeger, 1988), 98–120; Susan C. Schwab, *Trade-Offs: Negotiating the Omnibus*

Trade and Competitiveness Act (Boston, Mass.: Harvard Business School Press, 1994), 79–218; Sharyn O'Halloran, *Politics, Process, and American Trade Policy* (Ann Arbor, Mich.: Univ. of Michigan Press, 1994); and Susanne Lohmann and Sharyn O'Halloran, "Divided Government and U.S. Trade Policy: Theory and Evidence," *International Organization* 48 (Autumn 1994): 595–632.

3. E. E. Schattschneider, *Politics, Pressure, and the Tariff* (New York: Prentice Hall, 1935); Jeffry A. Frieden and David A. Lake, "Introduction: International Politics and International Economics," in Jeffry A. Frieden and David A. Lake, eds., *International Political Economy: Perspectives on Global Power and Wealth,* 3rd ed. (New York: St. Martin's, 1995), 1–16.

4. For the general argument, see Alexander Hamilton, *Report on the Subject of Manufactures,* vol. 10 of *The Papers of Alexander Hamilton* (New York: Columbia Univ. Press, 1966), 230–340. For an excellent intellectual history of the concept, see Douglas A. Irwin, *Against the Tide: An Intellectual History of Free Trade* (Princeton, N.J.: Princeton Univ. Press, 1996), chap. 8.

5. In October 1995, the Clinton administration proposed relaxing restrictions on the export of computers. See "U.S. Announces Major Reform of Computer Export Controls," *Dispatch,* 23 October 1995, 776. This move came back to haunt the administration, since China's access to American technology has led to congressional claims that Clinton's policies have jeopardized national security.

6. See chapter 7.

7. For his general statement on international trade, see Patrick J. Buchanan, *The Great Betrayal: How American Sovereignty and Social Justice Are Being Sacrificed to the Gods of the Global Economy* (Boston: Little, Brown, 1998).

8. H. Ross Perot with Pat Choate, *Save Your Job, Save Our Country: Why NAFTA Must Be Stopped—Now!* (New York: Hyperion, 1993), chaps. 3, 4.

9. David P. Levine, *Wealth and Freedom: An Introduction to Political Economy* (New York: Cambridge Univ. Press, 1995), 134.

10. For a concise, readable discussion of the benefits and costs of free trade, see Gary Burtless, Robert Z. Lawrence, Robert E. Litan, and Robert J. Shapiro, *Globaphobia: Confronting Fears about Open Trade* (Washington, D.C.: Brookings Institution and the Progressive Policy Institute; New York: The Twentieth Century Fund, 1998).

11. See, for example, Bhagwati, *The World Trading System at Risk* (Princeton, N.J.: Princeton Univ. Press, 1991); and Anne O. Krueger, "Free Trade Is the Best Policy," in Robert Z. Lawrence and Charles L. Schultze, eds., *An American Trade Strategy: Options for the 1990s* (Washington, D.C.: Brookings Institution, 1990), 68–96.

12. Burtless, et al., *Globaphobia*; Edward L. Hudgins, ed., *Freedom to Trade:*

Refuting the New Protectionism (Washington, D.C.: Cato Institute, 1997); Anne O. Krueger, *American Trade Policy: A Tragedy in the Making* (Washington, D.C.: American Enterprise Institute, 1995); and Bryan T. Johnson, "Why Free Trade Is Good for America," The Heritage Foundation, F.Y.I. No 127, 23 January 1997.

13. For summary discussion of these perspectives, see Rudiger W. Dornbusch, "Policy Options for Freer Trade: The Case for Bilateralism," in Lawrence and Schultze, eds., *An American Trade Strategy*, 125–34; and Robert Z. Lawrence, "Discussion," in Lawrence and Schultze, eds., *An American Trade Strategy*, 136–38.

14. Burtless, et al., chap. 7; Dani Rodrik, *Has Globalization Gone Too Far?* (Washington, D.C.: Institute for International Economics, 1997).

15. Laura D'Andrea Tyson, *Who's Bashing Whom? Trade Conflict in High-Technology Industries* (Washington, D.C.: Institute for International Economics, 1992), 17–28.

16. For a concise presentation of the logic behind managed trade, see Robert Kuttner, "Managed Trade and Economic Sovereignty," in Robert A. Blecker, ed., *U.S. Trade Policy and Global Growth: New Directions in the International Economy* (Armonk, N.Y.: M. E. Sharpe, 1996), 3–36.

17. Ibid.

18. Ibid., 32.

19. Robert B. Reich, *The Work of Nations: Preparing Ourselves for 21st Century Capitalism* (New York: Knopf, 1991), 171–84, 225–40.

20. Laura D'Andrea Tyson, "Managed Trade: Making the Best of Second Best," in Lawrence and Schultze, eds., *An American Trade Strategy*, 142–85.

21. John W. Kingdon, *Agendas, Alternatives, and Public Policies*, 2nd ed. (New York: HarperCollins, 1995); and Deborah A. Stone, *Policy Paradox: The Art of Political Decision Making* (New York: W. W. Norton, 1997).

22. See, for example, Richard W. Stevenson, "U.S. Trade Deficit Worsens, and Gap with China Grows," *New York Times* (Late New York Edition), 21 November 1996, A1.

23. United States Trade Representative, *1997 Trade Policy Agenda and 1996 Annual Report of the President of the United States on the Trade Agreements Program* (Washington, D.C.: U.S. Government Printing Office, 1997), 168–83.

24. This discussion is based largely on Stone, *Policy Paradox,* part II.

25. The discussion of symbols and numbers is taken from Stone, *Policy Paradox,* chaps. 6 and 7.

26. For example, see Robert D. Hershey, Jr., "Trade Gap Swells to Record; Japanese Auto Imports Cited," *New York Times,* 22 June 1995, A1, B2.

27. Most experts argue that trade policy alone cannot eliminate the trade deficit. Other macroeconomic factors, including the federal budget deficit, play an important role and must be addressed as well. For a straightforward discus-

sion of some of these issues, see Paul Krugman, *The Age of Diminished Expectations: U.S. Economic Policy in the 1990s* (Cambridge, Mass.: MIT Press, 1992), 35–50.

28. This discussion of solutions draws on Stone, *Policy Paradox*, part IV.

29. This discussion relies heavily on Kingdon, *Agendas, Alternatives, and Public Policies*, 71–195.

30. Destler, *American Trade Politics*, 11–38; 65–104; and Lohmann and O'Halloran, "Divided Government and U.S. Trade Policy."

31. See chapter 2.

32. Roger H. Davidson and Walter J. Oleszek, *Congress and Its Members*, 6th ed. (Washington, D.C.: CQ Press, 1998), 260.

33. Eichengreen's analysis of Smoot–Hawley is based on surprise at the absence of 100 percent voting and a search for why it did not occur. See Barry Eichengreen, "The Political Economy of the Smoot–Hawley Tariff," in Frieden and Lake, eds., *International Political Economy*, 3rd ed., 37–46.

34. Members of Congress tend to vote along party lines because they are members of the party and therefore agree with its policy positions, and because they look to fellow party members for voting cues. See John W. Kingdon, *Congressmen's Voting Decisions* (New York: Harper & Row), 105–26.

35. An excellent example is the relationship that developed between House Ways and Means Committee Chairman Dan Rostenkowski (D-IL) and Senate Finance Committee Chairman Bob Packwood (R-OR) during the creation of the Tax Reform Act of 1986. See Jeffrey H. Birnbaum and Alan S. Murray, *Showdown at Gucci Gulch: Lawmakers, Lobbyists, and the Unlikely Triumph of Tax Reform* (New York: Vintage, 1987).

36. Kingdon, *Congressmen's Voting Decisions*, 22.

37. The most important example of this type of analysis is Schattschneider's. See also Raymond A. Bauer, Ithiel de Sola Pool, and Lewis Anthony Dexter, *American Business and Public Policy: The Politics of Foreign Trade* (New York: Atherton, 1963), 321–99. Studies have also examined domestic economic forces, though not necessarily concentrating on interest groups as such. See Peter Alexis Gourevitch, "International Trade, Domestic Coalitions, and Liberty: Comparative Responses to the Crisis of 1873–1896," in Frieden and Lake, eds., *International Political Economy* (St. Martin's, 1995), 3rd ed., 90–109; and Jeff Frieden, "Sectoral Conflict and U.S. Foreign Economic Policy, 1914–1940," in G. John Ikenberry, David A. Lake, and Michael A. Mastanduno, eds., *The State and American Foreign Economic Policy* (Ithaca, N.Y.: Cornell Univ. Press, 1988), 59–90.

38. Bauer, Pool, and Dexter, *American Business and Public Policy*, 332–40.

39. See chapter 7. The American high-technology electronics industry is represented by at least ten major interest groups that frequently do not agree on public policy issues. See Philip A. Mundo, "Political Representation of the

U.S. Electronics Industries," presented at the annual meeting of the American
Political Science Association, Washington, D.C., 30 August 1991.

40. Bauer, Pool, and Dexter, *American Business and Public Policy,* 332–40.
41. This is the familiar distinction between the trustee and delegate interpretations of representation.
42. This assumption is the basis of public-choice analyses of congressional behavior. See, for example, Morris P. Fiorina, *Congress: Keystone of the Washington Establishment* (New Haven, Conn.: Yale Univ. Press, 1977; and R.
Douglas Arnold, *The Logic of Congressional Action* (New Haven, Conn.:
Yale Univ. Press, 1990).
43. Avoiding blame can be a powerful motivation for congressional action (or
inaction). See R. Kent Weaver, "The Politics of Blame Avoidance," *Journal of
Public Policy,* 6 (October–December 1986): 371–98.
44. Peter F. Cowhey, "'States' and 'Politics' in American Foreign Economic
Policy," in John S. Odell and Thomas D. Willett, eds., *International Trade
Policies: Gains from Exchange between Economics and Political Science*
(Ann Arbor, Mich.: Univ. of Michigan Press, 1990), 225–51.
45. Sharyn O'Halloran, "Congress and Foreign Trade Policy," in Randall B.
Ripley and James M. Lindsay, eds., *Congress Resurgent: Foreign and Defense
Policy on Capitol Hill* (Ann Arbor, Mich.: Univ. of Michigan Press, 1993),
283–303.
46. James M. Lindsay, "Congress, Foreign Policy, and the New Institutionalism," *International Studies Quarterly* (1994) 38: 291–92.
47. David A. Lake, "The State and American Trade Strategy in the Pre-
hegemonic Era," in Ikenberry, Lake, and Mastanduno, eds., *The State and
American Foreign Economic Policy,* 33–58.
48. For a discussion of the development of the USTR, see Destler, *American
Trade Politics,* 105–37; and Steve Dryden, *Trade Warriors: USTR and the
American Crusade for Free Trade* (New York: Oxford Univ. Press, 1995).
49. See chapter 6.
50. For a general discussion of organizations in politics, see James G. March and
Johan P. Olsen, *Rediscovering Institutions: The Organizational Basis of
Politics* (New York: Free Press, 1989). For an example of application of this
approach, see R. Kent Weaver and Bert A. Rockman, eds., *Do Institutions
Matter? Government Capabilities in the United States and Abroad* (Washing-
ton, D.C.: Brookings Institution, 1993). For a review of the recent theoretical
development of the new institutionalism, see Bert A. Rockman, "The New
Institutionalism and the Old Institutions," in Lawrence C. Dodd and Calvin
Jillson, eds., *New Perspectives on American Politics* (Washington, D.C.: CQ
Press, 1994), 143–61. For specific applications to trade policy, see Helen
Milner, "Maintaining International Commitments in Trade Policy," in
Rockman and Weaver, eds., *Do Institutions Matter?,* 345–69; Judith Gold-

stein, *Ideas, Interests, and American Trade Policy* (Ithaca, N.Y.: Cornell Univ. Press), chaps. 3 and 4; and O'Halloran, *Politics, Process, and American Trade Policy.*

51. Woodrow Wilson, *Congressional Government: A Study in American Politics* (New York: Houghton Mifflin, 1885).

52. Rockman, "The New Institutionalism and the Old Institutions," 147.

53. Karen Orren and Stephen Skowronek, "Beyond the Iconography of Order: Notes for a 'New Institutionalism,'" in Lawrence C. Dodd and Calvin Jillson, eds., *The Dynamics of American Politics: Approaches and Interpretations* (Boulder, Colo.: Westview, 1994), 311–30.

54. See, for example, Stephen Skowronek, "Presidential Leadership in Political Time," in Michael Nelson, ed., *The Presidency and the Political System,* 3rd ed. (Washington, D.C.: CQ Press, 1990), 117–61.

55. Rockman, "The New Institutionalism and the Old Institutions," 149–50.

56. Fiorina, *Congress: Keystone of the Washington Establishment,* 56–70.

57. Rockman, "The New Institutionalism and the Old Institutions," 153.

58. Hugh Heclo, "Ideas, Interests, and Institutions," in Lawrence C. Dodd and Calvin Jillson, eds., *The Dynamics of American Politics: Approaches and Interpretations* (Boulder, Colo.: Westview, 1994), 366–92.

59. Steven Pearlstein and Paul Blustein, "In the Best of Both Worlds, Consider a Third Option," *Washington Post,* 23 June 1997, A 12.

4

Domestic Politics and the GATT

During the 1980s and 1990s, the American economy began to feel the brunt of dramatic economic change. Because of stunning leaps in communication, technology, and manufacturing design, corporations increasingly spread their operations across national boundaries in search of the cheapest components and labor. At the same time, foreign firms challenged American companies in several key sectors in the American market as well as in other markets around the world.

The growing uncertainty in the international competitiveness of American industry resulted in two convergent developments in the U.S. trade policy. First, the institutions involved in the policy process adapted to the new challenge. Congress and the presidency, including executive branch agencies, changed the rules by which they process trade policy in light of heightened global economic competition. The adaptation is remarkable because it was done to meet the new challenge, while at the same time sustaining a commitment to trade liberalization, the dominant theme in U.S. trade policy since the end of the Second World War. Second, the policies themselves reflected the dual nature of the institutional adjustment. Still committed to multilateralism and the principle of the elimination of all trade barriers, the United States remained a major supporter of the General Agreement on Tariffs and Trade (GATT) and regional free-trade agreements. At the same time, recognizing the political consequences of economic hardship caused by foreign competition, U.S. trade policy incorporated measures designed to exact concessions from foreign governments that either engage in trade practices damaging to American economic interests or permit or encourage firms based within their borders to do so.

This chapter briefly reviews the history of U.S. involvement in the GATT along with short assessments of major trade legislation in the 1960s and 1970s. The discussion then focuses on the 1984 and, especially, the 1988 trade bills in themselves and in relation to the Uruguay Round of GATT negotiations. Although GATT negotiations are an international activity, Congress must give the executive the authority to enter such talks. The relationship between Congress and the president on this issue is the central institutional arrangement. More directly than dealing with the GATT, passing trade legislation is very much a matter of the domestic policy process. The institutional characteristics of Congress play a major role in determining the content of trade legislation.

While institutions comprise most of the story in these areas, ideas and interests play a significant role as well. By the 1970s, Democrats and Republicans had completed the task of trading places on the desirability of trade liberalization to the extent that neither would ever have a consistent position on the issue. Interest groups representing American firms adversely affected by trade began to mobilize during the 1970s. Textiles, steel, and automobiles were well-represented in Washington. In addition to working on trade bills, interest groups sought administrative relief as executive branch agencies implemented key provisions of U.S. trade law, like Sections 201 and 301.[1] (This pattern of interest-group behavior intensified in the 1980s and affected the contents of the 1988 trade bill and implementation.) On the other side were a growing number of interest groups supporting free trade. They pressed for trade liberalization, encouraging government officials to resist mounting protectionist pressure.[2]

The interaction between ideas and institutions underlay the overall institutional changes resulting from new economic conditions. Indeed, the institutional rearrangements grew out of a commitment to adhere to the principle of trade liberalization. The idea, in effect, had become so embedded in the institutions that when the institutions were forced to adapt, individuals within them sought to do so in a way that sustained the idea.[3] Beyond this intriguing durability of the idea of free trade, new solutions emerged to specific trade problems arising out of the uncertainty of the new domestic and international economies.

Background

The United States enjoyed political, military, and economic dominance immediately following the Second World War. From this position, American policy makers reckoned that the United States had every-thing to gain and little to lose by leading a massive economic recon-struction of the non-Communist world. Part of that effort was a plan to create an international trade organization—a supranational entity intended to promote global trade liberalization. Falling short of that, the same impetus created the GATT, something like a second-best alternative to a genuine supranational organization.[4] Created in 1948, the GATT went through several rounds of negotiations in the 1950s in which considerable progress was made in the reduction of tariffs. United States involvement in these negotiations required the passage of several major trade bills that gave the president authority to negotiate tariff reductions by stipulated rates and essentially incorporated GATT rules into U.S. law.[5]

U.S. trade policy changed in the 1960s, mainly with respect to the GATT. By the time John F. Kennedy moved into the White House, tariffs had been reduced so much that there was not much more to be gained by making them the center of future rounds of GATT negotia-tions. Continuing in the Wilsonian internationalist tradition, Kennedy sought to take bolder steps toward trade liberalization, a strategy continued by Kennedy's successor, Lyndon Johnson. The Trade Ex-pansion Act of 1962 reflected Kennedy's internationalist outlook. Go-ing beyond prior trade bills, which had given the president explicit but narrow authority to reduce tariffs, the 1962 legislation was the first trade bill to authorize the president to engage in multilateral negotia-tions through the GATT.[6] Behind American leadership, the GATT turned to nontariff barriers (NTBs) to trade, a considerably more nettlesome set of issues than tariffs.[7]

The 1970s: Chips, Datsuns, and Steel

American industry experienced a major shock to its collective psyche in the 1970s. Foreign competition in two manufacturing stalwarts—automobiles and steel—caused American firms' profits to drop (if not disappear altogether) and contributed to the closing of factories and the idling of thousands of blue-collar workers. American-made products could not compete with foreign manufacturers in terms of quality or price. For example, Japanese automobile manufacturers filled a new demand for small, fuel-efficient cars. The Big Four—Ford Motor Company, General Motors Corporation, Chrysler Corporation, and American Motors Corporation—had not planned for this shift in consumer preference, nor were they able to respond quickly to the new market.[8] American steel producers bent under the weight of foreign competition as well.[9] More surprisingly, the American semiconductor industry cried foul as Japanese chip makers flooded the American market with cheap dynamic random access memory (DRAM) chips.[10]

In addition to the dramatic reversal of fortune experienced by major American corporate champions, the U.S. economy was suffering from the confluence of several negative trends. Inflation was climbing, resulting in part from overspending in the 1960s and early 1970s to fund both expanded domestic programs and the Vietnam War. At the same time, baby boomers and women were entering the job market, straining the economy's capacity to create new jobs, and energy prices soared as oil producers limited supply to increase price in classic cartel behavior. Interest rates shot up, and policy makers first began to worry seriously about an out-of-control federal budget deficit. These related developments combined to create conditions of nerve-rattling economic uncertainty. Given all this, it is hardly surprising that the federal government tried to remedy economic woes. Among its efforts were new initiatives in trade policy.

The Policy Response

The Tokyo Round

The Tokyo Round of GATT negotiations grew out of the shortcomings of the Kennedy Round, the results of which Congress never formally approved. An ambitious Kennedy administration had attempted to expand the scope of the multilateral trade regime by placing NTBs on the negotiating table. In part because of congressional resistance, the Kennedy Round made little progress on NTBs.[11]

The negative economic conditions in the United States supplied another major part of the drive to initiate a new round of GATT talks.

Beginning the 1960s, U.S. policy makers became aware of the problems foreign competition was creating for American firms. Not surprisingly, these concerns first materialized in Congress, the governmental institution most in tune with particular interests in American politics. Recognizing the changing economic atmosphere, President Richard M. Nixon created the Commission on International Trade and Investment Policy (the Williams Commission) to investigate international trade and U.S. trade policy. The results of the report captured the growing uneasiness among American producers. It recognized the economic resurgence of the Japanese and European economies and recommended a multilateral approach to the new problems facing American firms.[12]

Throughout the 1972 presidential election year, Special Trade Representative (STR) William Eberle and his deputy, William Pearce, worked on a trade bill that would allow U.S. participation in a new GATT round. For his part, President Nixon favored a new round of GATT negotiations and agreed to pursue trade legislation that would grant him the authority to enter the negotiations. With a nudge from British Prime Minister Edward Heath, Nixon began building domestic support for a new trade initiative. The Watergate scandal soon consumed Nixon, leaving to the STR, cabinet officers, and other aides the task of supplying energy for the trade bill and new GATT talks.[13] Congress eventually granted the president negotiating authority for this round of GATT negotiations, but not until 1974, after Gerald Ford had replaced Nixon in the White House.[14]

The 1974 Trade Act

The 1974 Trade Act granted the president the authority to enter the Tokyo Round of GATT talks. Reducing the trade-inhibiting effects of such things as discriminatory government procurement policies and licensing requirements quickly proved to be much more difficult than the comparatively simple task of reducing tariffs. Consider the institutional arrangement that accompanied the march toward lower tariffs. Congress granted the executive the authority to negotiate tariff reductions by explicit percentages. The executive, then, could use that set figure as a target, fully aware that it could go no further. This made the executive's role simple; limits to the president's ability to lower tariffs sent clear signals to foreign leaders and gave U.S. representatives a straightforward task with clear parameters. When the tariff reductions were met, the president could return to Congress for another installment of negotiating authority to reduce tariffs still further, but again by a fixed amount.

Now, consider how making NTBs the central concern of multilateral trade negotiations affected the institutional arrangements. Since NTBs involved much more than numerical tariff reductions, U.S. representatives needed room within which to strike deals on difficult issues. To accommodate this new requirement, Congress introduced fast-track procedures in the 1974 trade bill,[15] which gave the president the authority to negotiate trade agreements with foreign countries, with the proviso that Congress would have the opportunity to accept or reject the deals. The president was required to inform Congress of his intent to enter negotiations and to keep Congress informed of the progress of the talks. To stop itself from amending trade accords, which would both scuttle agreements and undermine the president's negotiating position, Congress included in fast-track procedures a rule that allowed it to vote either yes or no on a trade agreement, with no opportunity for amendments. The fast-track procedures gave the executive more credibility in the eyes of foreign negotiators because the mechanism prevented Congress from adding all sorts of potentially damaging amendments to the deal.

In addition to introducing fast-track procedures, the Trade Act of 1974 included numerous provisions that reflected Congress's growing dissatisfaction with executive enforcement of U.S. trade law. The general thrust of these measures was both to give the president more tools with which to deal with trade issues and at the same time to limit the president's discretion in implementation.[16] For example, the 1974 bill created Section 301, which gave the president broad powers to address foreign countries' alleged unfair trade practices, including, for example, domestic laws and regulations that discriminated against American products. Congress changed Section 201, the escape clause originally included in the Trade Act of 1942, to make it easier for domestic producers to claim injury resulting from foreign competition. Finally, Congress strengthened antidumping and countervailing-duty provisions of U.S. trade law with the goal of increasing the likelihood that American petitioners would be granted administrative relief in response to foreign countries' subsidizing their industries.[17]

With the Trade Act of 1974, Congress attempted to address problems some legislators had perceived within the executive branch's trade apparatus. The bill changed the name of the Tariff Commission to the United States International Trade Commission (USITC) and changed the Special Trade Representative to the United States Trade Representative (USTR). The law gave more decision-making authority to these agencies with the goal of limiting presidential discretion in mind.[18]

Key committee chairmen played a major role in the relationship between Congress and the executive. With respect to trade policy, House Ways and Means Chairman Wilbur Mills (D-AR) and Senate Finance Committee Chairman Russell Long (D-LA) negotiated with the executive branch to create the 1974 bill. Nixon and Ford administration officials—including STR Eberle, Treasury Secretary George Schultz, Agriculture Secretary Earl Butz—worked closely with Mills and Long to create the legislation. Their task was made easier because these two powerful legislators, once convinced, could deliver the entire Congress.[19]

The executive, for its part, was hardly a focused, unified force leading the United States into the Tokyo Round. The STR competed for economic policy leadership with Nixon's Council on International Economic Policy and with Secretary of State Henry Kissinger. The former was set up to direct economic policy, and therefore fell instantly into a turf war with the STR, and the latter treated trade policy as secondary to foreign policy. Senator Long addressed these bureaucratic facts of life in the 1974 trade bill by giving the STR statutory authority, arguing that the trade agency should not be the president's "flunky."[20]

The institutional adjustments embodied in the Trade Act of 1974 are in part a response to changes in the global economy and the American position in it. The rules of the international trading system had graduated to a more complex level. Having reduced tariffs dramatically over the previous twenty-five years, and with further necessary tariff reductions easily within reach, economic leaders turned to the more difficult problem of NTBs. This sparked an adjustment in American political institutions as Congress gave the president the negotiating flexibility required to deal with these complex issues, at the same time eliminating its ability to alter agreements once they were in place. Congress did not abdicate its constitutionally based authority over trade policy altogether, of course; it created the fast-track procedure, which allowed congressional input at the beginning of negotiations and final say in an up–down vote at the end. In doing so, Congress kept its grip on the controls of U.S. trade policy, but limited its ability to steer.

Congress was in a grumpy mood as it considered the results of the Kennedy Round in 1967. From the perspective of many legislators, the executive had exceeded its authority in this round of GATT negotiations by agreeing to new antidumping accords and discarding the American Selling Price mechanism.[21] The congressional displeasure continued through the difficult years of 1968 through 1973, with trade policy being a secondary concern compared with the Vietnam War and other matters of presidential excess. With this as the backdrop, it is hardly surprising that President Nixon's 1973 request for negotiating authority for the Tokyo Round met with congressional opposition.

Congressional willingness to give negotiating authority to the executive at this time in history reflects the importance of economic changes for American political institutions. The year 1974 was not one in which to expect Congress to accommodate the executive. The Watergate scandal, which had engulfed the Nixon administration, was coming to its inevitable end as the embattled president resigned in the face of impeachment proceedings. With the unfolding deceptions of Watergate as the background, Congress responded to what many perceived to be ten years of presidential abuse of power by enacting the War Powers Resolution in 1973 and the Budget Act in 1974, both intended to rein in an out-of-control executive and at the same time reestablish congressional authority over military affairs and federal government spending.[22] In this atmosphere, it is surprising that Congress willingly turned over more authority to the president on trade policy. The most plausible explanation for this is that Congress, regardless of mood or relations with the president, could not ignore the realities of the changing global economy. The institutional response, which must have been galling to many legislators, was to do what seemed necessary to deal with these changes.

Congressional action on other aspects of U.S. trade law were more consistent with the congressional–presidential relations at the time. Not only did Congress restrict presidential discretion in implementing some key provisions of U.S. trade law, but also it reached into the top layers of the executive branch itself, seeking to alter the way the executive did business and giving itself a toehold in the executive trade policy apparatus. These were institutional responses to the pressure American producers were feeling from foreign competition. Congress appeased these interests by enacting measures to induce the executive to supply administrative relief to American producers claiming injury resulting from foreign competition, for whatever reason.

The Trade Agreements Act of 1979

The Trade Agreements Act of 1979 closed the deal on the Tokyo Round and continued the trends in the relationship between Congress and the president begun in the 1974 act. Using the fast-track procedure for the first time, Congress approved the results of the Tokyo Round with little difficulty, in no small part because the executive had kept Congress and the private sector informed of the negotiations.[23] The institutional arrangement embodied in the fast-track procedure successfully maintained the U.S. position, along with its obligations, in the international trading system.

The key player in the Carter administration was STR Robert Strauss. A long-time political operative in the Democratic Party, Strauss had helped to engineer Carter's 1976 election to the presidency. Strauss understood the ways of Washington; he knew Congress, knew how to negotiate, and perhaps better than any other, knew just what it would take to get Congress to agree to the Tokyo Round. On the international front, Strauss successfully worked out differences with the European Community (EC) and with Japan to get the stalled talks moving. Domestically, working with Senator Long and other key congressional leaders, Strauss secured support for the latest round of GATT negotiations. Going beyond Capitol Hill, Strauss wooed key interest groups—for example, those representing the steel and textile industries—to get their support, or at least acquiescence, for the Tokyo Round.[24]

With the 1979 bill, Congress continued its effort to make the executive more receptive to American producer interests. For example, it strengthened Section 301 of the trade law by changing the way unfair trade practices would be handled. Congress also required the president to reassign some trade policy authority within the executive branch; the Commerce Department, traditionally friendly to American business, took over antidumping and countervailing-duty responsibilities from the Treasury Department. In addition Congress made countervailing-duty investigations more receptive to complainants—American producers.[25]

All of these moves reflect continuing congressional dissatisfaction with the manner in which the executive had been implementing U.S. trade law. Congress sought to push the president and top executive branch officials to be more sympathetic to American producers, while at the same time protecting itself from protectionist pressure. The 1979 law, then, reflects the institutional embodiment of the American dual trade policy. The allocation of responsibilities between Congress and the executive permitted continued U.S. commitment to global trade liberalization by means of multilateralism, while simultaneously allowing the government to pursue the interests of complaining American producers.

The institutional arrangement that insulated Congress from protectionist pressure held during the 1970s. Although Congress was forced to respond in some fashion—mainly by changing administrative procedures and structures to encourage more enthusiastic enforcement of U.S. trade law—it did not succumb to unbridled protectionism.

Ideas

Even with this cursory look at the 1970s, it is clear that the idea of free trade has been remarkably durable. Having enjoyed economic dominance in the 1950s and early 1960s, supporting trade liberalization was an easy, painless position—Americans had everything to gain and little, if anything, to lose. Under economic pressure in the 1970s, however, it would be reasonable to expect the idea of free trade to fall by the wayside. It certainly took considerable heat, and U.S. trade policy began to incorporate a variety of means to allow the government to act in ways decidedly antithetical to trade liberalization. The principle of free trade, however, remained the North Star of U.S. foreign economic policy. From Kennedy's ambitious plan for the GATT to the Williams Commission's recommendation that trade problems be addressed in a multilateral, nonsector-specific fashion, to the uneventful approval of the Tokyo Round, the United States remained committed to trade liberalization in general, though specific lapses certainly occurred at an increasing pace.

The Run-up to the Uruguay Round:
The 1988 Trade Bill

The American economy was in turmoil at the beginning of the 1980s. President Jimmy Carter had the dubious honor of presiding over simultaneous high inflation and high unemployment,[26] an unfortunate situation that certainly damaged the president's reelection chances. The tax cuts pushed through Congress by President Ronald Reagan in 1981 reduced revenue to the federal government dramatically. Coming as they did without a compensating cut in federal government spending, the result was a ballooning federal budget deficit. The deficit increased at such an alarming rate that the president, an erstwhile supply-side devotee, found it necessary to support a modest "revenue enhancement" in 1981.[27] If this were not bad enough news, by 1982, the economy had been bogged down in the deepest recession since the Great Depression.[28]

The competitiveness of American industry did not provide a counterweight to the overall pall cast upon the American economy. Steel and automobiles continued to encounter difficulties resulting from foreign competition in both the domestic and foreign markets. The American semiconductor industry had not found relief from foreign competitors—mainly Japanese—and sought more help from government. Add to these woes a rapidly expanding trade deficit, which underscored the weak competitive position of some American producers. In addition to these now-familiar problems, some U.S. policy makers and private sector representatives pointed out the GATT's lack of provisions for service industries and intellectual property protection.[29] In an economy that increasingly relied on high technology and services for growth and more jobs, the absence of such international safeguards became increasingly unacceptable.

Taken together, these factors combined to form a new "issue context."[30] Conditions had changed to the point that the policy environment was ready for new initiatives, which came in the form of the

Uruguay Round of GATT negotiations and the Omnibus Trade and Competitiveness Act of 1988. The story of the 1984 trade bill is a precursor to these more significant developments.

Prelude: The Trade and Tariff Act of 1984

The 1984 trade bill did not involve major shifts in U.S. trade policy. It neither authorized the executive to enter a new round of GATT talks, like the 1974 bill, nor approved the results of recently concluded negotiations, as the 1979 bill did. The 1984 bill incorporated issues that had been nearing the trade policy agenda in the previous decade—such as intellectual property protection, trade in services, and trade in high-technology products.[31] Congress resisted efforts to include in the trade legislation measures intended to protect specific industries. It did, however, strengthen import relief sections of U.S. trade law, especially Sections 201 and 301.[32]

Overall, the 1984 bill sustained the basic institutional arrangement between Congress and the executive on trade policy. Trade policy was still confined to policy elites—mainly top administration officials and congressional committee chairmen. But in Congress's tightening of requirements on the executive, forcing it to gain congressional fast-track approval of future trade-liberalizing agreements, there was some evidence suggesting that Congress was increasingly inclined to seize a greater leadership role in the making of U.S. trade policy.[33] At the same time, even in the uncertain economic conditions of the early 1980s, Congress continued to shield itself from protectionist pressure, leaving to the executive the difficult decisions of who receives administrative relief.

The Omnibus Trade and Competitiveness Act of 1988

Encompassing both traditional trade measures and a package of trade-related provisions, the Omnibus Trade and Competitiveness Act of 1988 (OTCA) reached well beyond other pieces of trade legislation. The OTCA's content reflected the changes in the American position in the global economy and the attendant concerns of U.S. policy makers. The bill included so-called competitiveness measures—provisions intended to help American firms improve their ability to compete in foreign as well as the domestic market. Bearing a thinly veiled resemblance to industrial policy, these sections of the 1988 bill indicate, first, the extent to which policy elites had concluded that much of the country's economic difficulties could be remedied through trade policy, and second, the broadening of the definition of trade policy to include such things as efforts to encourage the development of new technologies.

The 1988 bill sharpened the teeth of U.S. trade law. It strengthened and expanded Section 301 of the 1974 trade bill, transferring authority to administer it formally from the president to the USTR in hopes that the latter's constant contact with groups with interests in trade would cause it to implement the provisions of Section 301 more aggressively than the president had. Moreover, Congress reduced discretion in the use of Section 301, again in hopes that doing so would cause it to be used more effectively. In addition to changes in implementation of Section 301, Congress added Super 301, which required the USTR to create a priority list of countries engaged in unfair trade practices and to take action to stop them, and Special 301, which deals with violations of intellectual property rights in foreign countries. Taken together, these actions reflected Congress's intent to get serious about perceived American trade problems.[34]

The passage of the 1988 trade bill illustrates the institutional characteristics of Congress and the presidency along with the dynamics of their interaction. As the story unfolds, it becomes clear how these institutional characteristics shaped the eventual legislation. The importance of ideas and interests are also clear in the passage of this bill. It is thus worthwhile to tell the legislative story in some detail.

Origins of the OTCA

The 1986 election returned the Democrats to majority status in the Senate and installed a group of new leaders, amenable to a trade bill, who joined the Democratic leaders in the House in support of a trade initiative. The Reagan administration, more aggressive in its trade policy at the time, was also open to the possibility of major trade legislation. The administration's attitude was in part attributable to increasing public pressure to take action in the area of international trade, but also because top officials believed that Congress would inevitably take up the issue.[35] Thus, Congress initiated the OTCA with the support of a willing administration.

The first move came in the House, as H.R. 3, the Trade Act of 1987, was introduced on 6 January 1987. As is the case for all trade legislation, the House Ways and Means Committee had primary jurisdiction over the bill, and its Chairman, Dan Rostenkowski (D-IL), would be a major player in shepherding the legislation through the labyrinth of House procedures.[36] Rostenkowski's game plan for maneuvering the legislation through this maze was clear:

> . . . if he addressed his key members' interests, kept the bill partisan, adopted language different from that expected in the Senate, and produced a text that would not immediately be labeled "protectionist" by the press, then he could get the measure through the House and still have enough maneuvering room in the House–Senate conference to achieve a signable bill.[37]

Rostenkowski adhered to this strategy throughout House deliberations over H.R. 3, although he did not succeed in every conflict. The chairman steered a careful course between the hard-line Democrats and Republicans on his own committee. The former favored strong antidumping and countervailing-duty provisions in the bill, while the latter wished to soften the provisions in the spirit of pursuing trade liberalization. The Gephardt amendment—a strident policy requiring severe retaliation against countries that engaged in unfair trade practices authored by Representative Richard Gephardt (D-MO)—was a major bone of contention. Opposing what he saw as an unnecessarily protectionist provision, Rostenkowski organized the mark-up of the trade bill with the conspicuous absence of the Gephardt amendment. Perhaps recognizing the difficulty of defeating Rostenkowski on his own turf, Gephardt chose not to fight for his amendment in subcommittee.[38] Even Rostenkowski's legendary power and legislative skill could not keep the Gephardt amendment out of the bill, however, as Gephardt introduced it during floor debate and, after spirited speeches, won its approval on a close vote.[39]

The Subcommittee on Trade of the House Ways and Means Committee reported out a bill that had bipartisan support. Rostenkowski's effort to steer the legislation toward the middle at the cost of losing hard-line Democrats, but with the benefit of winning over moderate

Republicans, succeeded. But Democratic opposition to the legislation was significant, as indicated by the fact that Speaker Jim Wright (D-TX) himself was displeased with it.[40]

The Ways and Means bill covered the predictable range of trade-related issues. It strengthened provisions on unfair trade practices, antidumping, and the escape clause, all of which reflected the growing concern among relevant interests that American producers were not competing on a level playing field with foreign firms. It also aimed to rearrange trade policy authority within the executive branch by shifting more responsibility to the USTR.[41] The logic behind this move was that the USTR was a product of congressional action, not presidential discretion. As such, it could be receptive to congressional influence and pressure from industries seeking relief from foreign competition or access to foreign markets. The USTR had the potential of being a congressional outpost within the administration more responsive to particular economic interest than the more free-trade–oriented presidency.

Rostenkowski's bipartisanship attracted a core of Democratic and Republican supporters to the bill, although each displayed different levels of enthusiasm. Leaving the Gephardt language out of the bill and deliberately seeking Republican input throughout the process earned Rostenkowski some support.[42] The House passed the bill, and the story moved across the capitol to the Senate.[43]

Effects of the House's Institutional Characteristics

The House's consideration of the 1987 trade bill involved several key developments that reflect the chamber's institutional character. The ambiguous relationship between committee chairmen and party leaders is evident in the contest among Chairman Rostenkowski, Speaker Wright, and Majority Whip Gephardt. Wright accommodated Rostenkowski's desire to make the bill a bipartisan effort, though not agreeing with it completely. Gephardt took the Chairman on with respect to his effort to add an amendment (in his name) to the bill that would dramatically strengthen the U.S. response to unfair trade practices. In spite of Rostenkowski's political clout, Gephardt won the day by narrowly achieving approval for his amendment on the House floor. The conflict between Gephardt and Rostenkowski on this issue was hardly acrimonious; indeed, each approached the debate with a great deal of respect for the other.

Partisanship was not the key determinant of the outcome of House consideration of the trade bill. Rostenkowski pursued Republican support from the start, mainly to provide some insurance in the event that hard-line members of his own party did not go along with the bill. Republican support—primarily in the person of Representative Bill Frenzel (R-MN)—was key to the bill's moving out of committee, although Frenzel dropped his support for the legislation on the final vote. This turn of events suggests that trade does not easily break down along partisan lines; ideology, constituent interests, and interest-group pressure may be more important than party in determining a legislator's vote on trade.

Business groups seeking to influence the trade bill found the going difficult. Rostenkowski's desire to create a moderate bill attractive to large parts of both parties locked out groups seeking special breaks for the industries that backed them, forcing lobbyists to give up on the House and turn to the Senate.

The Senate's Traditional Role

The conventional view of the Senate is that it tempers the excesses of the House. Representing an entire state and elected to six-year terms, senators are less immediately responsive to particular interests; with only one-hundred members and rules that provide ample opportunities for a determined minority to thwart a majority, the Senate arrests the majoritarian impulse in American politics. This general role of the Senate is evident in the Trade Bill of 1987, although not as dramatically as the conventional wisdom might lead one to believe.

The Senate bill was introduced in the Senate on 5 February 1987. The legislation contained provisions on a range of customary trade-related issues: fast-track authority, the escape clause, responses to unfair trade practices, and intellectual property protection, to name some of the most important ones. The Senate, of course, came under pressure from interest groups and the executive branch to alter the bill, but the changes that were made largely originated in the Senate. Shortly after the bill's introduction, the Finance Committee, under the guidance of Chairman Lloyd Bentsen (D-TX), held hearings involving administration officials—primarily USTR Clayton Yeutter. The dynamics of the interaction between administration officials and senators suggested a lack of trust.[44] A key sticking point in the negotiations was the extent of discretion the president would have in implementing U.S. trade law. The Senate wanted to limit discretion, forcing the president to respond to unfair trade practices with the full force U.S. law allowed. Not surprisingly, the administration saw the matter somewhat differently and wanted to maintain considerable discretion over how to respond to trade problems. This tension resulted in the clumsy language embedded in the Senate bill delineating how a president ought to deal with unfair trade practices using Section 301; the final language was that the president's response was "mandatory but not compulsory."[45]

Chairman Bentsen built support for the legislation within the Finance Committee by giving precedence to provisions with the greatest consensus. The Committee changed the bill in some key respects—for example, tightening restrictions on fast-track authority, introducing the idea of reverse fast-track procedure, relaxing escape clause requirements, increasing the scope of relief options available to the executive branch, and strengthening Section 301 and other provisions of the bill intended to address unfair trade practices.[46] The bill also included provisions on telecommunications, trade adjustment assistance (TAA), and miscellaneous tariff adjustments.

On 7 May 1987, the Finance Committee approved S. 490 19-1. The press thought the bill to be somewhat less strident than the House version, mainly because it lacked an equivalent of the Gephardt amendment. Committee members were confident that the bill would do well both on the Senate floor and in conference with the House trade bill.[47]

As was true for the role of the House Ways and Means Committee in the development of the House trade bill, the Senate Finance Committee had jurisdiction over only one part—albeit the largest and most central part—of the trade bill. Responsibility for other parts of what was becoming the "omnibus bill" was scattered over nine other Senate committees, including Agriculture, Banking, Judiciary, Governmental Affairs, Commerce, Small Business, Foreign Relations, and Labor and Human Resources. To put all these provisions into one omnibus piece of legislation, Senate Majority Leader Robert Byrd (D-WV) created an InterCommittee, under Bentsen's control, to stitch the various parts together.[48] On 16 June 1987, the Commerce, Science, and Transportation Committee, the last committee to deal with the bill, completed its work, sending the legislation to the Senate floor.[49]

Senate floor action began on 25 June 1987. The omnibus trade bill was among the most ambitious single pieces of legislation with which the Senate had ever dealt. Senators offered 160 amendments, 87 of which dealt with provisions originating in the Finance Committee and the rest with relatively nongermane issues like the federal budget deficit and the reflagging of Kuwaiti tankers in the Persian Gulf. The amendment strategy worked out by the bill's proponents was to come to a compromise, before the formal vote on the amendment, to avoid an embarrassing, time-consuming floor fight. Only a few amendments were intended to restrict trade, and for the most part, they were kept out of the bill. The most controversial amendment, which involved plant closings, became the focus of debate, ultimately becoming part of the Senate bill and the first trade bill emerging from conference.[50] In addition to plant closings, amendments dealing with oil and energy security and escape clause provisions caused serious disagreement. Finally, the Senate dealt with the Gephardt amendment with Super 301, a provision that was a less strident version of Gephardt's language.[51]

The Omnibus Trade Act of 1987 passed the Senate 71–27. Winning significant bipartisan support at this stage, the rest of the road remained hardly smooth. Of the nineteen Republicans who voted for the bill, sixteen had already expressed their reservations, assuming that they would be addressed in conference.[52] This set the stage for the effort of representatives from the House and Senate to hammer out differences in conference.

Consequences for the Trade Bill

The procedures and structure of the Senate affected the content of its version of the 1987 trade bill. In general, the Senate arguably produced a more temperate bill than the House did. The strongest evidence for this is the Senate's treatment of provisions delineating U.S. response to unfair trade practices. Unlike the harsh Gephardt language in the House bill, the Senate produced Super 301—a tougher provision than in earlier trade bills, but considerably less offensive than Gephardt's amendment to the House bill.

The behavior of Senate committee and party leaders differed from that of their House counterparts. Finance Committee Chairman Bentsen pursued the trade bill with as much enthusiasm as Rostenkowski had in the House, but he dealt with his committee differently. For example, Bentsen did not find it necessary to cobble together a bill that would gain the support of moderate Republicans on the committee to insure against hard-line Democrats' defections. He did not face the threat of disloyalty from members of his own party, nor was it necessary for him to work so hard to craft a moderate document, since that was the Senate's inclination anyway. Bentsen, finally, used a different strategy than Rostenkowski's to obtain agreement on disputed parts of the bill over which the Finance Committee had jurisdiction. Rather than taking on opposition, he started with measures on which there was considerable agreement and used the consensus to build toward compromise on the remaining contested provisions. Majority Leader Byrd deferred to the Finance Committee Chair in constructing the omnibus legislation. Unlike Speaker Wright, who created his own leadership substitute that encompassed all the provisions reported out of various House committees, Byrd turned over the task of stitching the legislation together by giving Bentsen control over the InterCommittee.

The result in the Senate was a bill that had the full support of its major architect, Senator Bentsen. How this, along with the differences in the two versions of the legislation, would affect the interaction between House and Senate conferees remained to be seen in the last legislative step.

Conference

Because the 1987 trade bill was one of the first pieces of omnibus legislation considered by Congress, its sheer size presented a coordination problem for House and Senate leaders as they went to conference. The conference was organized into seventeen separate subconferences, each dealing with a limited range of issues. Unlike routine conferences on other legislation "where trade-offs were possible throughout a piece of legislation, the atomization of (this) conference structure precluded compromise across issues and subconferences."[53]

The number of subconferences is somewhat misleading, however. In the end, only two seemed crucial to passage of the bill—those that involved key committee and party leaders from each chamber. The other subconferences, those dealing with more peripheral parts of the omnibus bill, fell into line after the first two reached agreement.[54]

The House conferees, headed by Rostenkowski, completed their work on "phase I" of the conference ahead of the Senate. The document (a major portion of the entire omnibus bill) settled disputes on noncontroversial items and dropped issues on which there was considerable disagreement. On their first consideration of the House offer, Senate conferees went to work looking for points on which they could compromise, making counterproposals, and agreeing to drop some issues on which agreement seemed unlikely. By the time the Senate conferees had finished their work, however, many House conferees had left Washington for a weekend. While Bentsen had a mandate from his conferees to negotiate the final agreement, Rostenkowski did not, and the two leaders could not cut a final deal.[55]

Phase II negotiations proceeded without a final accord on phase I matters. In the end, House and Senate conferees settled differences on several key issues, leaving only the most nettlesome to be resolved, including Section 301 matters, Super 301 and Gephardt's activities, transfer authority under Section 201, remaining antidumping and countervailing-duty issues, trade adjustment assistance, and more.[56]

Bentsen and Rostenkowski began the endgame by addressing the major controversies in both phases of the conference over which they had primary responsibility. Working with USTR Yeutter, the two congressional leaders successfully struck a deal on the entirety of the issues considered by subconference #1. The agreement won majority support of House conferees, with Gephardt, Ed Jenkins (D-GA), Frenzel, and Philip Crane (R-IL) opposing it. On the Senate side, Bentsen won unanimous approval of the deal.[57]

The Reagan administration hardly spoke with one voice on this complex bill. Top officials disagreed on the overall thrust of the legislation as well as on its various components. The USTR and Commerce Department clearly supported the bill. As the principal executive branch office for trade, it is hardly surprising that the USTR favored it. The administration needed fast-track authority to proceed with further international trade negotiations, and many aspects of U.S. trade law required modifications. For its part, the Commerce Department has traditionally acted in the interest of business. American firms found the Commerce Department an agreeable point in the executive branch to express its interests, many of which could be addressed in the omnibus trade legislation.

Opposing the trade bill were the Office of Management and Budget (OMB), the Council of Economic Advisors (CEA), and the National Security Council (NSC). For budgetary reasons, fears of protection, and the potential subordination of security to mere trade, these agencies weighed in against the bill. The State Department, always suspect when it comes to U.S. trade policy—its mission being diplomacy and foreign policy above everything else—generally sided with bill opponents. The Treasury Department remained uncommitted or supported the trade agencies on issues other than those within its immediate jurisdiction. Finally, the Agriculture and Labor Departments favored the legislation but were not major players in the conference deliberations.[58]

As the conference sorted through the complex bill, the administration developed a clear list of objections. Among them were provisions of Section 301, TAA, and other miscellaneous concerns.[59] These differences were reconciled fairly readily, leaving only the plant-closing notification provisions as the major obstacle to enactment of the legislation. After much haggling, this provision remained in the bill. On 21 April 1988, the House passed H.R. 3, the product of the conference committee, 312–107. The Senate followed suit on 27 April, passing the bill 63–36, a margin too small to protect the bill from a presidential veto.[60] As expected, President Reagan immediately vetoed the bill.[61]

In the fashion typical of the relationship between Congress and the presidency, all was not lost. Congress quickly reintroduced a "new" trade bill, identical to the 1987 bill but without the plant-closing provisions.[62] The bill raced through Congress in July 1988 as signed into law on 23 August 1988.[63]

Observations on the Conference

The single most striking aspect of the trade bill conference is its size. As noted above, this legislation was one of the first omnibus bills handled by Congress. Its volume and complexity required multiple subconferences (seventeen in all) to deal with it in a reasonable amount of time. Spreading responsibility in this novel way altered the usual dynamics of conference committees. Unsure of how differences among subconferences and between the conference and the administration would be reconciled, and not willing to be the ones to block the entire bill, subconference leaders sought agreement. A second important feature of the conference is the leadership roles played by Rostenkowski and Bentsen. While the conference was too large and the bill too complex to permit micromanagement by either chairman, each clearly dominated the proceedings and moved his chamber closer to the other on key points of disagreement. Without Rostenkowski's and Bentsen's commitment to enacting a major trade bill, the conference would certainly have had a lesser chance to succeed.

A third development that stands out in this conference is that there is limited evidence of the Senate's tendency to temper the House's excesses. On one hand, the Senate was successful in replacing the Gephardt language of the House bill with its own Super 301 provision. On the other hand, the plant-closing measure—among the more strident contained in the bill—was part of the final bill, eventually forcing a presidential veto. Moreover, some observers would hardly agree that Super 301 was a moderate provision; certainly less ambitious than the Gephardt amendment to the House bill, it still required dramatic presidential action in response to a determination of unfair trade practices.

Interest Groups

Several peak associations—the Business Roundtable, the Emergency Committee for American Trade, and the United States Chamber of Commerce—took positions somewhere between congressional hard liners and administration free traders, allowing them to influence the content of the legislation as Congress gathered their support. While preferring trade liberalization, the business community maintained its support for Section 301 of the trade bill, which allows the United States to respond unilaterally to unfair trade practices affecting American exports. Not surprisingly, business interests took a hard stand on the plant-closing provision in the bill, but ultimately lost. For its part, organized labor was unenthusiastic about the legislation, but strongly supported the Gephardt language included in the House bill and the plant-closing provision. Agriculture interests remained quiet.[64]

Interest-group activity on the trade bill suggests a considerable degree of disagreement among groups concerned with trade policy. Peak business associations vaguely supported trade liberalization, while groups representing specific industries opposed or supported the bill, depending on how it would affect their group members. Unions, predictably, opposed portions of the bill that would potentially leave workers exposed to the negative effects of foreign competition. Interest groups, moreover, were hardly the monolithic political powerhouses of Washington mythology. As Susan Schwab notes, business groups failed to organize effective opposition to the plant-closing provision because the responsibility for dealing with this issue fell to labor relations people, not the trade experts. They were less attuned to the dynamics of the trade bill and not part of the informal network of lobbyists working on the bill. Thus, they were unable to act effectively.[65] Agriculture groups did not fully recognize the implications in the trade bill for American farmers, not because lobbyists were not on top of the situation, but because the matter was so arcane as to be difficult to convey to members.[66]

While certainly important in the development of the trade bill, interest groups did not control it or determine its content. As other serious studies have found, there is a limit to interest-group influence over public policy.[67] In this case, lobbyists determined that the bill was going to pass in some form and sought only to influence its content within this context. Congress chose to pursue the bill; interest groups were left to modify it at the margin.

Ideas

The new ideas in the 1988 trade bill involved trade in services. The 1988 bill attempted to take account of the growing importance of services in the American economy and their potential importance in international trade. Industries such as construction, financial services, and legal services, some thought, could do well in foreign markets. Congress, for example, ordered an Office of Technology Assessment study on the topic to provide information to lawmakers and other interested members of the policy community.[68] At the same time, the United States was pursuing trade in services in the ongoing Uruguay Round of GATT negotiations.

Referring generally to government intervention intended to enhance the competitiveness of specific industries, "competitiveness policy" was a new label for some old ideas. The strategy has an inverse variation as well; government can intervene to ease the decline of certain industries by providing, for example, job training for laid-off employees. It should come as no surprise that this sounds suspiciously similar to industrial policy.[69] Taboo among conservative, mainly Republican, politicians, policy makers found it politically unwise to use the term "industrial policy." The idea survived, however, under its new label, competitiveness policy, capitalizing on the decline of the competitiveness of American firms at home and in foreign markets. Industrial policy did not take up a lot of space in the 1988 trade bill, but it did contribute to the establishment of the competitiveness council, a top-level government–business–labor clearinghouse for ideas on how to improve the competitiveness of American firms.

Finally, intellectual property protection became a major concern of U.S. trade policy in the development of the 1988 bill. High-technology industries—electronics, biotechnology, pharmaceuticals—require effective intellectual property laws to succeed. The cost of creating new products is high; having them stolen (i.e., reproduced without permission and compensation) wreaks havoc on high-technology industries like semiconductors and software. Thus, the 1988 trade bill addressed this problem by delineating U.S. response to violations of intellectual property protection. The issue remains a problem, however, because the U.S. found intellectual property protection in the Uruguay Round largely inadequate and foreign countries—namely, the People's Republic of China—brazenly disregard intellectual property rights.[70]

The Response to Globalization

The 1988 act goes well beyond trade issues in scope to include provisions on competitiveness, intellectual property protection, and education and training. The act is extremely specific in dealing with specific industries; for example, the language of the law explicitly discusses telecommunications.[71] Having retaken control of the Senate in 1986, a Democratic-controlled Congress reined in presidential authority on trade policy in part in response to the programs pursued by Republican President Ronald Reagan. The central thrust of the act was to force the executive to be more responsive to domestic industries damaged by international competition and to be more aggressive in curbing unfair trade practices abroad. Congress at the time clearly did not trust the president to behave in a way consistent with what the Democratic congressional majority wanted.

The 1988 act also went considerably beyond previous trade legislation. Its sweeping concerns—intellectual property protection, telecommunications, services, competitiveness, education and training—reflect the growing concern in the United States for the international competitiveness of American firms, both in terms of performance in foreign markets and meeting the challenge of foreign competition in the domestic market.

The politics of the passage of the act reflect the changing dynamics of trade policy in the United States. The fact that the 1988 act included such a breadth of issues, some of which bear only a tenuous link to trade policy narrowly defined, is attributable to the growing economic uncertainty among American producers. The confidence of the 1950s had been replaced by the doubt of the 1980s. As firms lost market share at home and abroad to foreign firms, and as workers lost their jobs because of failure to beat foreign competitors, Americans looked to government for a solution. What is most curious about this turn of events is that government's response to these concerns focused on trade policy. With explicit industrial policy taboo in the American political culture, competitiveness policy (the politically acceptable term for industrial policy) found its way into the basic U.S. trade law.

As the partisan debate on the 1988 act indicates, Democrats, the party of trade liberalization, had become the party of protection, whereas Republicans, who so much favored tariffs historically, became the ideological bulwark of free trade. To some extent, roles had been reversed. But it is important not to overstate partisan differences. As the debate over the North American Free Trade Agreement (NAFTA) five years later revealed, party does not necessarily predict position on trade policy. Interest groups had not disappeared, certainly. Producer groups fought hard for provisions in the most recent trade laws that made import relief easier to get. At the same time, pro–free-trade interest groups began to appear on the political scene, certainly not balancing the political pressure completely, but adding another novel force to the political debate.[72]

The legislative–executive relationship had also evolved considerably by the passage of the 1988 trade act. Congress had tightened the reins on the executive. The delegation of authority, begun in the Reciprocal Trade Agreements Act (RTAA) of 1934, was now granted only grudgingly. A Democratic-controlled Congress was less willing to relinquish authority to a Republican president.[73] The executive could negotiate trade agreements but was thoroughly hemmed in by clever bureaucratic reorganization and innumerable provisions requiring automatic response and strict limits on presidential discretion. The bureaucratic complexity adds to the need to examine the domestic underpinnings of trade policy. The ever-increasing limits on the president require further attention in the context of the diminishing power of the executive. It may be that there is less here than it seems. That is, the president remains supremely more nimble in trade policy than Congress. But the constitutionally-based authority of Congress over the issue gives it enduring power over the executive.

The Uruguay Round

The Uruguay Round of GATT negotiations was launched at a 1986 meeting of seventy-four nations in Punta del Este, Uruguay. The ambitious agenda included continued tariff reductions and international investment, trade in services, intellectual property protection, and trade in agriculture. After seven years of fitful negotiations, the final agreement was concluded on 15 December 1993. Signed by more than 177 GATT member nations by April 1994, "the pact generally accomplished its proposed goals by (1) reducing tariffs; (2) eliminating certain nontariff barriers and subsidies; (3) broadening GATT principles to areas such as trade in services, investment, and intellectual property rights (although services remained outside the formal GATT agreement); and (4) applying more effective disciplines to agricultural trade."[74] Among the achievements of the accord are a reduction in average tariffs worldwide from 6.3 percent to 3.9 percent and the creation of the instantly controversial World Trade Organization (WTO), a supranational organization intended to arbitrate international trade disputes among nations.[75]

The United States took a prominent position in initiating the Uruguay Round, but only after several years of disagreement between

Congress and the Reagan administration over America's trade priorities. While Reagan administration officials sought to engage in further multilateral trade negotiations through the GATT, Congress was mostly concerned with passing legislation to address the hardships faced by some domestic industries. While Congress focused on imports of manufactured goods from Japan and the European Community's (EC's) agriculture policies, the administration concerned itself with trade in services and initiating a new round of GATT talks.[76]

As early as 1982, USTR Bill Brock met with representatives of Japan and the EC at a ministerial conference to discuss a new set of talks. But the usual sticking points in international trade deals—for example, trade in agricultural products—frustrated Brock's efforts and stalled any progress toward a new round of negotiations for two or three years. The idea started moving again when USTR Clayton Yeutter, who had replaced Brock at the beginning of Reagan's second term, reached an agreement at a ministerial meeting in Geneva. As had become routine, the main obstacle involved the relationship between developed nations and less-developed ones, especially India and Brazil. The key action that resulted in agreement among these nations was Yeutter's willingness not to include service industries in the proposed round of GATT talks. Although this had been a major concern domestically in the United States and subsequently a goal of U.S. trade policy, Yeutter calculated that a new round of GATT talks without services was better than no new talks at all.[77]

Procedures

To approve the Uruguay Round agreement, Congress and the president had to agree on legislation that incorporated the components of the new pact into U.S. law. Congress usually creates the implementing legislation under fast-track rules, which only permits a single, up–down vote on the bill after its formal introduction. In fact, however, Congress deals with a mock implementing bill in much the same way as it processes any other piece of legislation. Congressional leaders dole out the legislation to various relevant committees, schedule the vote, and work with the executive to iron out points of disagreement. Committees hold mock mark-up sessions in which they write the final language of the bill. Throughout the process, legislators and administration representatives negotiate difficult parts of the bill to construct sufficient agreement to allow the bill to pass. Thus, the dynamics between Congress and the president, which typify the development of any major piece of legislation, applied to the implementing bill that formally adopted the GATT, albeit in its mock stage.

Budget constraints complicated the process for dealing with the GATT. The Budget Enforcement Act of 1990 (BEA) required Congress to make up for lost revenue either by raising new funds or cutting spending. Because lowering tariffs—as the Uruguay Round would do—reduced revenues to the federal government, Congress needed to compensate to comply with the BEA's "paygo" requirements.[78] The calculation for finding a substitute source of revenues or for cutting spending was spread out over ten years; that is, the balance sheet had to read zero, ten years after the GATT implementing bill became law.

The Senate imposed its own, more restrictive rules, complicating the budget issues still more. The Senate required a budget offset within five years, not the ten years required by the BEA. Since the implementing bill did not meet this requirement, a three-fifths majority vote was necessary to waive the budget rule before formal consideration of the implementing legislation. Thus, in effect, to win U.S. approval, the GATT would need a majority vote in the House and a three-fifths super-majority victory in the Senate.

The Politics of Congressional Approval

In spite of serious opposition, Congress eventually passed the implementing legislation that, in effect, ratified the GATT. Congress started down this path as early as May 1991 when it granted the executive—the Bush administration at the time—fast-track negotiating authority. This enabled the president to continue negotiations in the Uruguay Round talks with credibility and to begin negotiations on NAFTA. Led by Senator Ernest Hollings (D-SC) and Senator Byron Dorgan (D-ND), congressional opponents of fast-track authority argued that the measure would almost surely lead to an agreement. As Dorgan argued, "it strains reality to think that Congress would reject a trade agreement, even a bad one, once the president submitted it for approval."[79] After a protracted struggle with Congress, the Bush administration won the day when it "pledged not to accept any weakening of U.S. environmental laws and softened its opposition to adjustment benefits for U.S. workers who lose their jobs as a result of the Mexico talks."[80]

In general, the debate over approval of the Uruguay Round accord was not as heated as the NAFTA debate had been a year before. This is not to say, of course, that there was no significant disagreement, public posturing, and old-fashioned political horse trading. But the GATT debate did not take on the economic immediacy that NAFTA did. While more was at stake in the GATT than in NAFTA, the agreement was much more complex, thus making it difficult for its detractors to single out a particular aspect of it that promised dire consequences for Americans. Ross Perot would find it difficult to demonize the consequences of global tariff reductions embodied in the GATT in the same way that he labeled the dreaded results of similar components of NAFTA. Moreover, while NAFTA was a new idea, the GATT had a fifty-year history of successful international trade accomplishments that most would agree made Americans better off. Although the Uruguay Round certainly broke new ground—such as putting trade in services on the global negotiating table for the first time—it was not qualitatively something entirely new. Perhaps for this reason, then, opposition to the GATT remained at a somewhat lower temperature than it had for NAFTA.

Support for the GATT came from the usual sources. The Clinton administration, assuming the mantle of the free-trade executive, pushed hard for passage of the GATT implementing bill. In addition to the administration, certain business groups and industries supported the GATT. Those with something to gain in more exports and with little fear of competition from imports—like the American computer industry—strongly favored the further trade liberalization the conclusion of this round of GATT talks promised. Large, peak business associations—the U.S. Chamber of Commerce, the Business Roundtable, and the National Association of Manufacturers, to name the more prominent among them—threw their weight behind the GATT, as did service industries and industries concerned with intellectual property protection abroad—one being the software industry.

Opposition to the GATT came from several corners. Organized labor and some industries opposed the agreement because they feared that cheaper imports would drive American producers out of business, costing working Americans their jobs. In this group, the textile industry was most vocal, finding a clear, ringing voice in Senator Hollings. Hollings was not alone, of course. For his part, Senator Dorgan opposed the new GATT agreement because of its potentially adverse effects on American agriculture. Some rather surprising allies joined these opponents to the GATT. Environmentalists worried that the GATT, through its new supranational organization, the WTO, would impose changes on U.S. environmental laws and regulations. This was the same fear that some environmentalists had expressed in regard to NAFTA a year earlier. Political conservatives expressed a related, more general concern that the WTO would undermine U.S. sovereignty. Echoing some of the same concerns that some had voiced over the perceived growing power of the United Nations, these conservatives—Senate Majority Leader Robert Dole (R-KS) among them—worried that in its power to arbitrate trade disputes among GATT signatories, the WTO would impost international law on the United States. Dole carried this concern—with maximum political pay-off—into his personal negotiations with President Clinton over Senate passage of the GATT.

In addition to these objections, the budgetary requirement that losses in tariff revenue had to be offset, either by increased revenue from other sources or by spending cuts, generated considerable concern in Congress. Legislators representing agricultural states objected to reducing subsidies to compensate for lost revenue from tariff reductions. On the supply side, some legislators argued that there was no need to raise revenues at all; assuming freer trade actually delivered on its promise of greater prosperity, revenues would go up in any case as a result of faster economic growth.

House Democrats objected to the GATT out of concern for worker rights and the environment. Democratic leaders, such as House Majority Leader Gephardt, wanted assurances that environmental concerns would not be sacrificed to economic growth, and in particular, that the new WTO would not attempt to alter U.S. environmental law. Labor unions, along with their congressional allies, pressed for guarantees that worker rights would not be violated in foreign countries in order to keep costs down. Doing so would have two negative consequences from the unions' perspective: First, workers would be subject to harsh conditions, and second, cheaper labor would constitute unfair competition to the American worker.[81]

Closing the Deal

As the congressional debate over the GATT implementing legislation headed into the fall of 1994, the Clinton administration wanted to have a vote before the November congressional elections. For entirely different reasons, the House and Senate postponed the vote until after the election. In the Senate, Hollings, fearing for the textile industry based in his state of South Carolina, exercised his senatorial prerogative of placing a hold on the GATT implementing bill, which stalled action on the legislation for forty-five days, well after the elections.[82] House leaders—both Democrats and Republicans—agreed to delay the vote until after the elections, largely because of members' uneasiness about casting such a controversial vote so close to an election.[83]

The administration was left with little choice but to wait, and it is fairly clear that no one in the Clinton White House expected a Republican takeover of Congress. With the stunning outcome of the November elections, the future of the GATT vote was hardly certain. In the face of opposition led by Senator Jesse Helms (R-NC),[84] the administration successfully persuaded congressional leaders to vote before the new Congress was sworn in, based in part on the premise that this would be an opportunity to demonstrate the bipartisanship that would be necessary in the 104th Congress.

The final act involved a one-on-one deal between President Clinton and Senate Minority Leader Dole. To gain Dole's support, the administration had to satisfy the soon-to-be Majority Leader's concern about the WTO's potential effect on American sovereignty. To do this, the administration proposed a measure that would give the United States a clear path out of the WTO should it, in the view of U.S. officials, intrude upon American sovereignty.[85] Satisfied with this provision and persuaded to abandon his demand for a cut in the capital gains tax in exchange for his support for the implementing legislation, Dole agreed to support the bill.

By late 1994, in the aftermath of a devastating loss to congressional Democrats, the Clinton administration won support for the new GATT agreement. The legislative victory marked the White House's second major trade triumph, allowing it to point to trade policy as a significant area of Clinton accomplishments. But the administration's efforts to gain approval of the GATT implementing legislation did not win high praise. Unlike the White House's full commitment to NAFTA a year earlier, the Clinton administration seemed preoccupied with other major bills—health care reform being the largest among them. Suggesting that it had taken on more than was prudent, the White House, in the view of some critics, could not commit the resources necessary to any major bill. In spite of this handicap, however, the administration won a striking victory when it persuaded congressional leaders to allow a lame-duck Congress to vote on something with the long-term consequences of the GATT.

Conclusion: Ideas, Interests, and Institutions

The GATT is an old idea. Created by Western powers behind strong American leadership, the GATT has served the cause of trade liberalization for nearly fifty years. American policy makers and interested publics had become accustomed to the GATT by the time the Uruguay Round was initiated in 1986. There was little hand wringing over what this new round of talks would mean for American economic health. That is not to say, however, that the new talks were not accompanied by considerable controversy and disagreement.

The Uruguay Round introduced new ideas into the GATT structure. As in previous rounds, it sought to reduce tariffs still further and to address nontariff barriers. Unlike previous rounds, however, this set of talks attempted to take account of the increasingly important and equally intractable issues of trade in services, intellectual property protection, and trade in agricultural products. Doing so represented new ideas that grew out of the changes that had taken place in the global economy—as defined by producers who complained of infringement of intellectual property rights, stunted growth in trade in services, and stagnation in the progress of liberalization of agricultural trade. The potential solution existed in the GATT. It is hardly surprising that the international community, spurred on by the United States, turned to a new round of GATT talks to address these modern problems.

Although the ideas for innovation in the GATT came largely from international experience, the interests involved in the congressional approval of the accord were purely domestic. There is little unexpected about how interests lined up on the GATT. Labor unions, industries that stood to lose from import competition, and some environmentalists opposed the GATT. The populist impulse so prevalent in the anti-NAFTA forces was also present in the GATT debate, but it could not make as much of an impact on the outcome. The rhetoric of Ross Perot, Patrick Buchanan, and Representative David Bonior (D-MI) could not penetrate the complexity of the GATT and thus did not arouse public opprobrium as much as NAFTA did. Industries that wished to expand exports and were not terribly concerned with international competition supported the GATT. Articulated through such traditional bulwarks of unfettered capitalism as the United States Chamber of Commerce and the National Association of Manufacturers, these interests generally supported the new trade deal, even while seeking to protect some of their own particular concerns.

But interest does not explain all of the activity of these political and economic players. Even some of the most export-oriented industries had something to fear from increased penetration of American markets by foreign firms. They had to be driven to some extent by an ideological commitment to free trade. Whereas specific corporations may not have been so unqualified in their support for the GATT, the interest groups representing them, especially the peak business associations, were. This suggests something other than pure calculation of interest in the positions of these groups. Moreover, ideological think tanks like the Heritage Foundation provided ample support for the free-trade position. Interests, then, played a role in the congressional passage of the GATT implementing bill, but not without significant ideological grounding.

Congress and the presidency behaved in ways that typify the manner in which the domestic policy process deals with foreign economic policy. Whether Reagan, Bush, or Clinton occupied the Oval Office, the president fulfilled the traditional obligation of the free-trade executive. None of these chief executives opposed the GATT, and each sought the approval of Congress to enter into GATT negotiations. All three presidents favored free trade in principle, and all were aware of the real political limits of achieving it. Thus, Reagan compromised his principles when he negotiated import quotas with Japan,[86] and Clinton was willing to engage in some hard-ball politics tempered by the strategic use of concessions to achieve at least some agreement, if not the ideal one. But all three pushed trade liberalization farther than where it had been when they entered office, much as one would expect from the free-trade executive.

For its part, Congress served its core function of channeling numerous particular interests into the sweeping GATT implementing legislation. It would be unreasonable to expect a perfect bill, free of deals, narrow concessions, and the like. Members of Congress operate in the real world of electoral politics and are compelled to see to their constituents' interests and the interests of powerful interest groups that fund their election campaigns in order to keep their jobs. In the spirit of loyalty to one's state, therefore, Senator Hollings fought hard, using every trick at his disposal to derail the GATT legislation to protect the textile industry in his state, which would very likely be endangered by the increased trade liberalization the Uruguay Round promised. The product of this fundamental dynamic is a bill that draws together varied interests in perhaps inelegant ways.

In addition to the roles played by each of these major institutions, closing the deal on the implementing legislation of the Uruguay Round clearly demonstrates the relationship between Congress and the presidency on trade matters. Through the invention of the fast-track procedure, Congress delegates to the executive negotiating authority on the GATT, as well as other multinational trade agreements. This delegation serves two purposes: On the international level, it gives U.S. negotiators credibility at the bargaining table, where their foreign counterparts can be assured that the deal they cut in Geneva will not be watered down on Capitol Hill. On the domestic level, this ingenious invention allows members of Congress to enact trade-liberalizing policies under effective political cover. Although some legislators might find free trade a good idea in the abstract, voting for it in a piecemeal way typical of the routine legislative process would expose them to criticism that they were selling out workers and businesses in their constituencies in order to further some amorphous abstract principle. Delegating authority to the executive under the fast-track procedure puts a legislator in the position of having to vote for a good bill even though it might contain provisions harmful to the immediate interests of her constituents. Under these conditions, she can claim that while she knows the harm this act might cause, the overall good it will bring is worth the price. And besides, the way the rule works, she has no recourse but to support the bill. This is an ideal situation for a free-trade–minded, reelection-conscious member of Congress who seeks more than anything else to avoid blame.[87]

At the same time, the fast-track procedure gives Congress significant control over trade policy. Responding to increasing pressure from constituents feeling the pain of economic transformation, legislators can at least incorporate provisions into the implementing legislation that keep Congress in the game. Thus, for example, Majority Leader Dole insisted upon a somewhat improved escape route out of the WTO should the United States determine that the multinational panel was not acting in America's interests. And Senator Hollings was able to get some additional protection for his cherished textile industry as a result of the procedures used to create trade policy.

The institutional arrangements that characterize Congress and the president with respect to the GATT reflect a marvelous adaptation to domestic and international changes and pressure. It allows the United States to move toward freer trade with the understanding that this is better for the country as a whole. The United States can do so, moreover, in a credible way on equal footing with other nations with less porous domestic political systems. At the same time, the arrangement permits particular interests to be heard—certainly not as much as they would be under routine legislative procedures, but more than if they were completely locked out of the process. The overall effect is a balanced lurching forward of American policy on the GATT that is remarkably characteristic of the unique institutional arrangements of the American pluralist system.

Endnotes

1. Discussed in chapter 6.
2. I. M. Destler and John S. Odell, *Anti-Protection: Changing Forces in United States Trade Politics* (Washington, D.C.: Institute for International Economics, 1987).
3. Judith Goldstein, *Ideas, Interests, and American Trade Policy* (Ithaca, N.Y.: Cornell Univ. Press, 1993). Goldstein discusses this phenomenon in relation to trade policy before the Second World War.
4. See chapter 2.
5. For a discussion of trade policy politics during much of the 1950s, see Raymond A. Bauer, Ithiel de Sola Pool, and Lewis Anthony Dexter, *American Business and Public Policy: The Politics of Foreign Trade* (New York: Atherton, 1963).
6. Patrick Low, *Trading Free: The GATT and U.S. Trade Policy* (New York: The Twentieth Century Fund, 1993), 54–55.
7. See chapter 2.
8. For an excellent account of why American car companies could not compete with their Japanese counterparts, a penetrating comparison of Ford and

Nissan is provided by David Halberstam, *The Reckoning* (New York: Avon, 1986).

9. Michael L. Dertouzos, Richard K. Lester, and Robert M. Solow, *Made in America: Regaining the Productive Edge* (New York: HarperPerennial, 1989), 278–87.

10. For a discussion of this and subsequent events in the American semiconductor industry, see, for example, Thomas R. Howell, Brent L. Bartlett, and Warren Davis, *Creating Advantage: Semiconductors and Government Industrial Policy in the 1990s* (San Jose, Calif. and Washington, D.C.: Semiconductor Industry Association and Dewey Ballantine, 1992); Kenneth Flamm, *Mismanaged Trade? Strategic Policy and the Semiconductor Industry* (Washington, D.C.: Brookings Institution, 1996); and Clyde V. Prestowitz, Jr., *Trading Places: How We Are Giving Our Future to Japan and How to Reclaim It* (New York: Basic Books, 1988).

11. Low, *Trading Free*, 173.

12. Ibid., 175–76.

13. Steve Dryden, *Trade Warriors: USTR and the American Crusade for Free Trade* (New York: Oxford Univ. Press, 1995), 171–80.

14. Low, *Trading Free*, 177–78. Because of the standoff between Congress and the president, the U.S. entered the Tokyo Round without congressional authority. See also Sharyn O'Halloran, *Politics, Process, and American Trade Policy* (Ann Arbor, Mich.: Univ. of Michigan Press, 1994), 93.

15. Low, *Trading Free*, 56.

16. See chapter 6.

17. Low, *Trading Free*, 56–58.

18. Ibid., 58.

19. Dryden, *Trade Warriors*, 173–74, 177–79, 182–85; Gary Mucciaroni, *Reversals of Fortune: Public Policy and Private Interests* (Washington, D.C.: Brookings Institution, 1995), 79–95.

20. Dryden, *Trade Warriors*, 174–85.

21. The American Selling Price was the price of the domestic equivalent of an import in the American market. It was used to determine whether a foreign firm was violating antidumping rules. Low, *Trading Free*, 174; Dryden, *Trade Warriors*, 183.

22. For the most negative view on presidential authority at the time, see Arthur Meier Schlesinger, *The Imperial Presidency* (Boston, Mass.: Houghton Mifflin, 1973), chap. 7.

23. Low, *Trading Free*, 186. Low points out that, while Congress formally approved the new trade accord, the legislation it passed paralleled but was not identical to the language in the agreement. In fact, in some cases, the language of the U.S. law was inconsistent with that of the international pact. The primary significance of this is that U.S. law remains superior to interna-

tional law; thus, the president uses his discretion in determining when to abide by international trade law. See Low, *Trading Free,* 58–59.

24. Dryden, *Trade Warriors,* 207–53.

25. Low, *Trading Free,* 59–60.

26. Caused in large part by skyrocketing oil prices in the 1970s, this economic condition, which became known as stagflation, is characterized by "excess capacity and unemployment coexisting with inflation." See James S. Olson with Susan Wladaver-Morgan, *Dictionary of United States Economic History* (Westport, Conn.: Greenwood, 1992), 515.

27. In the face of the prospect of a ballooning budget deficit, Reagan proposed small tax increases, euphemistically called "revenue enhancements," which, in the end, did not become law. The better-known, perhaps, revenue enhancement was the Tax Equity and Fiscal Responsibility Act of 1982 (TEFRA). Spearheaded by Senate Finance Chairman Bob Dole (R-KS), the law raised excise taxes and closed loopholes. See Herbert Stein, *Presidential Economics: The Making of Economic Policy from Roosevelt to Reagan and Beyond,* 2nd revised ed. (Washington, D.C.: American Enterprise Institute), 274; and Timothy J. Conlan, Margaret T. Wrightson, and David R. Beam, *Taxing Choices: The Politics of Tax Reform* (Washington, D.C.: CQ Press, 1990), 34.

28. Some economists attribute the economic slump to Federal Reserve Board Chairman Paul Volker's relentless effort to get inflation under control by keeping interest rates high. The result was a grinding recession. See, for example, Paul Krugman, *The Age of Diminished Expectations: U.S. Economic Policy in the 1990s* (Cambridge, Mass.: MIT Press, 1992), 58, 83–84.

29. The Coalition of Service Industries (CSI), headed by top service industry executives (e.g., financial services), pressed for a greater concern for these growth industries in U.S. trade policy. ADAPSO (which later became the Information Technology Association of America), a trade association for software producers, was intent upon obtaining better intellectual property protection worldwide.

30. Mucciaroni, *Reversals of Fortune,* 95–96.

31. Low, *Trading Free,* 60.

32. Ibid., 61.

33. Susan C. Schwab, *Trade-Offs: Negotiating the Omnibus Trade and Competitiveness Act* (Boston, Mass.: Harvard Business School Press, 1994), 62–63.

34. Low, *Trading Free,* 62–66.

35. Schwab, *Trade-Offs,* 79–82.

36. Ibid., 83.

37. Ibid., 84.

38. John Cranford, "Trade Legislation Passes First Hurdle in House," *Congressional Quarterly Weekly Report,* 14 March 1987, 468–69.

39. Schwab, *Trade-Offs*, 86–88, 92.
40. Ibid., 88.
41. Cranford, "Trade Legislation Passes First Hurdle in House."
42. Schwab, *Trade-Offs*, 106.
43. John Cranford, "House Passes Comprehensive Trade Measure," *Congressional Quarterly Weekly Report*, 2 May 1987, 811–18.
44. Schwab, *Trade-Offs*, 129.
45. Ibid., 128–29.
46. Ibid., 131–38.
47. Drew Douglas, "Finance Committee Approves Trade Measure," *Congressional Quarterly Weekly Report*, 9 May 1987, 906–14.
48. Schwab, *Trade-Offs*, 143–44; Drew Douglas and David Rapp, "Foreign Relations, Judiciary, Labor Add to Trade Measure," *Congressional Quarterly Weekly Report*, 6 June 1987, 1181–83; and Drew Douglas, "Senate Panels Key on Exports as Trade Markups Wind Down," *Congressional Quarterly Weekly Report*, 13 June 1987, 1234.
49. Drew Douglas, "Trade Bill Heads to Floor Trailing Veto Threat," *Congressional Quarterly Weekly Report*, 20 June 1987, 1318–21.
50. Drew Douglas, "Senate Twice Retains Veto-Bait Provisions," *Congressional Quarterly Weekly Report*, 11 July 1987, 1511–13.
51. Schwab, *Trade-Offs*, 146–52.
52. Ibid., 154.
53. Ibid., 157.
54. While the conference proceedings were under way, the administration successfully won congressional approval for the U.S.–Canada Free Trade Agreement. The negotiations over the trade bill seemed not to affect the passage of the agreement. While the significance of this is difficult to determine, it is apparent that Congress separated the issues, or perhaps, Congress did not see the free-trade agreement as being as important as the trade bill in conference. See Schwab, *Trade-Offs*, 165–66.
55. Schwab, *Trade-Offs*, 183–84.
56. Ibid., 195.
57. Ibid., 197–98.
58. Ibid. 202–03.
59. John R. Cranford, "Odds Against Reagan in Trade Conference," *Congressional Quarterly Weekly Report*, 17 October 1987, 2527–28.
60. Elizabeth Wehr, "Trade Bill Passes Senate, Heads for Certain Veto," *Congressional Quarterly Weekly Report*, 30 April 1988, 1131.
61. Schwab, *Trade-Offs*, 214.
62. Stripped from the trade bill, the plant-closing provisions became a separate bill, which was passed by Congress and vetoed by the president.
63. Schwab, *Trade-Offs*, 217–18.

64. Ibid., 167–74.
65. Ibid., 170. For discussions of issue networks, see Hugh Heclo, "Issue Networks and the Executive Establishment," in Anthony King, ed., *The New American Political System* (Washington, D.C.: American Enterprise Institute, 1978), 87–124; Frank R. Baumgartner and Bryan D. Jones, *Agendas and Instability in American Politics* (Chicago: Univ. of Chicago Press, 1993); and Robert H. Salisbury, John P. Heinz, Robert L. Nelson, and Edward O. Laumann, "Triangles, Networks, and Hollow Cores: The Complex Geometry of Washington Interest Representation," in Mark P. Petracca, ed., *The Politics of Interests: Interest Groups Transformed* (Boulder, Colo.: Westview, 1992), 130–49.
66. Schwab, *Trade-Offs*, 171–72. It is interesting to note that Bauer, Pool, and Dexter made a similar observation in their classic study of the politics of the renewal of the Reciprocal Trade Act in 1954 and 1955. They observed that one of the most trying tasks for Washington-based lobbyists was explaining to the member of the groups they represented the intricacies of policy making in the nation's capitol. See Bauer, Pool, and Dexter, *American Business and Public Policy*, 330–31.
67. Jeffrey H. Birnbaum, for example, demonstrates both the influence and the failed efforts of business lobbyists. Birnbaum and Allan Murray illustrate how congressional leaders—curiously enough, Rostenkowski among them—resisted interest-group pressure in the passage of the 1986 tax reform bill. In both cases, as in this case, members of Congress acted against the will of interest groups, at times shutting them out of deliberations. See Jeffrey H. Birnbaum, *The Lobbyists: How Influence Peddlers Work Their Way in Washington* (New York: Times Books, 1992); and Jeffrey H. Birnbaum and Allan S. Murray, *Showdown at Gucci Gulch: Lawmakers, Lobbyists, and the Unlikely Triumph of Tax Reform* (New York: Vintage, 1987).
68. U.S. Congress, Office of Technology Assessment, *International Competition in Services*, OTA-ITE-328 (Washington, D.C.: U.S. Government Printing Office, July 1987).
69. For accounts of the development and application of the concept, see Richard D. Bingham, *Industrial Policy American Style: From Hamilton to HDTV* (Armonk, N.Y.: M. E. Sharpe, 1998); and Otis L. Graham, Jr., *Losing Time: The Industrial Policy Debate* (Cambridge, Mass.: Harvard Univ. Press, 1992).
70. The 1996 example is the virtually unfettered reproduction of American-made compact disks in China. While the Chinese government has made a show of destroying counterfeit CDs, the effort is largely cosmetic, and the United States in 1996 sought to get China to do more. See United States Trade Representative, *1997 Trade Policy Agenda and 1996 Annual Report of the President of the United States on the Trade Agreements Program* (Washington, D.C.: U.S. Government Printing Office, 1997), 165–66.

71. Ibid., 62–65.
72. I. M. Destler and John S. Odell, *Anti-Protection: Changing Forces in United States Trade Politics* (Washington, D.C.: Institute for International Economics, 1987); and Helen Milner, "Resisting the Protectionist Temptation: Industry and the Making of Trade Policy in France and the United States during 1970s," in Jeffry A. Frieden and David A. Lake, eds., *International Political Economy: Perspectives on Global Power and Wealth*, 3rd ed. (New York: St. Martin's, 1995), 368–86.
73. Susanne Lohmann and Sharyn O'Halloran, "Divided Government and U.S. Trade Policy: Theory and Evidence," *International Organization* 4 (Autumn 1994): 595–632.
74. Sondra J. Nixon, "GATT Puts U.S. on Latest Stretch . . . of the Long Road to Freer Trade," *Congressional Quarterly Weekly Report*, 3 December 1994, 3448–49.
75. Ibid., 3449.
76. Schwab, *Trade-Offs*, 61–62.
77. Dryden, *Trade Warriors*, 321–23.
78. The pay-as-you-go principle requires bills that increase spending or decrease revenues, provide offsets within the same program category, or be ruled out of order. G. Calvin Mackenzie and Saranna Thornton, *Bucking the Deficit: Economic Policymaking in America* (Boulder, Colo.: Westview, 1996), 93.
79. Quoted in David S. Cloud, "Lopsided Vote Seen Signaling Win for Bush on Fast Track," *Congressional Quarterly Weekly Report*, 18 May 1991, 1259.
80. David S. Cloud, "Hill Gives Bush Green Light to Negotiate Trade Pacts," *Congressional Quarterly Weekly Report*, 25 May 1991, 1358.
81. David S. Cloud, "Senate Finance OKs GATT Pact, Drops Fast-Track Extension," *Congressional Quarterly Weekly Report*, 6 August 1994, 2229.
82. Any senator may place a hold on a particular piece of legislation, perhaps to draw attention to his or her objections to the bill, or to serve as a bargaining chip for getting specific changes. This practice is in keeping with the Senate's tradition of giving each member considerable discretion over legislation. See Ellen Greenberg, *The House and Senate Explained: The People's Guide to Congress* (New York: W. W. Norton, 1996), 51.
83. Bob Benenson, "House Postpones GATT Vote in Last-Minute Drama," *Congressional Quarterly Weekly Report*, 8 October 1994, 2856.
84. Helms, an opponent of the GATT, argued that such an important decision should not be in the hands of a lame-duck Congress. See Bob Benenson, "In GATT Vote, Clinton Hopes to Avoid Another Nail-biter," *Congressional Quarterly Weekly Report*, 19 November 1994, 3349.
85. The provision was known as the "three-strikes" clause. It created the following procedure for American withdrawal from the WTO: A panel of U.S. judges would review all WTO decisions; if the panel found that the WTO had

acted arbitrarily against U.S. interests in three cases, it could propose a joint (congressional) resolution instructing the president to withdraw from the WTO; this would have to be signed into law or enacted over the president's veto. Although this measure allayed Dole's sovereignty concerns, it was not much different than the original text, which gave Congress the right to review U.S. membership in the WTO every five years and to recommend withdrawal if warranted. See Alissa J. Rubin, "Dole, Clinton Compromise Greases Wheels for GATT," *Congressional Quarterly Weekly Report,* 26 November 1994, 3405.

86. See chapter 7.
87. See the development of this concept in R. Kent Weaver, *Automatic Government: the Politics of Indexation* (Washington, D.C.: Brookings Institution, 1988).

5

The North American Free Trade Agreement

Congressional approval of the North American Free Trade Agreement (NAFTA) was a major achievement for the Clinton administration. With the help of congressional Republicans, a Democratic president successfully finished the task begun by his Republican predecessor of creating a sweeping free-trade area among the United States, Canada, and Mexico. The political battle that preceded congressional approval of NAFTA was a bare-knuckled brawl among contestants with starkly different economic interests. The political stakes were high, as a new president sought to win a major victory, albeit in an uncomfortable alliance with the opposition party.

NAFTA is partly about economics. It represents a commitment to freer trade within North America, and it is a step in the direction of global trade liberalization. From the U.S. perspective, NAFTA is also about foreign policy. It makes a great deal of sense to pursue a policy that will presumably help stabilize and enrich America's huge southern neighbor with which it shares a 1,500-mile border. Thus, the development of NAFTA, from conception to congressional approval, involved conflict over economic policy primarily, with foreign policy concerns not far below the surface. These issues exposed sharp political divisions based on intense economic interests, made all the more complicated and intractable by their foreign policy implications.

The principal message of this chapter is that the complex politics of NAFTA was essentially domestic in nature. Regardless of the foreign economic and political aspects of NAFTA, the agreement had to be approved through the domestic policy process. The central role played by Congress with respect to NAFTA placed the debate squarely in the domestic arena. Thus, to understand the politics of NAFTA, it is necessary to turn to the domestic policy process.

With this in mind, this chapter mainly examines NAFTA's development in the agenda-setting and adoption phases of the policy process, since it has not been in effect long enough to assess its implementation fully. The analysis then considers the importance of ideas, interests, and institutions in each of the steps of the policy process. The two paths of this assessment demonstrate the way the domestic policy process shaped NAFTA and how the agreement owes its basic character to it.

Ideas, Interests, and Institutions

Ideas, interests, and institutions are at the center of the politics of NAFTA. A blizzard of information swirled around the debate over NAFTA, as economic analyses of its effects, estimations of its foreign policy implications, and predictions of dire consequences filled popular and academic journals, newspapers, and the electronic media. In addition, ideology infused the entire debate, as free-trade advocates hailed the benefits of free markets, while NAFTA opponents challenged such claims with different perspectives on the fair allocation of resources. Much of the information relevant to NAFTA found its way in some form to the news media. The media popularized the discussion of NAFTA's consequences, disseminating both accurate analyses along with populist claims about what the agreement would do. Without the media, the populist opposition to NAFTA would have found little audience.

Obtaining congressional approval of NAFTA required a major political fight that included a vast array of participants acting on the basis of their economic interests. The potentially significant effects NAFTA would likely have on producers and consumers throughout the United States were lost on few; in response, interest groups staged massive campaigns to protect the interests of their members. NAFTA involved a complex partisan split between Republicans and Democrats; party, along with ideology and constituent interests, determined how members of Congress voted on NAFTA. Add to this orthodox expression of interests Ross Perot's populist appeal to oppose NAFTA on the basis of how it would hurt American workers.

Finally, American political institutions shaped the final product. This analysis examines how the institutional characteristics of Congress, the president, executive branch agencies, interest groups, and, by their absence, political parties determined the final version of NAFTA.

NAFTA's Main Components

In November 1993, after a great deal of debate and expense of political capital, not to mention angst, Congress approved NAFTA by convincing majorities in both houses. What exactly did Congress approve? NAFTA's basic goal is to reduce tariffs and other trade barriers among the United States, Canada, and Mexico. The initial agreement created a schedule by which tariffs would be reduced and nontariff barriers (NTBs) would be addressed (see figure 5.1). The simple goal of these actions is to increase trade among the three member countries.

As a result of pressure from environmental groups and organized labor in the United States, side agreements on environmental and labor issues accompany NAFTA.[1] Not part of the original text, President Clinton stipulated their creation as a condition of his support for NAFTA. The United States, Canada, and Mexico agreed to enforce their own environmental laws, thereby avoiding a situation where a country relaxed environmental regulation for the purpose of attracting industry. The side agreement established a multilateral commission to deal with environmental issues. The three members of NAFTA also agreed to monitor labor laws to prevent violations of provisions such as health and safety standards. A multilateral commission, similar in design to the one established for environmental issues, would deal with labor issues as they arose. In addition to these issues, the United States and Mexico agreed to establish a border commission to monitor the *maquiladoras,* assembly plants located just inside the Mexican border, mainly with Texas. The goal of this commission was to encourage the cleanup of the massive pollution that had built up in the area during its period of rapid, unregulated growth. The commission was also charged with the responsibility of monitoring labor laws in the region—for example, regulations on the use of child labor.

NAFTA was hardly a pure or simple agreement. In order to obtain congressional support, the Clinton administration offered various American producers concessions to protect them from NAFTA's po-

NAFTA's Main Components

Agriculture: The agreement converts nontariff barriers to tariffs and eliminates over 15 years' tariffs on U.S. products entering Mexico.

Automobiles: NAFTA reduces tariffs on cars and light trucks entering the Mexican market by half. Tariffs will be eliminated in five years for light trucks and ten years for cars.

Dispute Resolution: NAFTA provides for a three-step process: consultation, review by an international Trade Commission, and, if necessary, a decision by a five-member binational panel consisting of private sector industry experts.

Energy: The agreement opens the Mexican energy market to a significant extent. It allows for foreign investment in Mexican petrochemical industries, private electricity production, and direct sales of natural gas by U.S. and Canadian producers to Mexican consumers. Mexico still prohibits foreign ownership of its oil reserves.

Financial Services: NAFTA virtually opens the Mexican market. By 2000, limitations on establishing subsidiaries in Mexico will be eliminated, Canadians and Americans will be allowed to own 100 percent of insurance companies, and all equity and market-share restrictions will be eliminated.

Government Procurement: Mexican government projects will be open to Mexican, American, and Canadian firms equally.

Intellectual Property: NAFTA attempts to strengthen intellectual property protection as the signatories promised rigorous enforcement of domestic laws.

Investment: NAFTA gives national treatment to firms owned by Mexicans, Americans, and Canadians in any of the three nations.

Standards: Health, safety, and industrial standards will be set to the highest level available in any of the three countries.

Tariffs: Tariffs on most products will be eliminated in five or ten years. Some special products will lose their tariff protection over 15 years.

Textiles: NAFTA eliminates tariffs on more than 80 percent of American exports within six years. A rule of origin prohibits NAFTA from being used as an "export platform" for third countries trying to gain access to the American market. A "snap-back" provision allows a NAFTA member to take measures in the event of a surge in imports of NAFTA-made apparel.

Transportation: The agreement opens rail, bus, and truck transportation among the three countries before 2000.

Figure 5.1
Source: George W. Grayson, *The North American Free Trade Agreement: Regional Community and the New World Order* (Lanham, Md.: University Press of America, 1995), 101–05.

tential harmful effects. Thus, for example, fruit and vegetable growers in Florida and Louisiana won protection for their products from Mexican competition, as did the textile industry, located mainly in South Carolina and Georgia.

NAFTA proponents and opponents hotly debated the economic consequences of the trade pact. In general, opponents contended that NAFTA would cause American industries to move to Mexico to take advantage of cheaper labor and less-stringent environmental regulations. The result would be a dramatic loss of American jobs, which was perhaps most memorably captured in Ross Perot's phrase, "the giant sucking sound." NAFTA supporters, on the other hand, argued that freer trade with Mexico, while costing the United States some jobs, would result in economic growth on both sides of the border and consequently would create more jobs in the United States. A third, more disinterested position suggested that NAFTA was more foreign policy than economic policy; the economic consequences of NAFTA, according to this view, would be negligible, since most of what NAFTA proposed to do would happen anyway.[2]

At this writing, it is too early to tell whether NAFTA has proved to be the engine of economic growth promised by its proponents or the cause of environmental degradation and lost jobs, of which its opponents warned. Claims and counterclaims about NAFTA's consequences float about political debate, but only a few observations are possible. First, because of the severe economic crisis in Mexico and the attendant collapse of the *peso,* Mexico has not become the eager market for American products that NAFTA supporters had hoped for and predicted. Thus, the bilateral trade deficit with Mexico shows a dramatic increase since 1994. NAFTA is not likely to be the culprit in this turn of events. The weak *peso* buys less than it did when NAFTA was concluded, and many Mexicans have lost their jobs because of the economic crunch the country is experiencing. The consequences of these developments would have been felt in the United States whether NAFTA existed or not. Moreover, NAFTA did not cause a dramatic drop in U.S. tariffs; they were low before NAFTA. And Mexico had already embarked on a trade liberalization plan in the 1980s, well before NAFTA's enactment.[3] Second, little has been done to improve environmental conditions in Mexico, either in the nation's heartland or along its border with the United States, the location of the *maquiladoras.*[4] Third, NAFTA has displaced American workers, although the exact number is uncertain. The Clinton administration places the number between 32,000 and 99,497, while *The Economist* reckons 117,000 workers have applied for benefits owed to workers displaced by NAFTA.[5] Regardless of which number one believes, it falls considerably short of the 500,000 lost jobs that Perot predicted. Thus, both the trade pact's detractors and enthusiasts are wrong so far, though the former are considerably farther off the mark than the latter.

Finally, U.S. towns and cities along the Mexican border have not benefited from NAFTA. Instead of becoming burgeoning financial centers for growing Mexican enterprises or the beneficiaries of the creation of new, well-paying jobs, these communities have seen factories move to the Mexican side of the border, taking jobs with them. Meanwhile, public resources are stretched to deal with new Mexican immigrants.[6]

The next section of the chapter examines the development of NAFTA in the United States. The analysis follows NAFTA through agenda setting and program adoption and pays particular attention to the importance of ideas, interests, and institutions in each. The main part of the story occurs at the program-adoption stage of the policy process. Congressional deliberations and the relationship between Congress and the president are the key institutional factors in the approval of NAFTA. How NAFTA got on the policy agenda in the first place, however, is a less-publicized tale, but an important one nonetheless. The Bush administration's decision to pursue the agreement is where this part of the story begins. Finally, NAFTA's implementation is critical to its success. Whether American jobs go south, the environment collapses, or U.S. producers strike an export bonanza are all tied to the implementation of the agreement.

Setting the NAFTA Agenda

The central question here is how the idea of a North American free-trade agreement became a public policy issue. To answer this question, it is first necessary to pinpoint the origin of the idea—that is, when it was first articulated in a political setting. From this starting point, it should be possible to follow the development of the idea as it made its way to the policy agenda.

We can find the first serious proposal of a North American free-trade agreement in the 1980 presidential election bid of Ronald Reagan, free trader and firm believer in the market.[7] A free-trade agreement by the United States and its two neighbors was certainly consistent with Reagan's approach to foreign economic policy. But the idea of such a trade pact hardly occupied a central position in the campaign; indeed, it is difficult to find it in news coverage at all.

The Reagan campaign presumably did not invent the idea of a North American free-trade agreement. The fact that it found its way into the campaign suggests that economists had been considering the notion prior to the campaign. In any case, the notion of a trade pact for the United States, Canada, and Mexico has been in public debate at least since 1980, and probably in academic discourse before then.

The U.S.–Canada Free Trade Agreement (FTA) served as a precedent to NAFTA and perhaps gave the idea of such an agreement a measure of credibility. The practical experience provided by this trade pact suggested the possibility of expanding it to Mexico. As the two countries became accustomed to the agreement and experienced some of the benefits it provided, the prospect of including Mexico became more plausible.

As the precursor to NAFTA, the history of the FTA is instructive. The agreement was negotiated during the Reagan administration, but it was not the centerpiece of the administration's foreign economic policy game plan. Administration officials chose to act on the idea of a trade pact between Canada and the United States largely to score some victory in trade policy in the face of the inability of member nations to initiate a new round of General Agreement on Tariffs and Trade (GATT) negotiations. United States Trade Representative (USTR) Clayton Yeutter, with the support of Treasury Secretary James Baker, initiated the idea within the administration and shepherded it through the policy development process.[8] Although the FTA had not been one of the administration's top priorities, the logic that underlay it was certainly consistent with Reagan's free-trade, market-oriented ideology. Concluding the agreement with Canada gave the administration a tangible accomplishment in trade liberalization, and it mitigated to some extent the problem the United States was encountering in moving the GATT process forward.

The practical experience of creating and implementing the FTA laid the groundwork for its logical extension to Mexico. Comfortable with the trade relationship with Canada, experienced with its implementation, and enjoying its economic benefits, U.S. policy makers were prepared to take the next, logical step. Thus, although including Mexico in a free-trade area would represent a new challenge owing to the size and level of development of the Mexican economy, the concept was not altogether new.

Employing the same logic as its predecessor, NAFTA in effect extended the FTA.[9] Insofar as U.S. participation in the agreement is concerned, NAFTA was born in the Bush administration. Around February 1990, Mexican President Carlos Salinas suggested such an agreement to President Bush. Seeing enormous potential economic benefits and wishing to give more credibility to his efforts to restructure the Mexican economy, Salinas is responsible for originating the process that culminated in NAFTA.[10] Bush and Secretary of State James Baker "immediately accepted the idea, viewing it as a good chance to stabilize Mexico as a free-market, democratic nation, while providing trade expansion for American exports."[11] In summer 1990, with Salinas's proposal in play, USTR Carla Hills recommended that the president initiate negotiations for a North American free-trade agreement. Reminiscent of the origins of the FTA, Hills wanted talks on a North American trade pact in light of the fact that the Uruguay Round of GATT negotiations was stalled. Initiating a new trade agreement would allow the administration "to diversify America's trade options" in the spirit of moving U.S. foreign economic policy in the direction of trade liberalization.[12] With this in mind, in late February 1991, Hills, Baker, and Secretary of Commerce Robert Mosbacher held an unannounced meeting in Washington with senior Mexican officials in which they agreed to pursue negotiations on a bilateral free-trade pact. Canada entered discussions later.[13]

Several serious policy considerations underlay the Bush administration's decision to pursue a North American free-trade agreement. The specific issues concerned U.S. relations with Mexico. In part intending to improve the Mexican economy and stabilize its political system, and in part responding to Salinas's initiatives, administration officials saw considerable potential benefits from the trade pact.

Problems and Solutions

Putting NAFTA on the policy agenda addressed three problems. First, responding to Salinas's overtures to create a North American trade pact would improve U.S. relations with Mexico. In this sense, NAFTA was a matter of foreign policy intended to provide a partial solution to a long-term foreign policy problem. Second, NAFTA allowed the United States to make some progress toward trade liberalization. Although not a global deal, NAFTA supporters in the Bush administration could legitimately claim that the trade agreement was a step toward free trade.[14] Third, with the Uruguay Round of GATT talks going nowhere, the president needed to demonstrate leadership in this increasingly visible and important policy area; NAFTA provided just such an opportunity. While the idea originated with Salinas, Bush could take credit for putting it on the U.S. policy agenda. As Bush determined later, a victory on NAFTA could prove useful in his bid for reelection in 1992.

Thus, NAFTA provided a solution to three distinct, though related, problems. The political conditions of 1990 permitted the successful linking of the solution to these problems. The connecting of solution to problems here clearly illustrates the domestic nature of the development of NAFTA. International considerations were important, of course; long, sometimes difficult negotiations among the three member countries took place in order to create the agreement itself. But that agreement would mean little without American approval, which was channeled through the domestic policy process.

Connecting Solutions to Problems

Three factors contributed to the successful joining of the NAFTA solution to problems. First, the United States had experience with the FTA, NAFTA's predecessor. Based on this experience, the free-trade–oriented officials of the Bush administration could easily accept the argument that NAFTA would provide substantial economic benefits to the United States. Second, the Bush administration's immediate political problem called for something like NAFTA—a feasible, significant international agreement for which the president could take credit. Third, the stalled GATT talks created an opening for NAFTA. Though short of sweeping global change, NAFTA was arguably a step in the direction of trade liberalization.

In addition to these three conditions that allowed NAFTA, the solution, to be attached to the various problems, the policy environment was amenable to the trade pact. Accelerating the growth in the faith in markets that began with the deregulation of the 1970s, the

Reagan administration had introduced a free-market ideology into the American political mainstream. President Bush, though perhaps not the true believer his predecessor was, continued to advocate, at least rhetorically, free markets. Measures that enhanced trade liberalization are consistent with this general approach to economic policy. NAFTA, therefore, entered an agreeable political world.

Ideas

Ideas underlay the interplay between problems and solutions as NAFTA made its way to the policy agenda. The economic analyses that surfaced in the political debate did not necessarily represent mainstream economics. Most analyses suggested that NAFTA would have modest effects on the U.S. economy and potentially large consequences for the Mexican economy. The principal reason for the difference is that the American economy is many times larger than the Mexican economy.[15] Analyses anticipating that NAFTA would have dramatic consequences, either negative or positive, tended to have more ideologically oriented sources.[16]

In addition to the narrow focus on the anticipated consequences of the trade pact, NAFTA also fostered a broader discussion of the relationship between regional trade agreements and global trade liberalization. The central question was whether trade pacts such as NAFTA would lead to greater trade liberalization or would simply replace countries with regional alliances as the sources of protectionist policies.

Goals

The NAFTA debate involved two general goals: economic efficiency and the national interest. Freer trade is justified on the basis of efficiency. Greater efficiency leads to economic growth and better standards of living for everyone. Although NAFTA supporters frequently argued for the agreement in terms of efficiency, it is not clear that NAFTA, even if most successful, would have anything but a modest effect. The general consensus emerging from mainstream economic analyses was that NAFTA would increase trade somewhat, but the effect on the American economy would be negligible mainly because it is so large compared with Canada and especially Mexico. This is not to say, however, that efficiency was not part of the long-term U.S. goal. While NAFTA alone was not likely to produce massive gain in efficiency through free trade, it was, arguably, a step in that direction. Policy makers also intended NAFTA to benefit the national interest. To the extent that the agreement was a matter of foreign policy, it served the purpose of improving U.S. relations with Mexico.

Interests

Economic interests have traditionally played a significant role in major U.S. trade policies. In the case of NAFTA, however, economic interests, while present, were not the principal force behind placing the trade agreement on the policy agenda. Economic interests in the United States are expressed mainly through interest groups, and to a lesser extent through political parties. Economic groups usually represent producers, which are split on free trade; some stand to gain by opening foreign markets, while others stand to lose to foreign competition in the American market. The noteworthy aspect of the role interest groups played in placing NAFTA on the policy agenda is their absence.

Similarly, political parties had little to do with the initiation of NAFTA. Given the lack of clear partisanship in the subsequent battle over congressional approval of NAFTA, it is hardly surprising that parties were insignificant in the earlier stage of its development.

What is most interesting about the origin of NAFTA is that the government was responsible for it. Bush administration officials, for reasons discussed earlier, sought to put the trade agreement into play. Only after reaching the policy agenda did producer interests line up for or against the trade pact.

Although interest groups and political parties are the traditional means through which interests are given voice in American politics, class may have played a role as well. The application of this approach in the case of NAFTA claims that the state is in fact controlled by the business class (producer interests). Thus, in placing NAFTA on the policy agenda, the state is really acting in the name of corporate interests. Although an appealing argument, the evidence casts some doubt on it, at least at the agenda-setting phase. The Bush administration was not supported solely by business interests, of course, and policies that lead to freer trade have been supported by officials of both parties with dramatically different views on other economic issues.

Institutions

The lack of intense interest-group involvement may come as something of a surprise to most observers of American politics. After all, conventional wisdom places interest groups at the center of politics in the United States, usually in an extremely negative light. Here, the government originated a major policy change, a development that challenges the conventional wisdom. What happened in the NAFTA case is typical of trade policy initiatives in the United States; the presidency takes the lead in placing a major policy change on the agenda. The presidency—including the president and his extensive cohort of assistants—is in position to initiate controversial policies, ones that will inevitably cause harm to some in order to achieve a greater good. This is true to some extent for many issue areas, and it is especially the case with respect to trade policy. Bush administration officials combined foreign policy with economic considerations in their initiation of NAFTA. Unburdened by relatively parochial constituent interests, administration officials could take a broader, longer view on trade policy in devising NAFTA. Moreover, although any administration experiences conflict among its officials, the presidency can operate with a singleness of purpose unimaginable in Congress. Thus, the presidency enjoys the political independence and the ability to act that give it an institutional advantage over Congress in initiating trade policy in general, and NAFTA in particular.

Within the administration, several key agencies play a role in trade policy development. In the NAFTA case, the USTR led other officials in placing the agreement on the policy agenda. Once committed to the idea, the USTR, under the leadership of Ambassador Hills, carried the load. This, of course, makes a great deal of sense, since the USTR's sole purpose is to handle trade policy for the administration. Although created by Congress to give the legislature a presence in the executive branch, the USTR quickly became a creature of the presidency. The president appoints the head of the agency who then serves at the president's pleasure. In the case of NAFTA, the USTR served the interests of the president. Hills followed Bush's lead in getting the agreement on the policy agenda, and she and her successor, Mickey Kantor, played major roles in obtaining congressional approval of NAFTA.

The USTR's institutional significance lies in its singular charge and its close proximity to the president.[17] Because of its focus and presidential support, this lean agency is able to lead other executive branch agencies effectively with regard to trade policy. Thus, while the Commerce Department may wish to play a more significant role in trade policy development, it is relegated to a support position, as was the case for NAFTA.

Program Adoption: Turning NAFTA into U.S. Policy

There is no better place to illustrate the importance of the domestic policy process in the development of NAFTA than at the program-adoption stage. This story features a classic political battle within Congress and between Congress and the presidency. The defining factor of the formal adoption of NAFTA is the central role played by Congress, which derives from the authority the Constitution gives it over revenue (including tariffs) legislation and commerce.

NAFTA and Fast-track Procedures

Congress and the president have worked out a complex procedure for dealing with trade policy. The central problem is that constitutionally, Congress must enact policies, but the president is in position to negotiate them. This is another way to say that trade policy, including NAFTA, is a sometimes awkward marriage of foreign policy and domestic policy. To accommodate this cumbersome division of responsibilities, Congress historically has given the president the authority to negotiate trade agreements. Congress may add to its authorization a fast-track provision, which requires Congress to consider a trade agreement without amending it in a single up–down vote. Tying Congress's hands in this way avoids congressional attempts to change what the president negotiated, which would undermine the chief executive's credibility with foreign leaders.

On 1 March 1991, President Bush requested fast-track authority from Congress through 1 June 1993 for the Uruguay Round of GATT talks and for NAFTA. The congressional debate over granting fast-track authority to the president anticipated the political battle for congressional approval of the final agreement. At stake were environmental and labor issues as well as protection for industries that might be adversely affected by NAFTA. President Bush pressed Congress hard for fast-track authority, making commitments on four key issues that continued to be sources of contention throughout the development of NAFTA.[18] Environmental issues emerged as a major sticking point to the granting of fast-track authority. On 1 May 1991, the Bush administration addressed these concerns by agreeing to an action plan with Mexico to deal with environmental problems.[19] In addition, Ambassador Hills won the confidence of several major U.S. environmental groups; her good faith efforts in dealing with the National Wildlife Federation, the National Audubon Society, the Environmental Defense Fund, and the Natural Resources Defense Council earned their support for NAFTA.[20] Congress granted the authority establishing the pace of congressional action once the process was set in motion (see figure 5.2). Principal opposition to the measure came from the Northeast and parts of the South, where textile producers feared foreign competition that NAFTA might introduce into the American economy, from Blacks and Hispanics, who were concerned about potential job losses, and from farmers in the upper Midwest, who believed NAFTA would permit Canadian farmers to push them out of the domestic market.[21]

Once fast-track authority was in place, the Bush administration tried to make NAFTA a reality on both the foreign and domestic fronts. Central to the administration's effort was the USTR. Recognizing the need to gain congressional support, Hills developed close relationships with the House Ways and Means Committee and the Senate Finance Committee, the two committees with primary responsibility for trade policy. Hills's proximity to the president—Bush had elevated the USTR to cabinet level—gave Hills the necessary credibility and political clout to operate effectively on Capitol Hill.[22]

The USTR coordinated the U.S. negotiating effort with Mexico and Canada. It assigned responsibility for leading talks on certain issues to agencies throughout the executive branch; the USTR was the lead agency for seven categories, while other executive branch units took the lead in twelve additional areas under their jurisdictions. Disbursing

---

Fast-track Procedures for NAFTA

The president proves at least 60 days' notice to the House Ways and Means and Senate Finance Committees of his intention to commence trade negotiations with a foreign country;

The president informs the House of Representatives and the Senate of his intention to enter into an agreement at least 90 calendar days before he signs the accord;

After signing the agreement, the president submits it to the House and the Senate, along with an implementing bill crafted in concert with congressional leaders, a statement of administrative action proposed to implement the agreement, and detailed supporting information explaining how the agreement achieves the United State's negotiating objectives;

Provided the executive branch has met all procedural hurdles, the House (45 days in committees; 15 days on the floor) and the Senate (15 days in committees; 15 days on the floor) may take up to 90 legislative days to consider the legislation. Speech-making in each chamber is limited to 20 hours. Debate time in the House is split equally between proponents and opponents; in the Senate, the time is divided between the majority and minority leaders;

Finally, the House of Representatives votes first on the unamendable legislative package, which cannot be filibustered in the Senate.

Figure 5.2
Source: George W. Grayson, *The North American Free Trade Agreement: Regional Community and the New World Order* (Lanham, Md.: University Press of America, 1995), 62–63.

responsibility in this way allowed the USTR to build support within the bureaucracy and to tap the considerable expertise available in those agencies. The USTR coordinated the activities of these agencies throughout the negotiations. Lead agencies met every two weeks to assess progress and to adjust tactics. The White House Domestic Council and the National Security Council joined these sessions, adding to the overall coherence of the executive branch's activities. While all this activity was taking place within the executive branch, Hills maintained a constant link to Congress.[23]

Throughout the negotiations, the United States steered clear of several issues that were considered "sacred cows." The Jones Act, for example, which required U.S. flagged ships to carry cargo from one U.S. port to another, was untouchable. Similarly, the United States refused to negotiate its immigration policy. Certain "set-asides"—exceptions to NAFTA rules—were established as well. The United States would see to it that NAFTA did not adversely affect small business, minorities, and veterans.[24]

On 2 February 1992, the Bush administration produced the text of NAFTA as formulated by the three members' negotiators. The document embodied four basic principles that emerged from the administration's and the Congress's work on the pact:

> 1) complete elimination of all impediments to trade, 2) equal treatment in each country for all goods and services produced in North America, 3) a commitment not to erect additional commercial obstacles between and among the signatories once the pact was signed, and 4) the extension to North American partners of most-favored-nation treatment accorded a third country.[25]

NAFTA became a public matter in the middle of 1992 as the presidential election campaign heated up. At issue was whether Bill Clinton, the Democratic nominee, would endorse an agreement that seemed to be consistent with his New Democrat ideology but was crafted by his opponent, George Bush. For his part, Bush wanted to conclude negotiations with Mexico and Canada on NAFTA so that he could take credit for it in his bid for reelection. Still, he preferred to postpone the battle for congressional approval—with its likely airing of how NAFTA could hurt some constituents in the key electoral states of Michigan, Ohio, Illinois, and Pennsylvania—until after the election.[26]

Through the summer of 1992, Clinton indicated general support for the agreement, but withheld endorsement. In the face of Bush's accusations that Clinton was "waffling" on the issue, the future president chose to support NAFTA, provided certain conditions could be met. Clinton endorsed NAFTA in a 4 October 1992 speech at North Carolina State University. Expressing reservations on labor and environmental issues, Clinton nonetheless gave his support to the agreement but insisted on side agreements (i.e., outside the formal NAFTA text) to cover labor and environmental issues, as well as one to clarify provisions for compensating producers damaged by import surges.[27]

Meanwhile, Congress had been considering NAFTA. The main points of contention included the environment, job losses, and loss of major industries, like automobiles, to Mexico's cheap labor.[28] Potential opposition to NAFTA came from several sources. Legislators representing districts with heavy industries—the Rust Belt states of the Midwest and Northeast—had a great incentive to oppose NAFTA, since they feared the agreement might cost some of their constituents' jobs. The Congressional Black Caucus opposed NAFTA, while the general thinking at this time was that Hispanic members of Congress would support it. In addition to these specific concerns, the depressed state of the economy gave some members pause about voting for a trade pact that could damage some of their constituents. This was not time to take a seemingly bold economic move. Finally, Congress resisted the Bush administration's request for fast-track authority and continued to have doubts about NAFTA, in part out of a concern for its institutional authority over trade. Regardless of party, members of Congress think twice about conceding too much to the executive.[29] Congressional Democrats served notice to President Bush that they were serious about addressing these issues. Thus, "(w)ith accord on the North American Free Trade Agreement imminent, the House voted unanimously August 6 (1992) to warn President Bush that it would not tolerate any pact that would weaken U.S. health, safety, labor or environmental laws."[30] With this nonbinding resolution, Congress demonstrated that approval of NAFTA was by no means guaranteed. Around this time, congressional Democrats began to make it clear that they would not easily support NAFTA. At this point, House Majority Leader Richard Gephardt (D-MO) appeared willing to broker a deal between Clinton and Democratic lawmakers, but his support, as it turned out, was uncertain.[31]

1993: Clinton versus the Democrats

Clinton, the New Democrat, did not have the support of congressional Democrats on NAFTA. The president was forced to look to the Republican party to create a congressional majority to approve the agreement. The Clinton administration formulated a strong argument for NAFTA, focusing mainly on its positive overall economic effects.

The point man in the administration's campaign to get NAFTA approved was USTR Mickey Kantor. A successful Los Angeles lawyer and long-time Washington operative, Kantor played a key role in shaping Clinton's election campaign. Kantor's nomination for the USTR came as something of a surprise, but he rose to the challenge

impressively. Kantor brought tenacity, intelligence, and political durability to the trade agency, characteristics that fit nicely with its culture.
Assuming his role as the administration's top trade official, Kantor
became a persistent, tough negotiator for American interests.

Congress proved difficult to convince. Many members of the Democratic majority, particularly in the House, opposed NAFTA. Fearing
environmental degradation resulting from NAFTA, "green" legislators
either completely opposed the pact or demanded stringent provisions
in the environmental side agreement with Mexico before they would
give their support. Labor issues involved worker safety and, more
important, the prospect of American jobs going south to take advantage of lower wages. Both Democratic and Republican legislators
found problems with NAFTA's potential for damaging some U.S.
industries—textiles and automobiles, in particular.

Clinton's New Democrat ideology did not have overwhelming appeal among congressional Democrats who found NAFTA more in
line with the Republican party than their own. Thus, House Majority
Whip David Bonior (D-MI) strongly opposed NAFTA.[32] Representing Macomb County, the blue-collar suburb north of Detroit and
home to the now-famous Reagan Democrat, Bonior argued that
NAFTA would mean losing to Mexico automobile jobs on which
many of his constituents relied.[33] House Majority Leader Gephardt,
while an early fence sitter on NAFTA, came over to the opposition.[34]
Rekindling the protectionist fervor that fueled his 1988 run for the
Democratic nomination for the presidency, Gephardt supported
Bonior in leading the congressional opposition to NAFTA. Speaker
of the House Thomas Foley (D-WA) supported NAFTA, but remained aloof, unwilling to engage in a hard sell for the pact. Rank-
and-file Democrats in the House were hardly willing to cast their lot
with the president. Some sixty-three freshmen, concerned with reelection, feared supporting NAFTA would cost them dearly with their
constituents. To make matters worse the Congressional Black Caucus
(almost all Democrats) opposed NAFTA because of potential job
losses. Moreover, House Democrats knew that NAFTA was only one
of several major bills Clinton wanted passed. They believed that he
would not push them too hard on the trade pact since he would need
their support on an even more important piece of legislation—health
care reform.[35] Thus, with its leadership split, House Democrats were
hardly a reliable source of support for the president.

For their part, Republicans might agree that NAFTA is a good idea, but constituent pressures and a reluctance to help a president who opposed them on other major issues kept them from throwing their unqualified support to the president. House Minority Whip Newt Gingrich (R-GA) was certainly in no mood to support Clinton without getting something in return. Thus, Clinton faced a Congress that would approve NAFTA grudgingly and only after the administration generously heaped concessions on undecided members to get their votes.

To take on the enormous task of winning congressional approval of NAFTA, President Clinton brought in William Daley to be the administration's principal lobbyist. The brother of Chicago Mayor Richard Daley, and the son of their famous father, Richard Daley, William Daley brought with him impeccable political credentials as a fund raiser and as a loyal and practical Democratic operative. It is also no coincidence that Daley hails from the same political organization as House Ways and Means Committee Chairman Dan Rostenkowski (D-IL), whose support was critical in winning the day for NAFTA.[36] Clinton also enlisted the support of several Democratic members of the House. In addition to Rostenkowski, Representative Robert Matsui (D-CA) and Representative Bill Richardson (D-NM) worked with the administration in winning their colleagues' support.[37]

The Clinton administration's campaign did not get off to a fast start. One general reason for the lethargic beginning is that the president had other issues on his agenda that required attention. The administration was brand new, of course, and not prepared to take on several major policy initiatives at once. The White House was understaffed; Thomas F. "Mack" McLarty, the president's first chief of staff, seemed uneasy in his job; there were paralyzing battles between policy specialists and the political consultants; and Hillary Rodham Clinton was pressing hard to put health care at the top of the agenda.[38] Reflecting these organizational problems was Deputy Director of the National Economic Council W. Bowman Cutter's failure to set deadlines for executive branch agencies to complete their plans for NAFTA.[39]

After this sluggish start, the administration got into motion by the end of summer 1993. Daley organized a major lobbying effort by cabinet members. The State Department became heavily involved under the leadership of Secretary of State Warren Christopher; both he and Charles Gillespie, a State Department official and former envoy to Colombia and Chile, lobbied Congress heavily. In addition to this insider strategy, Daley created publicity events to generate public support for NAFTA.[40]

Congress would be difficult to convince. The administration had hoped public support of NAFTA would pressure members of Congress into supporting the agreement, but convincing Americans of the desirability of NAFTA would be tough. Americans feared job losses that NAFTA opponents claimed it would cause. Clinton faced the formidable task of convincing Americans that jobs would not go south and that, in fact, NAFTA would improve their overall economic conditions.[41] Legislators were under considerable pressure from NAFTA opponents to block Clinton's efforts. For example, labor cut campaign contributions to House Democrats who supported NAFTA.[42] Making matters worse for the administration, House Republicans, who found themselves in an uncomfortable ideological alliance with the president, were cautious in giving their support to NAFTA. They did not want to take a strong position on a deal that might pass the House anyway.[43] Finally, while agreeing on the policy, House Republicans were not terribly eager to help a Democratic president, particularly one who was constructing a health reform proposal that many Republicans would find unacceptable. Helping Clinton on NAFTA might strengthen his hand on health care. With these considerations in mind, House Republican leaders Robert Michel (R-OH) and Gingrich devised a plan to provide 110 Republican votes in the House for NAFTA if Clinton could deliver 110 Democratic votes. The objective here was to force the president to push wavering Democrats into the pro-NAFTA column.[44]

A turning point in the adoption of NAFTA was the nationally televised debate between prominent NAFTA opponent Ross Perot and Vice President Albert Gore, Jr. Perot had made many appearances throughout the 1993 NAFTA debate opposing the agreement and warning Americans of the impending lob losses signaled by the "giant sucking sound" coming from Mexico.[45] Perot's populist appeal damaged the administration's efforts to get NAFTA approved by Congress. With Perot dominating the public debate, swaying public opinion became a difficult, if not impossible, task. In this gloomy atmosphere, Vice President Gore rose to the challenge by offering to debate Perot on NAFTA before a national television audience. Although many NAFTA supporters feared Perot's homespun explanations and simplistic solutions would trump Gore's policy expertise and stiff presentation, precisely the opposite occurred. The Vice President humiliated

Perot with his command of facts, and Perot humiliated himself with his glaring gaps in knowledge and flagging references to scant statistics. The debate was an enormous victory for the administration and essentially eliminated Perot from the struggle over NAFTA. Equally important, Gore's success in convincing the public that NAFTA was a good thing gave House Republicans the political cover they needed to give their support to the president.[46]

Interest groups were as active in the struggle over congressional approval of NAFTA as in any major policy decision. Business groups generally supported the agreement, seeing tremendous potential in the undeveloped and untapped Mexican market. Thus, for example, high-technology electronics manufacturers looked forward to building market share in Mexico. In addition, major peak associations, such as the National Association of Manufacturers (NAM), the United States Chamber of Commerce, and the Business Roundtable, signed on for NAFTA.[47] Some industries opposed NAFTA because of the harm the agreement could cause to their prospects in the American market. This was particularly the case for some agricultural sectors that sought concessions from Congress and the president to protect their products from cheaper imports from Mexico. Labor unions took a united stand against NAFTA. Led by the AFL-CIO, organized labor stood firmly on the position that NAFTA would cause Americans to lose their jobs to Mexicans as U.S. firms moved south in search of cheaper labor.[48] Labor was resolute on the point, so much so that Clinton chose simply to oppose labor, his natural ally, rather than to attempt to woo union support.

The most intriguing interest-group story involves U.S. environmental groups. Dramatically demonstrating the point that American "greens" are hardly monolithic, environmental groups sharply split on NAFTA. Groups opposing the trade pact, like the Sierra Club, argued that it would lead to widespread environmental degradation in Mexico, where the government kept environmental regulations lax in order to attract American industry. These groups also feared that U.S. environmental regulations would be undermined by NAFTA if the international agreement superseded domestic law. In addition, NAFTA would likely exacerbate the environment problems caused by *maquiladora* factories and would present food inspection problems at the United States–Mexico border.[49] This position put environmentalists in an odd alliance with populists, like Ross Perot and Patrick Buchanan, who claimed that international trade agreements in general undermined U.S. sovereignty.[50] On the other side of the issues were a number of well-known environmental groups, including, for example, the Environmental Defense Fund and the Audubon Society. They argued that NAFTA would encourage better environmental policy throughout North America, provided a satisfactory side agreement on the issue could be reached.[51]

The stage was set for the administration's final push in fall 1993. Clinton used every weapon in his political arsenal to win congressional support for NAFTA, cutting deals with members of Congress on issues that were of particular concern to them. Representative Lewis F. Payne, Jr. (D-VA) won guarantees of protection for the American textile industry. Representative Esteban E. Torres (D-CA) extracted an administration commitment to spend more money on environmental cleanup along border regions. Going outside the normal array of demands, Representative E. Clay Shaw (R-FL) forced the administration to extradite a rapist from Mexico to face authorities in the United States. The administration's concessions were not limited to individual legislators; the Florida congressional delegation won protection for agricultural products, including, for example, lettuce, citrus, tomatoes, and asparagus.[52]

On 30 September 1993, the House Ways and Means Subcommittee on Trade approved a draft version of the NAFTA implementing legislation. In addition to approving the trade agreement itself, Congress had to pass legislation that changed U.S. policy in accord with NAFTA provisions. This involved an unusual legislative process. The fast-track provisions under which Congress was considering NAFTA provided that the implementing legislation could not be amended once it was introduced. Therefore, in order to deal with the usual adjustments necessary to any legislation, Congress handled the implementation bill as a draft. The House Ways and Means Committee and the Senate Finance Committee carried most of the load on the legislation, essentially drafting the bill. The president then reviewed the draft, offering few changes. Once it finished polishing the draft into its final form, it was then formally introduced as a piece of legislation to be considered under a strict timetable.[53]

To sum up, the build-up to the final deliberation over congressional approval of NAFTA was marked by some typical and some not-so-typical aspects of American politics. The administration's all-out effort to sway the American public on NAFTA and to persuade members of Congress to approve it is reminiscent of many major political battles. Consider, for example, Franklin Roosevelt's maneuvering a frequently hostile Congress, a remarkable time in the history of presidential–congressional relations. More recently, Lyndon Johnson held a clinic on getting tough legislation through Congress, the Civil Rights Act being perhaps the most memorable example. Clinton's working of Congress on NAFTA certainly warrants high marks for energy and skill. Using public pressure, concessions on specific requests, and a good measure of arm twisting, Clinton fought effectively for NAFTA's passage. In this regard, the NAFTA political battle was altogether typical of American politics.

The presence of numerous interest groups on both sides of the issues was also emblematic of American politics. The fact that the alliances were temporary and sometimes matched odd bedfellows is nothing new. Indeed, the pluralist ideal has coalitions forming around a certain issue, disintegrating, then reforming in entirely different ways around other issues. What was somewhat unusual, however, was the clear split among environmental groups. Perhaps not surprisingly, this divide indicates that environmentalism brings individuals together on "green" issues but not necessarily on others.

Yet NAFTA was strikingly unusual in one key respect: The president had to rely on the support of the opposing party to win congressional approval of NAFTA. Indeed, the strongest opposition to the trade agreement came from congressional leaders of the president's own party. In spite of the unusual partisan alliance, however, the interaction between a determined president and a resistant Congress remained essentially normal.

The Endgame

The final ratification of NAFTA was marked by intensive administration activity as well as a flurry of negotiations in Congress. Congress had to deal with several key issues in the implementing legislation. First, it had to compensate for lost revenues to the federal government resulting from NAFTA's tariff reductions. Second, Congress needed to create programs, or modify existing ones, to clean up pollution, especially along the Mexican border, and to provide funding to build sanitation infrastructure—for example, wastewater treatment plants. Finally, the implementing legislation had to specify in what form and how generous worker assistance would be to help American workers thrown out of their jobs because of NAFTA.[54] In the contest among congressional leaders, NAFTA supporters won. Led by Democratic Representatives Matsui and Richardson, along with members of the Republican leadership, the pro-NAFTA effort was much better coordinated than the opposition. Unaccustomed to exchanging information with the other party's whips, the Republican and Democratic anti-NAFTA efforts suffered from lack of communication in general, and inaccurate counts of supporters and opponents in particular. The pro-NAFTA team, however, effectively shared information on the status of the agreement among House members and, because of this more accurate information, was able to drum up and sustain support more effectively.[55]

Ultimately, NAFTA's passage depended on the voting decisions of individual members of Congress. Since partisanship was somewhat confused on the issue, a straight party vote was remote. Party, however, did play a major role in the vote, as a majority of Democrats voted against NAFTA, while a majority of Republicans voted for it.[56] Legislators had to turn to other criteria for their votes. For many, the decision was clear. Market-oriented, free-trade members supported NAFTA from the start, and members who found some usefulness in protection and who were less enamored of the ability of the market to make fair allocations of resources, opposed NAFTA from the beginning. But for members of Congress in the middle, the decision was agonizingly difficult.

The main issue for many fence sitters was how the vote would play among their constituents. The answer to that question was often muddled, and even if constituents seemed to have a clear interest, legislators found deciding how to vote difficult as other considerations crept into their deliberations. Representative Bob Inglis (R-SC), for example, opposed NAFTA for ideological reasons. Influenced by his connection to Perot, he opposed the trade pact, although his district was home to high-technology manufacturing. Representative John M. Spratt, Jr. (D-SC), on the other hand, supported NAFTA on ideological grounds even though textile producers in his district might be hurt by it.[57] Similarly, Senator Max Baucus (D-MT) supported NAFTA, while the state's only Representative, Pat Williams (D-MT) opposed it. Since their constituencies were the same, they likely disagreed on NAFTA on the basis of ideology.[58]

On 17 November 1993, the House of Representatives approved NAFTA 234–200. Three days later, the Senate voted 61–38 for NAFTA, and with that, the Clinton administration won its first major political battle. A Democratic-controlled Congress failed to thwart a Democratic president, and the odd alliance between Clinton and congressional Republicans foretold of future partisan shifts, yet did nothing to alter the routine interaction between Congress and the president.

The central issue became clear in the endgame. Underlying the entire NAFTA debate was a clash among economic interests. NAFTA exposed a fundamental conflict that had existed not far below the surface for many years. David S. Cloud of *Congressional Quarterly Weekly Report* put it well:

> By its promise to join the economy of the richest country in the world with a poor, but emerging neighbor, NAFTA has provoked a long-simmering debate and exposed deeply felt anxieties about job security and a broader transition under way in the U.S. economy.[59]

In the same article, Cloud outlines the two opposing visions of the future that were at loggerheads in the NAFTA debate. Clinton's vision sees NAFTA as a great opportunity to provide new jobs and to improve the standard of living in both Mexico and the United States. Opponents see NAFTA as a tool of corporate America—an exploitative policy written by and for wealthy investors. The agreement, in this unkind view, would drive down American wages, cost American jobs, and worsen already terrible working conditions in Mexico.[60]

In light of this characterization of the conflict over NAFTA, the odd breakdown of party alliances makes sense. Congressional Democrats held true to their traditional base—working-class, blue-collar Americans, environmentalists, and some industries, like textiles, for example. Congressional Republicans acted in a way consistent with their traditional source of support—corporate America. What is odd is that Clinton, a Democrat, sided with the Republicans. It appears that on trade policy a New Democrat behaves much like a traditional Republican.[61]

The Importance of Institutions in
Program Adoption

The institutional characteristics of Congress, the presidency (including top executive branch officials), and the relationship between them were critical in the NAFTA debate.

Congress

Congressional structure and processes affected the final version of NAFTA. In general, Congress is designed to insure widespread agreement on an issue before it acts. Disbursed power, innumerable procedural obstacles, and bicameralism make winning a majority on a bill sometimes a formidable task. In most cases, legislation that wins widespread approval is watered down in some respect as individual legislators demand concessions and special provisions in exchange for their support of the bill. This was certainly the case for NAFTA. Clinton granted numerous concessions to legislators, especially members of the House, to gain their support of the trade agreement.[62] The incorporation of such concessions into the implementing legislation would not have been possible had it not been for the bargaining, compromise, and negotiation that marks routine business in Congress. With each member of Congress enjoying a measure of power and autonomy, it is frequently necessary to accommodate a large number of individual interests. Congressional procedures permit and even encourage the creation of legislation that satisfies these particular interests. It is no wonder that the implementing legislation that accompanied NAFTA included so many provisions that chipped away at the basic thrust of the agreement.

Congress might easily be considered two separate institutions sharing a single roof. Elected for different terms of office and responsible to different constituencies, representatives and senators have good reasons not to see policy issues in the same way. The House and Senate certainly viewed NAFTA from different perspectives. The agreement spawned little controversy in the Senate, where support for the agreement was a foregone conclusion from the start. The Senate's benign acceptance of the trade pact is attributable to two factors: First, the constitutional requirement that the Senate ratify treaties has given it traditional responsibility for foreign policy in Congress. As foreign policy, NAFTA attracted early Senate approval. Second, because most senators represent larger constituencies than representatives, it is less likely that they will be moved by the complaints of a particular industry.[63]

The House of Representatives, on the other hand, was home to a lively, often contentious debate on NAFTA. Closer to the voters than senators, and never far from the next election, representatives are forced to consider the immediate electoral consequences of their decisions. Approving a trade pact that might harm workers or industries in one's district might be political suicide. The problem was made that much worse for many representatives because their districts did not present clear signals on NAFTA. Thus, no matter how the representative decided, it would cost him or her votes in the next election.[64]

Parties and committees are the two organizing principles of Congress. In the NAFTA episode, committees played their usual roles; the House Ways and Means Committee and the Senate Finance Committee took the lead in their respective chambers in drafting the implementing legislation. The more serious struggle took place in the House, and thus put the Ways and Means Committee in the center of the storm. The Clinton administration's selection of William Daley to shepherd NAFTA through Congress had the additional benefit of securing Ways and Means Committee Chairman Rostenkowski's support of NAFTA.

Even though committee behavior was normal, party activity was not. As noted earlier, both parties split on NAFTA, forcing Clinton to rely on Republican support in the House to secure its passage. The absence of party salience with regard to NAFTA is significant for American politics in general. It reflects the fact that conflict cut along economic lines that were not consistent with party identification. This complicated the congressional struggle over NAFTA and perhaps indicated deeper problems within the parties on economic issues that will require sorting out, possibly in the form of a realignment.

Finally, constituent interests were at the root of the congressional vote on NAFTA, especially in the House. With little partisan guidance, House members looked to constituent interests to determine their votes. This was not always an easy task. When constituents sent no clear preference, then representatives were forced to vote on the issue on other criteria—for example, ideology.

The Institutional Presidency

The institutional presidency encompasses a considerable number of officials and agencies. This discussion considers the president himself, his immediate staff and assistants, and top government officials, usually political appointees. A key point to keep in mind throughout this analysis is that the president rarely acts alone; he usually relies on an array of advisers to make decisions, and he is forced to rely on them to implement them.

The president enjoys a national view, broader than that of any member of Congress. Elected by a national constituency, the president can more easily take positions that benefit the country as a whole, even while damaging the interests of some groups. This freedom has allowed presidents historically to take a strong free-trade position, pushing for trade liberalization even in the face of stiff congressional resistance. Presidents have also been more directly involved in making foreign policy initiatives. Constitutionally responsible for negotiations with foreign governments and enjoying the flexibility of a unitary actor, presidents have led in foreign policy, with Congress becoming involved only after a policy has been set into motion. Although Congress must give the president prior authorization to negotiate trade agreements—as in the fast-track authority Congress gave President Bush to negotiate NAFTA—the president has considerable discretion in his interaction with representatives of foreign governments.

The experience of Presidents Bush and Clinton demonstrated these advantages on trade policy. Bush initiated negotiations on the agreement and began to seek congressional approval of it late in his term. Once he decided to sign on to NAFTA, Clinton used the singleness of purpose of his office to win passage in Congress. It is worth noting that Clinton's commitment to a pact that leads to trade liberalization had at least as much to do with being president as it had to do with his ideology or his being a New Democrat. In any case, even with numerous opportunities and good reasons to back away from his support of NAFTA, Clinton pursued the deal until its ratification.

In addition to the White House staff, the assistants closest to the president, several key administration players were central in getting NAFTA adopted, with the USTR the most significant among them. Responsible for trade policy and nothing else, this executive office agency spearheaded the administration's effort to make NAFTA a reality. As part of the Executive Office of the President (EOP), the USTR enjoys immediate access to the White House. The USTR is appointed by the president and, thus, has the president's ear on trade policy. On NAFTA, both Hills and Kantor took advantage of this position, each becoming the unambiguous spokesperson for the administration's trade policy.

Less involved but still important in the episode were the State Department, Treasury Department, the Environment Protection Agency (EPA), the Agriculture Department, and the Labor Department. Having been centrally involved in hammering out the details of the agreement with Mexican and Canadian officials, these departments continued to be at the heart of the NAFTA debate. Each of these agencies had some concern over different aspect of the trade accord. The State Department focused on foreign policy issues, mainly those with Mexico, while the Treasury Department examined the significance of NAFTA for the strength of the *peso* and the health of American investments in Mexico. The Labor Department played some role in the side agreement on labor, and in a less direct way, Labor Secretary Robert Reich's continuing effort to improve job training in the United States was consistent with the general thrust of NAFTA. Similarly, the Agriculture Department attended to the effects of NAFTA on American farmers, and the EPA played a significant role in the development of the environmental side agreement.

There is nothing unusual about the activities of these agencies. Each was responsible for issues that fell within its jurisdiction, working in concert toward the main objective of completing the side agreements, writing the implementing legislation, and obtaining congressional ratification. More interesting, perhaps, was the interaction between Congress and the presidency. The institutional relationship between the legislative and executive branches in large part determines the nature of policies. The discussion so far has examined the characteristics of each; how the two interacted during the debate and final approval of NAFTA tells the rest of the story.

Congress, the Presidency, and the Approval of NAFTA

The separation of powers remains a marvelous invention. It forces two authoritative parts of government with different sources of power to agree. That requirement sometimes slows the development of public policy to a snail's pace; at the same time, it provides a nearly insurmountable obstacle to reckless governance. The struggle to approve NAFTA pitted a reluctant Congress against a determined presidency.

The interaction between the two is emblematic of American politics and provides a great deal of the explanation of the final outcome.

The president pulled out all the stops to obtain congressional approval of NAFTA. Working inside the Beltway, President Clinton pressured and cajoled individual members of Congress, and provided concessions to individual legislators—especially members of the House—in exchange for their support of NAFTA. Clinton, in short, demonstrated considerable Washington skill in persuading Congress, especially in light of the fact that he could not rely on his own party's congressional leaders for help.

Clinton worked Congress outside the Beltway as well. Going public is the new art of presidential persuasion, and Clinton proved to be adept at it.[65] In speeches and other public appearances, Clinton hammered home the message that NAFTA would be good for everyone. Whether he won the public opinion battle is less important than his success in convincing undecided members of Congress that he had come close enough to give them political cover to vote for the agreement.

The result of the interaction between Congress and the presidency was implementing legislation that watered down NAFTA. The trade deal's basic goal of eliminating all barriers to trade among the United States, Canada, and Mexico was undermined by numerous exceptions delivered by the administration to members of Congress. Nevertheless, because of these concessions, NAFTA became policy. A classic case of public policy making in the United States, a major policy shift was made possible by small exceptions to it. Public policy changes in the United States, but not without compromise.

Interests and the Adoption of NAFTA

Interest groups were active on both sides of NAFTA. Most business groups and some environmentalists favored NAFTA, while some opposed it, along with organized labor and many environmental groups. Agriculture eventually came to support the agreement, but only after the administration had given guarantees to protect some key products.[66] The economic interests so much at stake in the fight found expression primarily through interest groups. Thus, an old-fashioned battle emerged pitting business against labor, with environmental groups split between the two camps.

The party split makes quite clear the economic class divide in the United States. While not a class-conscious society, and certainly not one whose political structures and dynamics are dominated by class, the United States is clearly confronting a major economic shift that could separate its citizens by economic condition. As the rich move farther from the middle, and as low-end jobs become increasingly dead-end jobs, the United States faces the unhappy prospect of being permanently divided into affluent, information-age professionals, on one hand, and poor, uneducated, low-skilled workers on the other. NAFTA certainly has not caused this turn of events, nor will it determine whether it continues. But it embodies the emerging conflict and all the social and economic woes that accompany it. This explains why NAFTA, an otherwise esoteric international agreement that may have little effect in any case, drew so much political attention, kindled so much class-based ideological fire, and caused so many to fear for their economic future and, more basically, their way of life.

The NAFTA debate was, in a sense, a slice of the broader debate about the international competitiveness of American industry. NAFTA represented a step in the direction of free trade and more intense international competition, which would create new winners and losers in the American economy. One's view of economic uncertainty largely determined one's position on the agreement.

The less traditional groups involved in NAFTA focused on different issues. Environmental groups that opposed NAFTA wished to avoid environmental degradation in Mexico and the undermining of U.S. environmental regulations that NAFTA might inadvertently bring on. The "greens" split, but the fact that they mattered at all reflects their established presence in American politics.

Ideas in the Adoption of NAFTA

NAFTA was wrapped in ideology and information. There was no shortage of economic analyses of the effects of the agreement, ranging from dire consequences to stunning economic growth.[67] For supporters, NAFTA promised increased trade with Mexico, new Mexican markets, and greater access to Mexican-made products. For opponents, NAFTA meant lost American jobs and the elimination of traditional manufacturing industries in the United States. Antagonists took sweeping positions based on these arguments. What is critical for purposes here is that there was considerable uncertainty about what exactly NAFTA's effects would be. This is typical of complex policies; like it or not, policy makers operate in a contingent world, and their decisions can be justified only in part on the basis of analysis.

Both sides used and misused information to make their points. Perot characterized his view, that jobs would go south, in the phrase, "the giant sucking sound." A Mississippi broom factory became the symbol for lost jobs; the workers' lives would be disrupted, to say the least, as the factory moved to Mexico to take advantage of cheaper labor.[68] On the other side of the debate, the Clinton administration cited the new jobs that NAFTA would create, along with the growth of both the American and Mexican economies. Perhaps no symbol characterized the NAFTA debate more than the *maquiladoras*. Poor working conditions located in what can only be called an environmental disaster captured what NAFTA opponents feared. NAFTA would create more *maquiladoras*. Because of the successful use of this symbol, the Clinton administration and its allies were forced to promise to address the problems embodied in the *maquiladoras*.

Given the uncertainty that surrounded NAFTA, participants were forced to rely on ideology as at least a partial guide to how they should view the agreement. Neoliberalism, which features free trade, among other things, might characterize the ideologies of NAFTA supporters. Faith in markets domestically, and a desire to open the world economic system logically lead to a pro-NAFTA stance. Populism and old-style liberalism produce the opposite conclusion. Exaggerated fears based on hyperbolic claims about NAFTA draw Americans fearful for their jobs and their economic security to the populist flame. Protection of traditional manufacturing jobs pull organized labor and blue-collar workers in general into the liberal camp.

Information and ideology, then, played a major role in the NAFTA debate. The former became the currency of the debate, while the latter became the last recourse in a world of uncertainty.

Implementation

It is impossible to say much about NAFTA's implementation at this point. But it is possible and even useful to anticipate the issues that will need to be addressed as officials in the three member countries try to make the agreement work. Three categories of inquiry come to mind.

First, how will bureaucrats implement NAFTA? There is little to be concerned with in the routine reduction of tariffs, customs assessments, and the like. But there is considerably more to worry about when it comes to the side agreements on the environment and labor. U.S. officials must monitor the progress on these agreements and make adjustments and policy recommendations to address shortcomings as they arise. At this writing, two main problems have caught public attention: There seems to have been little progress in the improvement of working conditions in Mexico, and there is little evidence that living and working conditions are any better in the *maquiladoras* than they were before NAFTA went into effect.

The Clinton administration claims that progress has been made on both fronts. The North American Agreement on Labor Cooperation, established to implement the labor side agreement, has forged ahead on important labor issues, according to the administration. The successes, however, are limited at this early date to the creation of a complaint process and a forum for debate on major issues. Since NAFTA's inception, claims the administration, Mexico has increased oversight and enforcement of its labor laws.[69] The three NAFTA nations have also begun the effort to implement the side agreement on the environment. These efforts have been limited to continuation of bilateral programs between the United States and Mexico: the U.S.–Mexico Border XXI Program, which sets five-year plans for meeting environmental goals along the border; the Border Environment Cooperation Commission and the North American Development Bank, which help funnel funds to communities to run environmental programs. Along with these established bilateral efforts, the United States, Mexico, and Canada established an environmental body, the Commission for Environmental Cooperation, to deal with environmental issues across North America.[70]

American officials cannot act alone on these matters, of course, but they must see to the fulfillment of the agreement from the American perspective to the extent possible. This will require political will; without enthusiastic support from the Clinton administration, there is little reason to believe that American bureaucrats, however well intentioned, will have much success.

Second, congressional oversight is likely to serve the dual purpose of encouraging bureaucrats to implement NAFTA properly and to shed public light on problems. Tied up with a fierce ideological struggle fomented mainly by Speaker Gingrich and House Republicans, there has been little oversight of NAFTA—certainly none that has resulted in any action. If this continues, future American officials may find it necessary to take dramatic action to see to the enforcement of the provisions to which the United States agreed.

Finally, interest groups will affect the successful implementation of NAFTA. Environmental groups, in particular, have an interest in monitoring environmental developments, mainly in Mexico, and seeing to it that the United States does not weaken its environmental regulation to accommodate industries that wish to be more competitive in the Mexican market.

Conclusion

NAFTA clearly demonstrates the domestic roots of U.S. trade policy. The international agreement required American approval, not simply as a treaty ratification, but by means of the domestic policy process. Business, labor, and environmentalists joined the debate, seeking to protect their perceived interests, the result of which was an old-fashioned political brawl. In this episode, institutions shaped the final outcome, interests informed but did not dominate the debate, and ideas provided the tie-breaker for many undecided legislators as well providing the idea of a NAFTA from the beginning. A Democratic president won the support of congressional Republicans over the objections of members of his own party. Although foreign policy considerations were at work in the NAFTA debate, the agreement is fundamentally a product of domestic processes.

Endnotes

1. Office of the President of the United States, *Study on the Operation and Effects of the North American Free Trade Agreement* (Washington, D.C.: U.S. Government Printing Office, 1997), chaps. 3 and 4.
2. Paul R. Krugman, "The Uncomfortable Truth about NAFTA: It's Foreign Policy, Stupid," *Foreign Affairs* 72 (Nov/Dec 93): 13–19.

3. "When Neighbours Embrace," *The Economist*, 5 July 1997, 21–22.

4. Ibid., 23.

5. "When Neighbours Embrace," *The Economist*, 5 July 1997, 21. The president's figures are reported in the *Study on the Operation and Effects of the North American Free Trade Agreement*, 1997, 21–22. This study reports that 99,497 workers were certified under the North American Free Trade Agreement Transitional Adjustment Assistance program (NAFTA-TAA), but that "certification does not require that NAFTA be the cause of the dislocation or risk." (21) Only 12,193 workers applied for NAFTA-TAA benefits during this time. Add to this number some 20,000 workers who were certified under this program and the regular trade adjustment assistance program, but whose benefits came from the latter. According to the study, the roughly 32,000 workers accounted for in this way represent the low possible number, while the 99,497 who were certified under NAFTA-TAA account for the high number. The report indicates that the actual number lies somewhere between these extremes.

6. Sam Howe Verhovek, "Free Trade's Benefits Bypass Border Towns," *New York Times*, 23 June 1998, late New York edition, A1.

7. Steve Dryden, *Trade Warriors: USTR and the American Crusade for Free Trade* (New York: Oxford Univ. Press, 1995), 340.

8. Dryden, *Trade Warriors*, 340–43.

9. NAFTA was not technically a mere extension of the U.S.–Canada Trade Agreement. It was formally an altogether new document that had to be negotiated in its entirety by the United States, Canada, and Mexico.

10. Dryden, *Trade Warriors*, 369.

11. Ibid., 369–70.

12. George W. Grayson, *The North American Free Trade Agreement: Regional Community and the New World Order* (Lanham, Md.: Univ. Press of America, 1995), 55.

13. Dryden, *Trade Warriors*, 370.

14. The effects of free-trade areas on global trade liberalization are in dispute. Free-trade areas might lead to trade liberalization as the areas grow to include an increasing number of countries. On the other hand, they could too easily become trade blocs complete with their own high tariff walls. In effect, multinational regional trade blocs replace individual countries in a downward spiral of protectionism. Needless to say, NAFTA supporters preferred the former interpretation. See Rudiger W. Dornbusch, "Policy Options for Freer Trade: The Case for Bilateralism," in Robert Z. Lawrence and Charles L. Schultze, eds., *An American Trade Strategy: Options for the 1990s* (Washington, D.C.: Brookings Institution, 1990), 125–33; and Anne O. Krueger, "Free Trade is the Best Policy," in Lawrence and Schultze, eds., *An American Trade Strategy*, 91–93.

15. For an overview of the general consensus among economists about NAFTA's likely effects, see Timothy J. Kehoe, "Assessing the Economic Impact of North American Free Trade," in M. Delal Baer and Sidney Weintraub, eds., *The NAFTA Debate: Grappling with Unconventional Trade Issues* (Boulder, Colo.: Lynne Rienner, 1994), 3–33. See also Gary Clyde Hufbauer and Jeffrey J. Schott, *NAFTA: An Assessment* (Washington, D.C.: Institute for International Economics, 1993).

16. Ideological support for NAFTA came from several corners, the Heritage Foundation among them. See, for example, Michael G. Wilson, "The North American Free Trade Agreement: Ronald Reagan's Vision Realized," The Heritage Foundation Executive Memorandum #371, 23 November 1993. For an opposition tract, see H. Ross Perot with Pat Choate, *Save Your Job, Save Our Country: Why NAFTA Must Be Stopped—Now!* (New York: Hyperion, 1993).

17. Michael P. Ryan, *Playing by the Rules: American Trade Power and Diplomacy in the Pacific* (Washington, D.C.: Georgetown Univ. Press, 1995), 45–46.

18. The four issues included health and safety standards for agriculture imports from Mexico, transition periods of more than ten years for some U.S. tariffs, worker adjustment programs, and exclusion of labor mobility and immigration laws from the negotiations. Grayson, *The North American Free Trade Agreement,* 64–66.

19. Dryden, *Trade Warriors,* 370.

20. Grayson, *The North American Free Trade Agreement,* 67.

21. Ibid., 68–70.

22. Ibid., 73–75.

23. Ibid., 78, 86, 89.

24. Ibid., 82.

25. Ibid., 90.

26. Davis S. Cloud, "White House Pushes Trade Pact, Blasts Democrats' Bill," *Congressional Quarterly Weekly Report,* 16 May 1992, 1330; and David S. Cloud, "Free-trade Pact Buffeted by Election-year Forces," *Congressional Quarterly Weekly Report,* 12 September 1992, 2699–701.

27. David S. Cloud, "Clinton Endorses NAFTA, Outlines Reservations," *Congressional Quarterly Weekly Report* 10 October 1992, 3137. Grayson, *The North American Free Trade Agreement,* 122–31.

28. Cloud, "Free-trade Pact Buffeted by Election-year Forces," 2700–01.

29. Howard J. Wiarda, "The U.S. Domestic Politics of the U.S.–Mexico Free Trade Agreement," in Baer and Weintraub, eds., *The NAFTA Debate,* 131–33.

30. John R. Cranford, "House Signals Concerns on Free-trade Pact," *Congressional Quarterly Weekly Report,* 8 August 1992, 2334.

31. David S. Cloud, "Warning Bells on NAFTA Sound for Clinton," *Congressional Quarterly Weekly Report,* 28 November 1992, 3710–13.
32. David S. Cloud, "Clinton Team on Attack for NAFTA Support," *Congressional Quarterly Weekly Report,* 4 September 1993, 2335–36.
33. Beth Donovan, "Anti-NAFTA: Essential for Bonior," *Congressional Quarterly Weekly Report,* 11 September 1993, 2374.
34. David S. Cloud, "Defection of House Leaders Reflects Deeper Concerns," *Congressional Quarterly Weekly Report,* 11 September 1993, 2373–75.
35. Grayson, *The North American Free Trade Agreement,* 190–92.
36. Cloud, "Clinton Team on Attack for NAFTA Support."
37. Cloud, "Defection of House Leaders Reflects Deeper Concerns."
38. For an excellent account of the administration's first year, see Elizabeth Drew, *On the Edge: The Clinton Presidency* (New York: Simon & Schuster, 1994).
39. Grayson, *The North American Free Trade Agreement,* 197–98.
40. Ibid., 203–05.
41. David S. Cloud, "Clinton Enlists Big Guns in Push for NAFTA," *Congressional Quarterly Weekly Report,* 18 September 1993, 2436–39.
42. Thomas Galvin, "PACs: Silence Speaks Volumes," *Congressional Quarterly Weekly Report,* 18 September 1993, 2437.
43. David S. Cloud, "GOP Wants to See Democrats' Hand . . . before Getting into the Game," *Congressional Quarterly Weekly Report,* 18 September 1993, 2438–39.
44. Cloud, "GOP Wants to See Democrats' Hand."
45. This argument was stated most clearly in Perot, *Save Your Job, Save Our Country.*
46. Grayson, *The North American Free Trade Agreement,* 213.
47. Wiarda, "The U.S. Domestic Politics of the U.S.–Mexico Free Trade Agreement," 121–22.
48. Ibid., 124–27.
49. David Vogel, *Trading Up: Consumer and Environmental Regulation in a Global Economy* (Cambridge, Mass.: Harvard Univ. Press, 1995), 232–34. The list of environmental and other citizen groups opposed to NAFTA included Environmental Action, Friends of the Earth, Greenpeace, the Natural Resources Defense Council, Sierra Club, Center for Science in the Public Interest, Community Nutrition Institute, Consumer Federation of America, National Consumer League, Public Citizen, and Public Voice. See Wiarda, "The U.S. Domestic Politics of the U.S.–Mexico Free Trade Agreement," 127.
50. Wiarda, "The U.S. Domestic Politics of the U.S.–Mexico Free Trade Agreement," 129.
51. Ibid., 121–22.
52. David S. Cloud, "Administration Pressed to Deal to Win NAFTA Converts,"

Congressional Quarterly Weekly Report, 2 October 1993, 2620–21; Grayson, *The North American Free Trade Agreement,* 214.

53. The timetable is as follows: 45 days for House Committee consideration; 15 days for House floor activity; 15 days for Senate Committee consideration; 15 days for Senate floor activity. See David S. Cloud, "NAFTA on the Fast Track," *Congressional Quarterly Weekly Report,* 2 October 1993, 2621.

54. Cloud, "Administration Pressed to Deal to Win NAFTA Converts."

55. Grayson, *The North American Free Trade Agreement,* 215.

56. This outcome does not meet the test of a straight vote, which normally means at least 80 percent of one party must vote against 80 percent of the other. However, party cohesion was present in the NAFTA vote, although the fact that congressional Democrats were aligned against a Democratic president confused the issue. For an analysis of the importance of party in the NAFTA vote, see Charles F. Doran, "The NAFTA Vote and Political Party: A Partial Test," in Charles F. Doran and Gregory P. Marchildon, eds., *The NAFTA Puzzle: Political Parties and Trade in North America* (Boulder, Colo.: Westview, 1994), 247–64.

57. Phil Duncan, "Traditional Factors Little Help in Predicting Member's Vote," *Congressional Quarterly Weekly Report,* 6 November 1993, 3018–19.

58. Dave Kaplan, "Even When Voters are the Same, Pact Can Split Delegation," *Congressional Quarterly Weekly Report,* 6 November 1993, 3020–21.

59. David S. Cloud, "'Undecideds' are Final Target in Battle over Trade Pact," *Congressional Quarterly Weekly Report,* 6 November 1993, 3011.

60. Ibid., 3011–13.

61. Clinton's claim to being a New Democrat originates in the 1986 founding of the Democratic Leadership Council (DLC), of which Clinton is a charter member. These moderate-to-conservative Democrats wished to chart a new course for their party, away from the traditional labor union, big government base. Clinton agrees at times with this course of action, but not always. Whether Clinton and other DLC members truly represent the new age of the Democratic Party remains to be seen, of course, but if they do, their success could signal a party realignment and a significant shift of the political center of gravity in the United States to the right.

62. The various promises of protection were incorporated into the implementing legislation, not the trade agreement itself.

63. This is not always the case, of course. Note, for example, Senator Ernest Hollings's (D-SC) opposition to NAFTA in his tireless effort to protect his state's textile industry from foreign competition.

64. Davis S. Cloud, "'Undecideds' Are Final Target in Battle Over Trade Pact," 3011–13.

65. See Samuel Kernell, *Going Public: New Strategies of Presidential Leadership,* 3rd ed. (Washington, D.C.: CQ Press, 1997).

66. David Orden, "Agricultural Interest Groups and the North American Free Trade Agreement," in Anne O Krueger, ed., *The Political Economy of American Trade Policy* (Chicago, Ill.: Univ. of Chicago Press, 1996), 345–52, 370.
67. See, for example, Perot *Save Your Job, Save Our Country;* and Hufbauer and Schott, *NAFTA: An Assessment.* For a survey of the estimates of NAFTA's effects on jobs, see Robert A. Blecker, "The Political Economy of the North American Free Trade Agreement," in Robert A. Blecker, ed., *U.S. Trade Policy and Global Growth: New Directions in the International Economy* (Armonk, N.Y.: M. E. Sharpe, 1996), 142–46.
68. Barnaby J. Feder, "Tiny Industry Fears NAFTA's Reach," *New York Times,* 24 September 1993, late New York edition, D1–D2.
69. *Study on the Operation and Effects of the North American Free Trade Agreement,* chap. 3.
70. Ibid., chap. 4.

6

The Politics of Administrative Relief

Administrative relief is a mainstay of U.S. trade policy. Under competitive pressure, it has become an attractive trade remedy to industry as well as to government officials. In the domestic and international political context of the 1980s, blatant protectionism was not a viable option. Domestically, the Reagan administration's free-market orientation, with its emphasis on deregulation and tax cuts, did not provide an agreeable environment in which to introduce unvarnished protectionist policies. Government intervention of this sort did not square with the laissez faire principles that had become predominant in the eighties. Internationally, the widespread acceptance of the General Agreement on Tariffs and Trade (GATT) among industrialized nations, coupled with America's historical leadership role in multilateral trade liberalization, made it difficult for U.S. officials to back protectionist policies. These political conditions forced the U.S. government to justify its claims against foreign competition in terms of unfair trade practices. The policies that it developed from this premise have allowed members of Congress to advocate free trade while still offering protection to their constituents. The United States, then, remains above blatant protectionism in its rhetoric and in its rationale for acting, but reaps the benefits and suffers the costs of protection nonetheless.

A productive way to examine administrative relief is to think of it as a matter of implementation. Located in the executive, implementation involves the usual political participants in a different way from the agenda-setting or legislative process. Its peculiar organizational characteristics and political dynamics allow government and the private sector to use implementation to achieve protectionist objectives where legislative activity would most certainly fail. Thus, the analysis presented here demonstrates how a responsive government deals with political pressure by channeling it through accommodating institutions.

It is also helpful to think of administrative relief as regulation. U.S. trade law provisions intended to encourage market operations—presumably the intent of administrative trade remedies—serve roughly the same function for international trade as domestic laws do for economic activity within the United States. The laws are not the same, but the intent of each is similar.[1]

Ideas, Interests, and Institutions

Institutions are pivotal in administrative remedies to trade problems. How bureaucracies implement these programs determines in large part their effectiveness and usefulness to certain industries; bureaucratic politics is therefore central to administrative relief.

Interests and ideas play a clear role in the development and use of administrative trade remedies. Producer interests pressured the national government into providing protection from foreign competition. Recognizing how politically unpalatable old-fashioned protection was, these interests helped push policy makers into developing administrative trade remedies.

None of this would have mattered unless these remedies were available in the first place. The ideas on which they were based were embedded in U.S. trade law before the 1980s, during which policy entrepreneurs and pragmatic politicians transformed them into more aggressive policy instruments to quell the demand for protection.

Overview of the Main Types of Administrative Relief

U.S. trade law prescribes six types of administrative actions intended to address difficulties experienced by American industries resulting from foreign competition. Five of the provisions deal with imports in the

U.S. market, while one concerns American exports to foreign markets. The design and use of these forms of administrative relief reflect an increasing acceptance of the value of international trade. Participants in the development of U.S. trade policy understand that going back to more protectionist policies is as unlikely politically as it is undesirable economically.

Of the six administrative trade remedies considered here, the escape clause is the most plainly protectionist. It was intended to provide relief, usually in the form of higher tariffs, to industries that could prove injury resulting from imports. Trade adjustment assistance (TAA) was later added to the escape clause, the goal of which has been to provide companies, workers, and later, communities, with government assistance if they have been negatively affected by imports. The relief is temporary and intended only to give recipients time to adjust—such as through worker retraining—to new economic realities.

Three forms of administrative relief are based on the concept of unfair trade practices. Antidumping (AD) provisions of the U.S. trade law allow the U.S. government to retaliate against foreign firms if they "dump," or sell at below fair market value, products in the American market. Roughly parallel to the domestic practice of predatory pricing, dumping is considered unfair according to international trade rules. The United States may also respond to a foreign government's subsidizing its producers that export to the American market. Again, considered unfair, the United States may apply a countervailing duty (CVD) to neutralize the effect of the foreign government's subsidy. According to Section 337 of the U.S. trade law, if a foreign exporter to the United States violates U.S. copyright and patent laws in the production of the good or service, then the United States may retaliate by excluding certain foreign-made products from the American market. This too is considered an unfair trade practice, a violation of the spirit free trade.

Finally, the United States has taken measures to open foreign markets to American exports. Arguing that some governments protect domestic producers from American competition, in 1974 Congress created Section 301 of the U.S. trade law, which allows the U.S. government to identify such unfair trade practices and to retaliate against the guilty government by placing high tariffs on selected imports from that country.

Administrative Relief, Managed Trade and Free Trade

The logic underlying the main components of administrative relief reflects the contemporary tension between free trade and managed trade. Each of these provisions involves some level of government intervention in the market, which in itself is inconsistent with the fundamental principle of free trade. The escape clause, which was based on the peril point provision embedded in nineteenth-century U.S. trade law, grew out of the mercantilist tradition. Intended to be temporary, the escape clause is unapologetic government action designed to save an American industry from injury caused by foreign competition. There is no requirement to justify the action as being warranted by unfair trade practices on the part of the foreign competitor; the fact that imports are damaging the American firm is enough.

Although there is no need to demonstrate the existence of unfair trade practices, TAA is consistent with trade liberalization. The goal of TAA is to provide temporary assistance to companies, workers, and communities to allow them to adjust to new economic conditions. Moreover, the amount of aid recipients may obtain is relatively small and tightly constrained, underscoring the limited goals of the program.

Countervailing duty, antidumping, Section 301, and Section 337 of the U.S. trade law are all predicated on competitors' engaging in unfair trade practices. The rationale for U.S. government action is that, since American firms are victims of the unfair practices of foreign governments and corporations, it is necessary to neutralize somehow the effects of those activities. The goal is to establish the conditions under which market forces may properly operate, removing from foreign producers the unfair advantage they get by virtue of either their own activities or those of their governments. Roughly put, CVD, AD, Section 337, and Section 301 aim to establish a "level playing field" among competitors in the global market.

This reasoning is at the root of the school of managed-trade policy, which incorporates all of these forms of administrative relief.[2] It is important to note, however, that the theory did not precede the specific policies; AD, CVD, Section 337, and some version of Section 301 existed before trade policy elites ever spoke of level playing fields and managed trade. Instead, the managed-trade approach grew out of experience over the last two decades as a rationale for government intervention in international trade. Once conceptualized, the approach incorporated the already existent administrative relief provisions.

Overview of Implementation

The institutional arrangement of American bureaucracy is not a given; the policies it produces are dependent in large part on its peculiar structure, political power, and relationship to other governmental institutions. Knowing something about executives' and bureaucrats' decision making, interaction, and relationship to Congress will go a long way toward explaining the policies they produce.

As I. M. Destler and other students of U.S. trade policy have noted for years, Congress has delegated considerable authority to the executive in implementing administrative trade relief.[3] Intended at least in part as a way for Congress to remain free-trade–oriented in broad policy while leaving room for the executive to protect American industry through the implementation process, congressional willingness to deny itself some considerable decision-making power in this area has been a defining characteristic of American trade policy since the 1970s.[4] The question, then, is what does the executive do with a relatively large delegation of congressional authority.

Executive decisions fall in two categories. The president and his top political appointees make the broad, policy-oriented decisions. Given wide latitude by Congress, these officials can reshape public policy through their interpretations of statutes. In trade policy, the president and the United States Trade Representative (USTR) enjoy (or bear the burden of) such discretion in implementing the escape clause, TAA, and Section 337. Thus, the president can choose to provide relief to American producers damaged by foreign competition under the escape clause and TAA, or can use his discretion to decide not to do so. In any case, the president becomes the focus of political debate on the issue, inevitably bearing the brunt of the criticism from those who disagree with his decision. In giving the executive this sort of discretion over implementing decisions, Congress denies itself a measure of control over policy, but at the same time avoids blame for tough decisions.

Bureaucrats make implementing decisions as well. Less visible than those made by the president and top executive officials, middle-level civil servants routinely make decisions as they implement the often technical side of laws. Technical decisions require choices that affect the content of the program. Bureaucrats base these decisions on several factors: the formal rules of the agency; organizational mission and tradition; and political influence. Agencies certainly prescribe procedures for dealing with routine decisions. Bureaucrats nominally follow these procedures, which may or may not be appropriate to the task at hand.[5] But it is difficult, if not impossible, to define the entirety of bureaucratic decision making in a set of standard procedures. Bureaucrats also rely on the historical traditions of the agency in which they work and the informal norms of behavior that have evolved over time.

In making administrative decisions, Commerce Department officials, according to some critics, use analytic techniques biased in favor of American producers. This is hardly surprising when one takes into account the department's general mission, which is to do things that benefit American business. Political actors compete with agency rules, tradition and norms, and codes of professional conduct for the attention of bureaucrats. While formally in charge of the federal bureaucracy, the president and his political appointees cannot expect bureaucrats to fall automatically into line with their policy preferences. Bureaucrats' decisions are influenced by factors other than the wishes of their legal bosses. Thus, the administration must somehow prevail over those other influences, and the method is usually a political exercise.

In addition, Congress and interest groups seek to influence bureaucrats' behavior. Through congressional oversight, members of Congress call bureaucrats to task for their actions and attempt to alter their decisions to bring them more into line with congressional wishes. Congress may also control bureaucrats by manipulating an agency's budget, rewarding desired decisions with more budget dollars, and punishing uncooperative bureaucrats with budget cuts.[6]

These general principles apply to trade policy as much as to any other issue area. Decisions made by the United States International Trade Commission (USITC), the USTR, and the Department of Commerce, especially its International Trade Administration (ITA), implement various provisions of U.S. trade law. The behavior of bureaucrats and political appointees in these agencies conforms to the general patterns of bureaucratic activities outlined above. In addition, their relationships with Congress, the presidency, and interest groups confirm the conventional wisdom about bureaucratic decision making in American politics.

The President and Administrative Trade Relief

The president is ultimately responsible for the implementation of administrative trade relief. The USTR and the Commerce Department are directly under the chief executive's jurisdiction, and the USITC escape clause and TAA decisions mean nothing unless the president acts on them. One would expect that the president's activities in this regard would be similar to administrative actions in other areas—for example, implementation of environmental laws. To some extent, this is the case, but because of the fact that trade policy involves foreign as well as domestic issues, the constraints surrounding the president's actions and their potential consequences are different than they would be for ordinary domestic policy.

International trade is one component of foreign policy whose importance varies according to what policy makers view as critical to U.S. relations with other countries. To take a persistent problem, for example, U.S. trade policy runs into constant conflict with the American position on human rights. Should the United States continue to pursue trade opportunities with China, or should it use trade as a way to induce the Chinese government to change its domestic policies that affect (according to the United States) human rights? A less pointed example, perhaps, has been U.S.–Japanese relations since the 1960s. While the United States continues to spar with the Japanese on trade policy, the broader strategic and diplomatic relationship between the two countries remains unchallenged. No American policy maker wishes to undermine this rock-solid alliance by pursuing too aggressively problems in U.S.–Japanese economic relations.[7]

In addition to foreign policy considerations, the president must take account of general economic conditions in the United States. Trade deficits—the focus of concern in economic hard times—do not attract much negative attention when the economy is growing at a steady pace. The record bilateral deficit with China in 1996, for example, went mostly unnoticed in the context of robust economic growth. But trade deficits can become the focus of media attention when the economy is sluggish. Whether it is possible for government to reduce the trade deficit with trade policy, or whether it even matters is not the point. The trade deficit becomes the symbol of American economic weakness, and addressing it (more accurately perhaps, appearing to address it) is required of public officials, mainly the president.

The president, like all policy makers in this area, must grapple with public opinion on trade. The overwhelming problem is that most Americans know little about international trade, and many of them occasionally blame it for American economic problems.[8] To take measures that increase trade but harm particular interests is politically perilous for presidents. Conversely, from the perspective of the Oval Office, it is tempting to accommodate vocal industries in need of protection rather than pursue policies that would benefit an unappreciative public.

The health of trade-sensitive sectors of the economy is likely also to influence the president's judgment regarding the use of administrative trade remedies. Firms in troubled industrial sectors can attempt to sway the president directly on their own and through their trade associations, or indirectly by pressuring Congress. A president chooses to respond to an industry's complaints based on its political effectiveness, its importance in the president's supporting political coalition, and its importance in the economy. So, for example, President Reagan complied with the wishes of the American semiconductor industry because of its effective lobbying through the Semiconductor Industry Association (SIA), Reagan's reliance on business for political support, and the significance of the semiconductor industry in the growing high-technology sectors of the American economy. The procedures involved in implementing the escape clause, TAA, and Section 337 are intended to give the president a way to avoid caving to protectionist interests, but presidents have not always chosen this path.

Automatic Trade Relief

Antidumping, countervailing duty, and Section 301 decisions do not involve presidential discretion. In the case of Section 301 claims, the USTR must act according to fairly clear congressional guidelines. Antidumping and countervailing duty cases permit somewhat more discretion. Commerce Department officials are inclined to favor American producers in their determination of AD and CVD claims. This occurs in part, no doubt, because of the analytic guidelines issued by Congress. It is also likely, however, that the traditional link between the Commerce Department and American business predisposes bureaucrats to favor their chief clientele group. Since political appointees are likely to have close connections to business as well, there is little internal resistance to this inclination.

The USITC presents a different bureaucratic picture. As an independent regulatory agency, the USITC operates in a tradition that stresses political insulation and analytic neutrality. Congress influences the USITC by setting forth analytic criteria, and the president appoints the commissioners with the consent of the Senate. Thus, both Congress and the president have ways to influence the USITC, but both are somewhat formal and observable. It is, of course, unlikely that any agency in the U.S. government is completely apolitical, and it is certainly true that regulatory agencies in the past have become the pawns of the very segments of society they were supposed to regulate.[9] The USITC, however, has maintained a reputation for sticking close to analytic criteria in its determinations of trade-related injury to American producers.

Congressional Action in the 1980s

Certain sectors of the U.S. economy fared poorly during the 1980s. While the economy grew overall after 1982, industries such as steel, automobiles, and textiles suffered setbacks. Representatives of these industries asked the federal government for help by, among other things, persuading members of Congress to enact legislation intended to make economic life easier for them. Using trade policy to solve the economic woes of certain American industries was by no means the only choice available to Congress. Indeed, a large number of economists believe that trade policy alone cannot do much for American firms' competitiveness or the general problem of the U.S. trade deficit. Reducing the ballooning federal budget deficit, according to many economists, would have done more to alleviate these problems than manipulation of trade policy.[10] But Congress relied on trade policy nonetheless; largely because the policy area is easily manipulated, it allowed members of Congress to respond to the particular interests of their constituents, and it demonstrated legislators' commitments to defending the public's well-being.

While legislators may prefer free trade in principle, Congress's institutional design and electoral connection to the public prevent otherwise free-trade law makers from turning back protectionist forces. At the same time, legislators want to satisfy the demands of constituents and well-heeled business groups. For this reason, in the 1980s, Congress restricted executive discretion in the implementation of administrative relief, especially in regard to AD, CVD, and market-opening initiatives.[11] Congress intended this move to force the Reagan administration to pay more attention to the economy.[12] From the perspective of some legislators, President Reagan's approach to economic policy during his first term was one of benign neglect. After cutting taxes sharply in 1981, raising them in 1982, allowing the budget deficit to soar, and doing nothing to weaken the strong dollar, there was considerable doubt about the administration's grasp of economic policy.[13] At the same time, American producers were feeling the pinch of macroeconomic policy. The strong dollar made American exports less competitive in foreign markets, and the Federal Reserve Board's efforts to reduce inflation meant higher interest rates, which made borrowing by producers and consumer purchases more costly. It was not until 1985, when James Baker became Secretary of the Treasury, that the administration addressed the problem of the strong dollar. The budget deficit, however, remained essentially unmanaged.

A major part of the congressional response to the difficulties experienced by American producers was to put more teeth into U.S. trade policy. This was an interesting, and perhaps ill-conceived tactic in light of the limited usefulness of trade policy as a tool for addressing major economic shortcomings.[14] The consensus view of the dismal science aside, Congress chose to demonstrate its resolve through trade policy, largely because it was the most easily changed of American economic policies.

To sum up, the congressional response to the economic problems of the early 1980s was to use the policy most easily manipulated, that attended to particular interests, and that demonstrated legislators' willingness to defend their constituents' interests. While opening the door to protectionist policies, Congress put itself in position to enjoy the advantages of both the worlds of protectionism and free-trade advocacy.

The Agencies

The agencies involved in the implementation of administrative relief are a contrast in size, mission, history, and decision-making styles.

Each is responsible for a different part of administrative relief, which in itself is an interesting arrangement. Rather than placing all responsibility for implementing these provisions of U.S. trade law in one agency, Congress chose to spread them across three agencies. Doing so reflects the historical development of the trade policy machinery in the U.S. government. The USITC is the oldest of the three agencies. Its traditional responsibility of conducting economic analysis of the effects of trade distortions continues in its determination of whether foreign trade practices result in injury to American producers.

United States Trade Representative

The USTR is the lead agency on trade policy in the federal government. Located in the Executive Office of the President, the cabinet-level position is the principal vehicle through which the United States articulates major trade policies. Created in the 1960s as the Special Trade Representative, then upgraded to its current title during the Carter administration, the USTR negotiates trade agreements with foreign governments and is involved in several aspects of administrative relief.[15]

The Omnibus Trade and Competitiveness Act of 1988 gave the USTR the main responsibility for implementing Section 301 of the U.S. trade law. The 1988 act also charged the USTR with the responsibility of implementing so-called Super 301—an aggressive, unilateral mechanism for identifying and sanctioning countries that were engaged in general, not necessarily product-specific, unfair trade practices. Finally, the USTR implements Section 337 of the U.S. trade law, which deals with intellectual property infringements in the export of goods to the United States.

The most important characteristic of the USTR with respect to its role in administrative relief is its proximity to the president. The agency is small and filled with highly qualified trade experts.[16] Its mission is to advance American commerce abroad—making foreign markets more open to American products by reducing foreign trade barriers bilaterally and multilaterally, and as in the case of Section 301, unilaterally. The USTR serves at the pleasure of the president; to the extent there is discretion in carrying out its statutory tasks, the USTR is most responsive to the president's preferences.[17] This relationship distinguishes the

USTR from other agencies involved in administrative trade relief, as the law requires them to act under certain prescribed conditions.

In its original form as the Special Trade Representative, the USTR was intended to provide a central nexus for trade policy within the executive branch. The contemporary USTR does just that, though perhaps not quite in the way Congress had originally intended. As the principal voice of U.S. trade policy and as an access point for private interests to seek to influence trade policy, the USTR was the logical agency in which to place the responsibility for high-profile government actions, like those connected to implementation of Section 301 and Super 301 of the U.S. trade law.

Commerce Department

The Commerce Department's main responsibility in the implementation of administrative relief is to determine whether foreign governments and companies have engaged in two types of unfair trade practices: subsidization of producers and dumping of products in the American (or third country) market. Through activities collectively called import administration, the Commerce Department's International Trade Administration determines whether such practices are taking place to warrant initiation of countervailing duty proceedings in the case of subsidization, or antidumping measures if dumping is the problem.

Several of the Commerce Department's organizational characteristics bear on the agency's carrying out of its administrative relief responsibilities. The Commerce Department traditionally has been close to American business—a relationship Congress intended when it created the agency and one that has continued uninterrupted throughout the department's history. The agency was designed to promote American business at home and abroad, so it is hardly surprising that its decisions connected to administrative relief tend to favor American business.[18]

The department's decisions are not simply responses to pressure from the agency's traditional clientele, however; the fact that decisions are based on fairly clear technical criteria make the connection between them and American business interests somewhat more complicated than what immediately meets the analytic eye. The ITA relies on technical criteria for its determinations of subsidization and dumping. Applying these criteria, which favor American producers, should be a straightforward exercise involving data collections and analysis. What is more interesting, though, is that even when Congress changed the criteria to be less dramatically biased toward American business, ITA officials continued to apply the old, American business-friendly standards. This odd turn of events remains unexplained,[19] although the Commerce Department's organizational characteristics might offer some clues.

Congress moved the task of determining whether subsidization or dumping occurred in connection with CVD and AD investigations from the Treasury Department to Commerce for the deliberate purpose of finding an agency more sympathetic to American business interests.[20] The Treasury Department had this responsibility originally because of its jurisdiction over tax policy, and since trade sanctions frequently involve tariffs, which in effect are a form of taxation, the Treasury Department claimed jurisdiction. The Commerce Department's original mission and history of being friendly to business made the move sensible to members of Congress who wanted government to be more responsive to producer interests.

United States International Trade Commission

The USITC is the third agency involved in the implementation of administrative relief. This agency is, on the face of it, the least political of the three. Originally established as the United States Tariff Commission, then rechristened the USITC in 1974, the organization is a nonpartisan independent regulatory agency, sharing a legal status much like that of the Federal Communications Commission and the Federal Trade Commission. As an independent agency, the USITC is directly responsible to neither the Congress nor the president. Its six-member commission, consisting of no more than three members from one political party, who serve for fixed, staggered terms, is free to make decisions based on the criteria established by Congress.[21] Based on these arrangements, it seems that the commission, then, is relatively well insulated from domestic political pressure. One analysis, however, suggests that this political insulation may be as much a result of a self-selection process undertaken by American producers. If corporate leaders do not believe their companies have a good chance to prevail in USITC deliberations, they may choose not to pursue administrative relief at all.[22]

Regardless of the extent of the USITC's political insulation, the agency's activities are clearly defined and restrained. Its decisions, first, are based on clear technical criteria determined by Congress. Second, the agency determines only the extent to which imports have injured an American producer. The results of these investigations go either to the president, in escape clause, TAA, and Section 337 cases, or to the Commerce Department, in AD and CVD cases. The USITC itself does not decide whether to issue sanctions against foreign countries on the basis of its findings. Its analyses, however, are important nonetheless; without a positive finding of injury resulting from imports, no escape clause, TAA, AD, CVD, or Section 337 proceeding can go further.[23]

The Track Record of Administrative Relief

The use of administrative relief as a way to address trade problems is a rough indicator of the health of American producers. How much each type of remedy is used is partly a function of industries' expectations of the likelihood that they will receive trade relief. Use of the escape clause, which provides straightforward protection against imports regardless of whether they were traded fairly, has declined in recent years. Claims based on unfair trade practices, on the other hand, have generally increased.

Escape Clause

The escape clause is rooted in the peril point provision of nineteenth-century U.S. trade law. First appearing in a 1945 trade agreement between the United States and Mexico, it was intended to prevent imports from Mexico from causing injury to American manufacturers. An executive order in 1945 made the escape clause part of U.S. trade policy, and Congress included the provision in U.S. trade law in 1951.[24] Now codified as Section 201 of the U.S. trade law, the escape clause gives an industry the opportunity to petition the government for assistance in dealing with imports that have caused injury. The aid is temporary—five years with a possible extension of three years—and is intended to help American business adapt to competition that follows naturally from increased international trade. In recognition of the political reality of the need to protect domestic industries under some circumstances, Section 201, and its equivalent in other countries, is legal under Article XIX of the GATT.

Under Section 201, domestic producers must demonstrate only that they have been injured by imports to justify government action, usually in the form of tariffs. Unlike other administrative relief provisions in the trade law, the escape clause does not require a finding that a foreign government or firm has engaged in some sort of unfair trade practice, such as dumping, in the American market. Its justification was straightforward protectionism in the mercantilist tradition. The national government had the responsibility to protect the nation's industries from foreign competition; the escape clause was one way to do so.

The USITC evaluates Section 201 petitions to determine if the claimant—an American producer—has been injured by foreign competition. If the USITC finds that there is no injury, the process ends. If the USITC finds that injury has occurred, then the president may choose to act or not to act based on the USITC analysis. By statute, the president must take into consideration not only the USITC's findings, but broader national concerns in his decision concerning sanctions. This provision politicizes the process far more than other administrative relief provisions. Since the 1980s, the president has chosen in the vast majority of instances not to sanction the offending country, much to the consternation of the American petitioners. If the president does not act, then Congress can by joint resolution instruct the president to follow the USITC's recommendations. The president may veto the resolution, which can then be overridden by two-thirds majority vote in both houses of Congress.[25]

During the 1980s, escape clause petitions made up a small proportion of total claims for administrative relief (see table 6.1). Numbering only twenty for the entire decade, the number was highest in 1984 (seven),[26] perhaps because petitioners believed that President Reagan, eager to secure support for his reelection bid, would be more likely to authorize sanctions against their foreign competitors. In the two decades prior to the 1980s, escape clause petitions were filed at a rate that followed the tightening and relaxation of the requirements to qualify for aid. Following the enactment of the 1962 stricter requirements, the

Table 6.1
Section 201

Year	No. of Investigations	Year	No. of Investigations
1979	4	1989	0
1980	2	1990	1
1981	1	1991	0
1982	3	1992	1
1983	0	1993	0
1984	7	1994	0
1985	4	1995	1
1986	1	1996	3
1987	0	1997	1
1988	1		

Sources: I. M. Destler, *American Trade Politics*, 3rd ed. (Washington, D.C.: Institute for International Economics, 1995; New York: The Twentieth Century Fund, 1995), 166; United States International Trade Commission, *The Year in Trade 1997* (Washington, D.C.: U.S. International Trade Commission, 1998), 127; *The Year in Trade 1996*, 129; *The Year in Trade 1995*, 71; *The Year in Trade 1994*, 119; *The Year in Trade 1993*, 123; *The Year in Trade 1992*, 92.

average number of escape clause petitions per year from 1963 to 1974 dropped to three from eleven per year from 1958 to 1963. The number rose to an average of ten per year from 1975 to 1978, resulting from the looser restrictions Congress adopted in 1974. Throughout this period, the inclination of the president to accept a positive finding by the USITC did not change much, holding around a quarter of the time or less.[27] Although the law gives Congress a means to force the president to act on positive USITC findings, on only two occasions has it chosen to ask the USITC to investigate claims, both of which resulted in presidential action.[28]

Use of the escape clause declined precipitously in the 1980s, with the exception of 1984, for two reasons. First, the American economy was doing better by the mid 1980s. Although the federal budget deficit continued to climb, the dollar declined abroad, making American exports cheaper and imports into the United States more expensive. Second, the president has never been terribly cooperative in adopting USITC recommendations for relief. Considering other factors that concern the nation as a whole, the chief executive has more often than not chosen to let the suffering industry deal with its own problems. Because of this, the escape clause looks increasingly unattractive, especially in light of the existence of much more useful alternatives available under the unfair trade practices provisions of the U.S. trade law. The record in the 1990s bears this conclusion out, as the USITC conducted only six escape clause investigations from 1992 to 1997.[29]

Trade Adjustment Assistance

Created by Congress in the Trade Expansion Act of 1962, the initial purpose of trade adjustment assistance was to retrain and provide financial benefits to workers and companies damaged by foreign competition. The original idea apparently appeared under the auspices of the Council on Foreign Relations during World War II.[30] It was subsequently presented in a policy paper by David J. McDonald, then president of the United Steel Workers, to the Randall Commission during the Eisenhower administration.[31] Staying alive during the Eisenhower administration, the idea found a friendly ear in the Kennedy administration.[32]

The USITC initially had jurisdiction over TAA. Petitions are filed with it, and it determines the legitimacy of the claim. An affirmative finding goes to the president, who has the final decision whether to implement it. The criteria for TAA are essentially the same as those for the escape clause, and the two programs go hand-in-hand. But the logic underlying one provision was antithetical to the logic of the other. Trade adjustment assistance was intended to promote free trade, providing companies and workers a means to adjust to changes in the American economy resulting from global changes. Escape clause relief had protectionist overtones, quite the opposite in purpose from TAA. But since the eligibility criteria for both were the same, the USITC could not be liberal without TAA doing the same for the escape clause.[33]

Congress expanded TAA in the Trade Act of 1974 by relaxing eligibility requirements, extending assistance to communities as well as to corporations and workers, and making the Labor Department responsible for cases involving workers and the Commerce Department responsible for industry petitions.[34] This change, along with hard economic times for American auto workers in the late 1970s, caused the use of TAA to increase. The cost of the program in 1980s was $1.6 billion, six times greater than the previous high.[35]

Unlike his predecessor, President Reagan was not sympathetic to the use of TAA. A General Accounting Office analysis indicating that the program was in fact not helping workers move into new jobs gave the administration the justification it needed to cut the program, one of the many cuts included in the Omnibus Budget Reconciliation Act of 1981. Thus, funding for TAA dropped in 1981 and has remained low since.[36] Funds for displaced workers were limited to the rate of regular unemployment and could only be drawn after unemployment had run out. Moreover, recipients had to be in the process of retraining in order to qualify for assistance.[37]

In spite of these changes, the number of TAA petitions went up through 1989. Judith Goldstein reports that from 1963 to 1974, the average number of corporate petitions per year was five, and the annual average of worker petitions was 19. Reflecting changes in the 1974 Trade Act, these numbers jumped to eight and 882 respectively from 1975 to 1978. From 1979 to 1981, the numbers continued upward; corporations filed 623 petitions, and workers filed 2,071 petitions. So far, these trends are consistent with the changes in the law and the extent to which officials were receptive to the use of TAA. However, even after the 1981 budget cuts, the use of TAA continued at a high level. From 1982 to 1989, corporations filed an average of 251 each year, and workers made an annual average of 1,311 claims. What is more striking about the record of TAA use is the acceptance rate. By the 1980s, the acceptance rate for industry petitions was 0.97, and for workers, 0.47, both up from any previous time period, including the one immediate following the Trade Act of 1974.[38]

The discrepancy between funding for TAA and its relatively successful use can be explained by the amount of assistance that was actually handed out under the program. For example, from 1982 to 1989, assistance to corporations amounted to approximately $160 million (in grants and loans) per year,[39] hardly enough to break the federal budget. In addition, although Reagan was unsympathetic to the program, the administration found it a useful way to deflect protectionist claims in the United States; it could respond positively to TAA cases while maintaining a generally liberal stance on trade policy.[40]

The statute remained on the books and was reinvigorated in 1994 in response to the possibility that the North American Free Trade Agreement (NAFTA) would displace workers. Funding levels remained low—$200 million annually. From 1992 to 1994, fewer than half the number of petitions were certified.[41] Relatively small numbers of workers qualified for the program during this time. For example, in 1994, only 65,000 workers received assistance.[42] The picture changed in the next two years, however, as both the number of petitions and the certification rate increased. In 1996, for instance, 1,588 petitions were filed, with over 1,100 receiving certification. The numbers declined in 1997, however, as 1,354 petitions were filed and 857 were certified.[43] (Also see table 6.2.)

Countervailing Duty

U.S. trade law permits the executive to respond to foreign government subsidies of companies that export to the United States. The sanction involves placing duties on imports from subsidized firms to compensate for, or countervail, the effect of the subsidy. The idea of a countervailing duty first appeared in U.S. trade law in 1909, when the United States was allowed to implement the higher of a two-tariff schedule on imports from countries engaged in a variety of unfair trade practices, including the use of subsidies. The 1913 Trade Act gave the Secretary of the Treasury the authority to issue countervailing duties on subsidized imports as well. The current form of CVD was originally included in the 1930 trade legislation.[44]

While the underlying logic of the escape clause is that government has a legitimate responsibility to protect American producers while they adjust to new foreign competition, the premise of CVD is that

Table 6.2
TAA Cases

Year	No. of Petitions or Investigation	Certification	Partial Certification
1997	1,354	857	1
1996	1,588	1,086	3
1995	1,635	1,182	2
1994	1,245	602	8
1993	1,336	581	9
1992	1,442	700	3

Sources: United States International Trade Commission, *The Year in Trade 1997* (Washington, D.C.: U.S. International Trade Commission, 1998), 128; *The Year in Trade 1996,* 130; *The Year in Trade 1995,* 72; *The Year in Trade 1994,* 120; *The Year in Trade 1993,* 124; *The Year in Trade 1992,* 90.

foreign firms and countries are not playing fair and that government action is necessary to compensate for the consequences of that. Thus, in large part, "leveling the playing" field is the impulse that has driven the creation and use of CVD.

The Commerce Department's ITA determines whether a subsidy exists, and the USITC assesses whether American producers are injured as a result of it. The process is automatic; if both the USITC and the ITA find in the affirmative, then the American producer is entitled to relief by means of a CVD. The president is not part of the process, and therefore cannot impose other political considerations on the decision to level trade sanctions against the offending country, as he can in the use of the escape clause.

Administration of countervailing duties encounters the same general difficulties that affect antidumping actions. Defining a subsidy is problematic, and measuring it presents serious methodological hazards. Both issues are the subject of considerable debate, as critics charge that U.S. government officials are too quick to find a subsidy in the practices of foreign governments.

The use of CVDs increased markedly during the 1980s (see table 6.3), during which the Commerce Department initiated 345 CVD cases, 140 of which occurred in 1982.[45] Petitioners enjoyed a fair

Table 6.3
CVD and AD Cases

Year	No. of AD Cases	No. of CVD Cases	Year	No. of AD Cases	No. of CVD Cases
1979	26	40	1989	23	7
1980	21	14	1990	43	7
1981	15	22	1991	51	8
1982	65	140	1992	99	43
1983	46	22	1993	42	5
1984	74	51	1994	43	7
1985	66	43	1995	14	2
1986	71	27	1996	20	1
1987	15	8	1997	15	6
1988	42	11			

Sources: I. M. Destler, *American Trade Politics,* 3rd ed. (Washington, D.C.: Institute for International Economics, 1995; New York: The Twentieth Century Fund, 1995), 166; U.S. International Trade Commission, *The Year in Trade 1997,* (Washington, D.C.: U.S. International Trade Commission, 1998), 139 (1995–97).

measure of success; of the 258 petitions carried through the full process, 135 were successful, resulting either in the imposition of duties or termination of the subsidy. Destler explains the 1982 spike in the number of petitions as a result of the American steel industry's efforts to pressure President Reagan into negotiating import restraint agreements with the governments of major foreign competitors, which in fact it did.[46]

The number of CVD cases filed between 1974 and 1979 was considerably smaller than after the changes in the trade law legislated in 1979. The 1974 law made proving government subsidies somewhat easier, but left the responsibility for administering CVD in the Treasury Department, its historical home. As a result of the 1974 law, CVD petitions increased from one in 1973 and five in 1974, to 38 in 1975.[47] The success rate for CVD petitions, however, was low; of 35 affirmative findings by the Treasury Department between 1976 and 1978, 19 did not result in imposition of duties. The reason for this is that the 1974 law included a provision that permitted the Secretary of the Treasury to waive sanctions if the offending country was taking measures to reduce the subsidy's effect and if imposing a duty would damage the successful progress of ongoing multilateral trade negotiations.[48] Thus, while CVD petitions were not subject to the president's political discretion, they were hardly cut and dried during the 1970s, as the Secretary of the Treasury retained authority to waive sanctions based on extenuating circumstances.

Congress sought to address the problem associated with housing CVD responsibility in the Treasury Department in the 1979 law and, for the first time, made clear the criteria and procedures for determining whether to impose a CVD. Growing out of the Tokyo Round in 1974, Congress authorized the executive to negotiate an international agreement to limit the use of subsidies by foreign governments. To obtain such an agreement, the United States agreed to establish a material injury criterion in its determination of whether to issue a CVD. Congress incorporated this provision into the 1979 trade law.[49] A condition of enacting the trade bill was reorganization of the executive branch on trade policy, giving CVD authority to the Commerce Department, an agency correctly perceived to be more business-friendly than the Treasury Department.[50] With these measures, Congress codified the CVD procedure, making it more a technical decision based on clear analytic criteria. At the same time, Congress placed

CVD authority in an agency that was more likely than not to find in favor of petitioning American producers. Doing so, however, did not guarantee that petitioners would always find a receptive agency in the ITA. In making CVD determinations, one analysis indicates that the agency was influenced by national interest concerns more than interest-group pressure.[51]

The number of CVD petitions declined in the late 1980s and into the early 1990s, with the exception of a dramatic one-year total in 1992.[52] Excluding 1992, an average of five petitions was filed each year from 1990 to 1997, with a high of eight in 1991 and a low of one in 1996.[53] The reasons for this decline probably have to do with the improving state of the American economy, higher competitiveness of American industry, and declining subsidization abroad. Throughout this period, however, CVD was a much more popular means of achieving administrative trade relief than the escape clause. Addressing alleged unfair trade practices and cloaked in quasi-judicial administrative procedure, petitioning for a CVD became more politically acceptable. After all, the petitioner was not asking for protection from a superior foreign competitor. Rather, that competitor enjoyed an unfair advantage over the domestic producer owing to government support. Either neutralizing the government support with a duty or eliminating it altogether seemed like reasonable sanctions against this unfair play and would do no more than to put the American producer on an equal footing with its foreign competitor.

Antidumping

Dumping generally refers to the practice of foreign producers' selling products in the American market at prices less than fair market value, which is defined and measured in a variety of ways. U.S. trade law has contained antidumping provisions since the 1920s, but their use in the last two decades has increased as they have become a favorite option for industries seeking relief from foreign competition. The concept originated in the 1914 Federal Trade Commission Act, which declared unfair forms of competition unlawful. The 1921 antidumping legislation was based on its domestic counterpart, intended to address such unfair practices on the international level.[54]

Government action to stop alleged dumping in the American market raises the issue of how producer and consumer interests conflict.

However it is defined and measured, dumping means consumers can buy products at lower prices from foreign producers than from domestic producers. From the consumer's perspective, this is a good deal, as long as there is a reliable supply of the desired products. In trade matters, government action is almost always intended to help producers, however. Thus, the stage is set for a political conflict between consumers and producers of a product that is allegedly being dumped. This is precisely what occurred in the semiconductor case;[55] implementation of antidumping provisions cannot be properly understood without bearing in mind this fundamental political dynamic.

Any American firm may file an AD petition. The USITC determines whether the import in question has injured American industry, and the Commerce Department's ITA assesses whether the foreign firm in question has engaged in dumping its products in the American market. If both agencies find in the positive, then the United States applies a duty on the product sold at prices above the fair price in proportion to the dumping margin.[56]

The number of AD cases climbed after passage of the 1974 Trade Act. The average number of AD petitions per year jumped to 42 during the period from 1975 to 1978, up from 24 (1963–74) and 28 (1958–62). From 1979 to 1991, the average number of annual AD petitions was 40.[57] The use of AD increased in the 1980s. From 1980 to 1993, petitioners filed 673 AD claims, ranging from a low of 15 in 1981 to a high of 99 in 1992. Of the 539 cases that were completed, the ITA concluded that dumping had occurred in 278 (52 percent). However, the USITC found that the American industry in question had not been injured by the dumped import in 234 cases (43 percent).[58] The acceptance rate of AD cases increased more dramatically than the number of petitions, however. It climbed from 4 percent from 1958 to 1962, to 38 percent for 1979 to 1991.[59] The increase reflects the extent to which the AD process responded to American producers. It may also reflect the agency's vulnerability to political pressure from American producers and their interest groups.[60] During roughly the same period, AD cases outnumbered CVD cases 742 to 455. In the 17 years from 1979 to 1997, only two saw more CVD investigations initiated than AD investigations. Escape clause cases trailed far behind petitions based on unfair trade practices, totaling only 25 for the same time period.[61]

Measuring Dumping

The analytic problems associated with identifying dumping abound, and according to most observers, the way Congress and the ITA have solved them biases the process in favor of American producers. The first problem involves data collection. In the AD procedure, the ITA requires a foreign firm to provide a great deal of information to be used in the dumping determination. This places a costly burden on these firms—meeting deadlines, using the acceptable format, and the like. This is one reason why foreign firms do not provide such information. When this occurs, the ITA is authorized to use the best information available (BIA), which usually means information about the foreign producer supplied by the American petitioner. In addition, the agency uses average prices rather than marginal costs. Robert E. Baldwin and Michael O. Moore demonstrate that this practice results in dumping margins for firms filing information to be much lower (27.9 percent) than those for firms whose margins are determined using BIA (66.7 percent).[62]

The information itself, then, can create a bias in the ITA's calculations. The analytic techniques used by agency officials tip the scales still further in favor of American producers. The ITA must compare the foreign market value of a product with its domestic market value. To do this, it uses an average of foreign sales with each sale in the American market. Each sale in the United States above or equal to average foreign market value is counted as zero. Each sale below average foreign market value is counted as the percentage the U.S. price is below average foreign market value. As Destler summarizes the arrangement, "the law encourages the (ITA within the) Commerce Department to exclude from the calculation of the 'foreign market value' of a product (the foreign producer's home market average price) any sales that are below his average costs and to ignore in the calculation of the average price at which he sells in the United States any sales that are above the foreign market value."[63] Baldwin and Moore conclude that "this obviously yields the absurd result that, as long as prices vary over the sample period, a positive dumping margin can be found even if prices in the two countries are *identical* on every day."[64]

The bias in ITA calculations extends to investigations where only a sample of firms is included in the dumping calculations. In this instance, analysts apply an average derived from the sample to firms not included in it. This in itself is a reasonable practice. However, in doing this, the Commerce Department excludes negative and *de minimus* rates and includes positive rates determined using BIA, in effect extending the bias inherent in BIA to these firms.[65]

When the ITA cannot obtain information from foreign firms, it conducts its analysis using "constructed value" of the product sold in the firm's home market. This number is based on an estimate of the average cost of production plus eight percent to cover overhead profit. If the selling price in the United States is below this figure, then the ITA concludes that the firm is guilty of dumping. The practice of using a constructed value based on this calculation makes it extremely difficult *not* to be found guilty of dumping in the American market. An especially controversial aspect of the analysis is the required addition of an eight percentage-point margin for overhead and profit, a rate higher than what might be expected of domestic American firms.[66] It makes it impossible for foreign firms to sell below an eight percent margin, one that would be considered excessive in many cases.[67] Indeed, to make a profit, a firm need only sell above marginal costs, not necessarily eight percent above them. So, the U.S. standard runs counter to common business practice.[68] Allowing so much for overhead is also questionable; assuming that a firm will always incur this cost eliminates the possibility of technological and other efficiency improvements.

In the face of all this criticism, a case can be made that U.S. antidumping laws serve a valuable function and should not be discontinued. First, dumping is usually associated with protection. Firms can pursue a long-term strategy of dumping in foreign markets only if they enjoy favorable government policies at home. Government subsidies, a protected home market, and government sanctioning of cartels all permit a firm to exact profits from sales at home that it might lose by selling cheap abroad. Challenging dumping is one way to take on a larger array of unfair trade practices that otherwise might escape U.S. government action. Second, as nonmarket economies or economies in transition increase exports to the United States, antidumping may be the best way to prevent American producers from being injured by dumping. Third, U.S. firms are subject to antidumping claims abroad. To the extent that the adjudication of these cases falls short of an open and fair process, cutting back U.S. antidumping law will do little toward encouraging foreign governments to make their procedures more fair. Finally, and more broadly, the fact that antidumping laws may raise consumer prices may be a reasonable price to pay for maintaining the health of American producers.

Protecting Intellectual Property

The prospect that a foreign government will allow domestic producers to copy American products indiscriminately and export them to the American market is a major concern to American companies and policy makers. Software companies, CD producers, and pharmaceutical companies, to name a few, have sought assistance in these foreign markets. The administrative remedy for this problem is encoded in Section 337 of the U.S. trade law. This provision permits American producers to petition the U.S. government to sanction foreign countries in which intellectual property is not adequately protected and that export products based on American technology to the American market. It is patterned after domestic patent and copyright law and thus applies U.S. standards abroad. The USITC decides on the appropriate remedy,[69] and the president may waive the sanction for broader policy reasons.[70] If the USITC finds in the affirmative—that is, that unfair practices have been used in the importation and sale of products in the United States—then the president may issue an exclusion order, which keeps these products out of the American market.[71]

Section 337 is essentially an extension of U.S. law that is rooted in the Constitution. Compared with other forms of administrative relief, it is the most legalistic, using adjudicatory proceedings under the Administrative Procedures Act.[72] Its original injury standards were comparatively mild, even before they were relaxed by the 1988 law, and consequently, American producers have found it an agreeable way to address trade problems through administrative relief.[73]

From 1980 to 1990, there were 245 Section 337 cases, with the number peaking in 1983 at 43.[74] The pace remained the same in the 1990s (see table 6.4); the USITC conducted 80 investigations from 1992 to 1997.[75] Prior to the 1980s, the number of Section 337 petitions was considerably lower, averaging one per year from 1958 to 1962, four per year from 1963 to 1974, and twelve per year from 1975 to 1978. Given the legalistic nature of these cases, many are settled before the USITC reaches a finding. The president has waived few of the USITC's affirmative findings owing first to the fact that American

Table 6.4
Section 337 Investigations

Year	No. of Investigations	Year	No. of Investigations
1991	13	1995	12
1992	12	1996	12
1993	15	1997	15
1994	14		

Sources: United States International Trade Commission, *The Year in Trade 1997* (Washington, D.C.: U.S. International Trade Commission, 1998), 140; *The Year in Trade 1996,* 141 (1995–97); *The Year in Trade 1994,* 125 (1994–93); *The Year in Trade 1992,* 93 (1991–92).

technology has been stolen abroad, violating established practices and norms of business behavior, and second, to the USITC's technical and presumably therefore convincing analysis.[76]

Observations

As many critics have pointed out, the Commerce Department's ITA is predisposed to favor American business. With a mission that encourages it to help American companies, it is hardly surprising that the ITA's unfair trade practices procedures fit comfortably with the organization's central purpose. Indeed, Congress recognized this point when it engineered the transfer of CVD investigative authority from the Treasury Department to the Commerce Department. But the department's business-friendly attitude does not entirely explain its user-friendly AD and CVD procedures. It is important to keep in mind that Congress has specified the parameters for these procedures. Congress tightened and relaxed access to AD- and CVD-based relief in the trade bills passed in 1962, 1974, and 1979. International Trade Administration officials have discretion to operate within those parameters, but they do not set the general tone or direction of administrative relief policy. What remains unexplained is why these bureaucrats have not used Congress's instructions on revising rules to make administrative relief based on unfair trade practices somewhat more difficult to obtain. In this instance, the agency has acted, not necessarily in defiance of congressional will, but at least more in compliance with the organization's traditional role as the part of the executive branch most accommodating to American business interests.[77]

The president does not play a direct role in either AD or CVD investigations, keeping political decisions based on electoral politics and broader national issues—broader, at least, than the interests of certain American producers—out of these decisions. This, of course, is good news for American business. One of the main reasons the escape clause dropped into near disuse is that the president has proven unwilling to issue sanctions based on positive findings by the USITC. The automatic nature of the unfair trade practice petitions eliminates this problem. This same automatic quality gives AD and CVD proceedings a judicial, apolitical quality. Owing to the global march toward freer trade through the GATT and now the World Trade Organization (WTO), and in light of the impossibility of resorting to old-fashioned protectionism, obtaining trade relief under the umbrella of impartial, internationally acceptable administrative rules is less onerous.

The implementation of Section 337 is a more straightforward process than AD or CVD procedures. The president chooses whether to issue sanctions based on the law and tends to follow USITC recommendations. The commission's technical expertise, the legalistic nature of the disputes, and the fact that most disagreements are settled before a ruling limit the importance of bureaucratic politics.

The importance of the Commerce Department's role in AD and CVD determinations illustrates one side of bureaucratic politics. A politically-charged executive branch agency, undeterred by presidential leadership and encouraged by congressional oversight, behaves in predictable ways. The USITC provides another, contrasting aspect of bureaucratic politics. An independent agency, such as the USITC, is not immune to political influence. Its commissioners are appointed by the president and confirmed by the Senate; presumably the president chooses people who view trade policy much as he does. Limiting to three the number of commissioners from a single party avoids partisan imbalance to some extent, but it does not extract ideology from USITC decisions.

The most important characteristic of the USITC is the analysis performed by its staff. Commission staff consist of professional economists and lawyers with expertise in trade policy. Their analyses adhere to statutory guidelines on what counts as injury to an American producer. Congress has relaxed and tightened these rules from time to time, and the USITC's analyses conform to the changes. As the closest thing to a neutral arbiter in the implementation of administrative trade remedies, the USITC holds the line on the doling out of trade relief. The Commerce Department may be fairly likely to find that a foreign firm is engaged in unfair trade practices, but without an USITC determination that the American producer has been injured by the unfairly traded import, no trade sanction goes into effect. This does not mean, of course, that administrative relief based on unfair trade practices is unattractive to American producers. But it might mean that because of the USITC's unwillingness to approve every petition, the floodgates of administrative relief have not opened.

Opening Foreign Markets

American producers need foreign markets to thrive; this has been so for many years, of course, but it is especially important now as American firms look abroad to sell their products. In spite of the considerable progress since World War II toward eliminating tariffs—at least among rich countries—trade barriers in the form of nontariff barriers (NTBs) exist to varying degrees in every country. While such barriers benefit American producers in their home market, they are an obstacle in foreign markets.

Recognition of the significance of NTBs to the health of American exporters led to the creation and subsequent strengthening of administrative measures designed to pry open foreign markets to American products. The principal lever for doing so is the U.S. government's threat to close some part of the American market to the offending country's exporters in retaliation for the existence of the NTB in its market.

Such is the logic of Section 301 of the U.S. trade law originally enacted by Congress in the 1974 Trade Act. The law is vague, requiring the president to take action against "unjustifiable" or "unreasonable" foreign actions that discriminate against U.S. commerce and to take actions to enforce any trade agreements. As Goldstein summarizes, "(f)or the most part, the statute has been aimed at the practices of foreign governments and corporations that hurt American exports, although the law covers any foreign violation of GATT and thus could be expanded to include imports."[78]

Under Section 301, as revised in 1979 and 1984, the president can change any trade concession the United States maintains in response to a violation, and the president can raise tariffs and nontariff barriers on the products in question.[79] Its underlying logic of reciprocity is not altogether new to American trade policy history. The United States frequently offered to open the American market to foreign products if a foreign country did the same for American products. In this way, reciprocity was a mechanism for directly increasing trade. The Section 301 version of reciprocity, however, works in the opposite direction. Unless a country complies with U.S. government wishes concerning its NTBs, then the U.S. government closes part of the American market. It is reciprocity, certainly, but the direct outcome is to close, not open markets. Critics eagerly point this out, as they also note that Section 301 is of questionable legality within the GATT framework. The main problem, according to the critics, is that a Section 301 sanction amounts to a unilateral action, which runs counter to the spirit, and probably the letter, of GATT regulations.[80] Proponents counter that, although this may be the immediate outcome, the long-term consequence is that the foreign government takes action to open its market to American products, thus advancing the cause of free trade. The outcome, though perhaps not the means, is certainly consistent with the ongoing pattern of freer trade launched after the Second World War.[81] Section 301 can also be defended on the grounds that it is intended to encourage multilateral negotiations, since in cases involving violations of WTO regulations, the president is required to seek a resolution through the multilateral trade dispute settlement process. The threat of applying sanctions under Section 301 can also lead to resolution of a dispute. Finally, some areas lie outside the purview of the WTO, and the United States may be left with no multilateral option.[82]

The Omnibus Trade and Competitiveness Act of 1988 and the Uruguay Round Agreement Act of 1994 added a provision to Section 301 intended to address abuse of intellectual property rights in foreign countries. Special 301, as it came to be known, requires the USTR to "identify those countries that deny adequate and effective protection for intellectual property rights or deny fair and equitable market access for persons that rely on intellectual property protection."[83] The goal of Special 301 is to prevent intellectual property rights violations from undermining American exports. In accordance with the statute, on 30 April 1996, the USTR identified 35 countries that violate intellectual property rights, placing eight of them on a priority watch list and 24 on a watch list. The U.S. will focus increased bilateral attention on countries making it onto the priority list.[84] (See also table 6.5.)

Section 301 has been joined by a beefed-up companion commonly referred to as Super 301, which Congress added to the U.S. trade law in the Omnibus Trade and Competitiveness Act of 1988. This relatively short-lived provision required the USTR to identify priority countries that engaged in unfair trade practices that impeded American exports based on the "number and pervasiveness" of such activities.[85]

As in the case of Section 301, Super 301 attracted critics. The main objections had to do with the consistency between Super 301 and the GATT. First, the timetable prescribed by the U.S. law was shorter than that prescribed by the GATT, meaning that if a dispute could be resolved under the GATT, there would likely be insufficient time to do so. Second, the United States would be the sole arbiter of what counted as an unfair trade practice, creating the possibility that the U.S. would identify practices that were not illegal according to the GATT. Third, the Congress enacted Super 301 while the Uruguay Round of GATT negotiations was under way, thereby undermining the effectiveness of those meetings. Fourth, the USTR had overwhelming authority over the implementation of Super 301; it determined what was an unfair trade practice, accused countries of engaging in them, and then "try"

Table 6.5
Section 301 Cases

Year	No. of Cases Initiated	Year	No. of Cases Initiated
1980	2	1989	4
1981	-	1990	3
1982	1	1991	4
1983	1	1992	1
1984	1	1993	1
1985	9	1994	4
1986	9	1995	5
1987	3	1996	9
1988	15	1997	6

Sources: (1980–90) Anne O. Krueger, *American Trade Policy: A Tragedy in the Making,* 40; United States International Trade Commission, *The Year in Trade 1997* (Washington, D.C.: U.S. International Trade Commission 1998), 130; *The Year in Trade 1996,* 131; *The Year in Trade 1995,* 73; *The Year in Trade 1994,* 121; *The Year in Trade 1993,* 124; *The Year in Trade 1992,* 91; *The Year in Trade 1991,* 151.

the country according to USTR rules. There was no bureaucratic check on the USTR's authority, which is disagreeable enough in itself. Add to this the susceptibility of the agency to protectionist pressures in the United States, and the probability of increased American protectionism rose.[86] Proponents of Super 301 assert that the law is not as aggressive or unilateral as its detractors claim. It is merely a logical extension of Section 301, and in any case, has not been used to an overwhelming extent.[87] All of this became less controversial as Super 301 expired, by statute, after two years, and Congress has not chosen to reenact it.

The number of Section 301 cases does not match the number of AD, CVD, and Section 337 cases. From 1980 to 1990, 48 cases were processed.[88] The number of petitions filed averaged four per year from 1975 to 1979, and five per year from 1980 to 1991.[89] From 1980 to 1990, the majority of cases that produced a determinable effect resulted in trade liberalization (19), and the remainder (5) brought on retaliation.[90] Between 1974, when Section 301 was created, and 1996, the USTR has initiated 116 Section 301 investigations, 26 of those coming during the first five years of the Clinton administration.[91] Whether the overall effect of Section 301 cases is trade liberalization or not remains in dispute. Michael P. Ryan's analysis, however, suggests that the scorecard reads in favor of liberalization, much in the spirit of the GATT.[92]

United States Trade Representative Carla Hills implemented Super 301 for the first time in 1989. Finding it politically unpalatable to name European agriculture practices as being in violation of U.S. trade law and wishing to avoid naming South Korea and Taiwan, two major trading partners of the United States, Hills identified Japan, Brazil, and India as the priority nations in violation of Super 301. Hills limited the indictment to six specific industries, areas with which the United States had been concerned prior to the implementation of Super 301. With respect to Japan, Hills went beyond Super 301, suggesting the initiation of a bilateral series of negotiations—the Structural Impediments Initiative—to address trade problems between Japan and the United States.[93]

Super 301 was not renewed in 1990, but in March 1994, President Bill Clinton issued an executive order—called a Super 301 executive order—that aimed to sharpen the implementation of Section 301 by identifying specific practices, not countries, the United States found objectionable. Clinton took this action, which met with congressional approval, in relation to ongoing talks with Japan. In the end, the USTR issued no executive Super 301 findings, as the intent of this move had been incorporated in the pending GATT implementing legislation.[94]

Conclusion

Administrative relief is essentially a process of implementation of U.S. trade law. As such, it involves factors normally associated with bureaucratic politics. One of the most fundamental questions that arises in implementation is the amount of discretion bureaucrats have in their decisions; that is, to what extent are bureaucrats constrained by rules embedded in the statute and by political control, mostly from the White House? On balance, the answer to this question is that bureaucrats' discretion was limited—the extent of the limits depends on the agency. USITC officials operate within the constraints of clear statutory guidelines. Commerce Department officials conduct their business in a similar fashion, although there appears to be at least one instance where bureaucrats continue to use an old set of decision rules rather than new ones issues by Congress. Because they are in the Executive Office of the President and are therefore responsive to the chief executive's policy goals, USTR officials take a leading role in U.S. trade policy. In this position, following prescribed decision rules has little relevance, as the USTR is constantly engaged in attending to the nation's trade policy and advancing the president's particular goals.

The organizational characteristics of the agencies involved in administrative relief affect their performance as well. The USITC is essentially a regulatory agency, patterned after other agencies created in the late nineteenth and early twentieth centuries. It enjoys a measure of independence from both Congress and the White House. There are limits to the independence, however. Congress has changed trade policy statutes to alter the USITC's findings on some types of trade relief petitions. At the other end of Pennsylvania Avenue, the president influences the USITC by nominating the commissioners. Although no more than three commissioners may come from a single party, the appointment power gives the president some inroad into USITC decisions.

The Commerce Department's behavior is certainly influenced by its basic mission, which is to promote American business at home and abroad. This explains the business-friendly atmosphere in Commerce Department dealings with industry on administrative relief, and it also explains why Congress shifted analytic responsibilities from the Treasury Department to Commerce.

As the lead agency for U.S. trade policy, the USTR is more concerned with policy change than with routine implementation and administrative procedure. A small, lean agency with a highly defined mission of seeing to the nation's trade interests, the USTR has become highly responsive to the president's trade policy goals.

The three agencies provide a contrast in organizational decision making, mission, and norms of behavior. In spite of these differences, however, they are all involved in reinvigorating the trade policy process by providing feedback on the implementation of major U.S. trade policies. The policy process involves constant interaction among the three main steps—agenda setting, program adoption, and implementation. Administrative relief illustrates this point. As agencies process relief petitions at various times, all of the political actors involved "learned"; that is, depending on how satisfied they were with the outcome of the process, they sought to change it. Thus, Congress repeatedly altered analytic criteria for implementation of all forms of administrative relief in order to fine tune policy outcomes.

Institutional Response

The development and use of administrative relief captures the response of American political institutions to change, both domestic and foreign. Economic change—the increase in the volume of international trade, the associated developments within the American economy, and the resultant decline in low-skill jobs—caused political changes in the United States. As new interests developed, they found political voice through the usual means: interest groups and elections. The political pressure was substantial, beginning in the 1970s and certainly in the 1980s and 1990s. Congress, the political institution most receptive to particular interests, responded by redesigning an administrative system to give relief to industries damaged, for whatever reason, by foreign competition. Administrative relief, moreover, had a certain appeal. It has a quasi-judicial quality, giving it the appearance, at least, of being outside politics. The genius of the strategy was that by using administrative relief to deal with pressure from powerful interest groups and constituents, members of Congress were able to deflect the task of responding to protectionist pressures to the executive branch, while maintaining commitment to trade liberalization.

This is more than blame avoidance. Members of Congress as individual politicians benefited from taking the pressure off of themselves to enact protectionist measures. But looking at the event in terms of the reaction of the entire political system rather than individuals in it, one gets a different view. From this perspective, the American political system found a way to continue free-trade policies while defusing protectionist demands. A porous democratic system like that of the United States cannot reject strong, intense, especially economic interests. The flexibility of its design, however, allows it to placate those interests while holding true to a plan that, according to most, would benefit more people in the long run.

To sum up, economic change of the sort faced by the United States since the 1970s is inevitable; even if the globalization of the economy is overstated, economic change within the United States has serious political consequences. The connection between politics and economics requires the government to respond to the new competitive pressures on American producers. From the self-interested politician's perspective, the way to deal with this was to pass along the tough decisions to the executive branch under the cloak of policy implementation and administration, allowing the politician to take credit for protection, avoid blame for the problems it creates for economic growth, and continue to support trade liberalization. From a systemic perspective, the solution was no less ingenious. It allowed the political system to placate powerful interests, while at the same time adhering to a steady policy of movement toward free trade.

Endnotes

1. See Pietro S. Nivola, *Regulating Unfair Trade* (Washington, D.C.: Brookings Institution, 1993).
2. For a statement of managed trade as a policy approach, see Laura D'Andrea Tyson, "Managed Trade: Making the Best of the Second Best," in Robert Z. Lawrence and Charles L. Schultze, eds., *An American Trade Strategy: Options for the 1990s* (Washington, D.C.: Brookings Institution, 1990), 142–94. For a theoretical analysis of managed trade, see Paul R Krugman, "Is Free Trade Passé?" *Journal of Economic Perspectives* 1 (Fall 1987): 131–44; and

Robert Kuttner, "Managed Trade and Economic Sovereignty," in Robert A. Blecker, ed., *U.S. Trade Policy and Global Growth: New Directions in the International Economy* (Armonk, N.Y.: M. E. Sharpe, 1996), 3–36.

3. Cornelius M. Kerwin, *Rulemaking: How Government Agencies Write Law and Make Policy* (Washington, D.C.: CQ Press, 1994).

4. I. M. Destler, *American Trade Politics,* 3rd ed. (Washington, D.C.: Institute for International Economics, 1995), chap. 4.

5. Bureaucratic rigidity is at the root of much of the criticism of large organizations, both public and private. For a spirited defense of bureaucracy, see Charles T. Goodsell, *The Case for Bureaucracy: A Public Administration Polemic* (Chatham, N.J.: Chatham House, 1994). For a straightforward solution to such problems, see J. D. Thompson, *Organizations in Action* (New York: McGraw-Hill, 1967).

6. Kerwin, *Rulemaking,* chap. 6; and Morris S. Ogul, *Congress Oversees the Bureaucracy: Studies in Legislative Supervision* (Pittsburgh, Pa.: Univ. of Pittsburgh Press, 1976).

7. President Clinton has elevated trade policy in his administration's overall foreign policy objectives. However, even in its most strident posturing vis-à-vis the Japanese, the administration has carefully sustained the broader relationship.

8. Ellen L. Frost, "Gaining Support for Trade from the American Public," in Geza Feketekuty and Bruce Stokes, eds., *Trade Strategies for a New Era: Ensuring U.S. Leadership in a Global Economy* (New York: Council on Foreign Relations, 1998), 66.

9. Marver H. Bernstein, *Regulating Business by Independent Commission* (Princeton, N.J.: Princeton Univ. Press, 1955).

10. Rachel McCulloch, "United States–Japan Economic Relations," in Robert E. Baldwin, ed., *Trade Policy Issues and Empirical Analysis* (Chicago, Ill.: Univ. of Chicago Press, 1988), 305–21.

11. Destler, *American Trade Politics,* chaps. 4 and 6.

12. For a discussion of congressional motives to accommodate domestic interests by means of administrative relief, see Douglas Nelson, "Domestic Political Preconditions of US Trade Policy: Liberal Structure and Protectionist Dynamics," *Journal of Public Policy* 9 (January–March 1989): 83–108.

13. George Hager and Eric Pianin, *Mirage: Why Neither Democrats Nor Republicans Can Balance the Budget, End the Deficit, and Satisfy the Public* (New York: Times Books, 1997), chap. 4.

14. Rachel McCulloch, "United States–Japan Economic Relations," in Robert E. Baldwin, ed., *Trade Policy Issues and Empirical Analysis* (Chicago, Ill.: Univ. of Chicago Press, 1988), 305–37.

15. For a history of the USTR, see Steve Dryden, *Trade Warriors: USTR and the American Crusade for Free Trade* (New York: Oxford Univ. Press, 1995).

16. Michael P. Ryan, *Playing by the Rules: American Trade Power and Diplomacy in the Pacific* (Washington, D.C.: Georgetown Univ. Press, 1995), 31–36.
17. Ibid., 45–46.
18. "The Commerce Mission Statement," <http://www.doc.gov/bmi/BUDGET/STRTDRFT/strtntro.htm> (3 November 1997).
19. Pietro S. Nivola, "Comment," in Richard Boltuck and Robert E. Litan, eds., *Down in the Dumps: Administration of the Unfair Trade Laws* (Washington, D.C.: Brookings Institution, 1991), 281–84.
20. Patrick Low, *Trading Free: The GATT and U.S. Trade Policy* (New York: The Twentieth Century Fund Press, 1993), 55, 60.
21. Wendy L. Hansen, *Regulatory Theory and Its Application to Trade Policy: A Study of ITC Decision-making 1975–1985* (New York: Garland, 1990), chap. 1.
22. Wendy L. Hansen, "The International Trade Commission and the Politics of Protectionism," *American Political Science Review* 84 (March 1990): 21–45.
23. United States Trade Representative, *1997 Trade Policy Agenda and 1996 Annual Report of the President of the United States on the Trade Agreements Program* (Washington, D.C.: U.S. Government Printing Office, 1997), chap. 8; and United States International Trade Commission, *The Year in Trade 1996* (Washington, D.C.: U.S. International Trade Commission, 1997), chap. 5.
24. Judith Goldstein, *Ideas, Interests, and American Trade Policy* (Ithaca, N.Y.: Cornell Univ. Press, 1993), 186.
25. Ibid., 189, 209.
26. Destler, *American Trade Politics,* 166.
27. Goldstein, *Ideas,* 209.
28. Ibid., 189.
29. United States International Trade Commission, *The Year in Trade 1992* (Washington, D.C.: U.S. International Trade Commission, 1993), 92; *The Year in Trade 1993* (Washington, D.C.: U.S. International Trade Commission, 1994), 123; *The Year in Trade 1994* (Washington, D.C.: U.S. International Trade Commission, 1995), 119; *The Year in Trade 1995* (Washington, D.C.: U.S. International Trade Commission, 1996), 71; *The Year in Trade 1996,* 129; *The Year in Trade 1997* (Washington D.C.: U.S. International Trade Commission, 1998), 127.
30. Destler, *American Trade Politics,* 23.
31. Goldstein, *Ideas,* 190.
32. Destler, *American Trade Politics,* 23.
33. Goldstein, *Ideas,* 190–91.
34. Destler, *American Trade Politics,* 143; Goldstein, *Ideas,* 192.
35. Destler, *American Trade Politics,* 153.

36. Ibid., 319.
37. Ibid., 153.
38. Goldstein, *Ideas*, 211.
39. Ibid., 211.
40. Ibid., 193.
41. United States International Trade Commission, *The Year in Trade 1992*, 90; *The Year in Trade 1993*, 124; *The Year in Trade 1994*, 120.
42. Destler, *American Trade Politics*, 153–54; United States International Trade Commission, *The Year in Trade 1994*, 120.
43. United States International Trade Commission, *The Year in Trade 1995*, 72; *The Year in Trade 1996*, 130; *The Year in Trade 1997*, 128.
44. Goldstein, *Ideas*, 203–04.
45. Destler, *American Trade Politics*, 166.
46. Ibid., 154, 157; 159–61.
47. Ibid., 145.
48. Ibid., 148.
49. Goldstein, *Ideas*, 204.
50. Destler, *American Trade Politics*, 150.
51. Wendy L. Hansen and Kee Ok Park, "Nation-State and Pluralistic Decision Making in Trade Policy: The Case of the International Trade Administration," *International Studies Quarterly* 39 (1995): 181–211.
52. Forty-three petitions were filed in 1992.
53. United States International Trade Commission, *The Year in Trade 1996*, 140; *The Year in Trade 1992*, 92; *The Year in Trade 1993*, 129; *The Year in Trade 1997*, 139.
54. Goldstein, *Ideas*, 198.
55. See chapter 7.
56. Anne O. Krueger, *American Trade Policy: A Tragedy in the Making* (Washington, D.C.: American Enterprise Institute, 1995), 43.
57. Goldstein, *Ideas*, 217.
58. Ibid., 168.
59. Ibid., 217.
60. Hansen and Park, "The International Trade Commission and the Politics of Protectionism."
61. Destler, *American Trade Politics*, 166; and United States Trade Representative, *1998 Trade Policy Agenda and 1997 Annual Report of the President of the United States on the Trade Agreements Program* (Washington, D.C.: U.S. Government Printing Office, 1998), 246–47.
62. Robert E. Baldwin and Michael O. Moore, "Political Aspects of the Administration of the Trade Remedy Laws," in Richard Boltuck and Robert E. Litan, eds., *Down in the Dumps: Administration of the Unfair Trade Laws* (Washington, D.C.: Brookings Institution, 1991), 269–70.

63. Destler, *American Trade Politics*, 169.
64. Baldwin and Moore, "Political Aspects of the Administration of the Trade Remedy Laws," 271, emphasis in original. Baldwin and Moore note that the Trade Act of 1984, in response to Commerce Department officials' recognition of the unfairness of this practice, permitted the department to use average U.S. prices in the calculation of dumping rates. According to the authors, the Commerce Department has not chosen to do so.
65. Baldwin and Moore, "Political Aspects of the Administration of the Trade Remedy Laws," 271.
66. Ibid., 45–46.
67. Krueger, *American Trade Policy*, 46.
68. Destler, *American Trade Politics*, 169.
69. Prior to the 1988 law, the USITC was required to determine injury. See Nivola, *Regulating Unfair Trade*, 23.
70. Ibid., 23.
71. Goldstein, *Ideas*, 207.
72. United States Trade Representative, *1998 Trade Policy Agenda and 1997 Annual Report*, 248–49.
73. Goldstein, *Ideas*, 208.
74. Ibid., 217.
75. United States International Trade Commission, *The Year in Trade 1993*, 129; *The Year in Trade 1994*, 125; *The Year in Trade 1996*, 141; *The Year in Trade 1997*, 140.
76. Goldstein, *Ideas*, 217–18.
77. Nivola asks the same question. See Nivola, "Comment," in Boltuck and Litan, *Down in the Dumps*, 281–84.
78. Goldstein, *Ideas*, 194.
79. Ibid., 194.
80. Jagdish Bhagwati and Hugh T. Patrick, *Aggressive Unilateralism* (Ann Arbor, Mich: Univ. of Michigan Press, 1990).
81. See Ryan, *Playing by the Rules*.
82. Greg Mastel, *American Trade Laws after the Uruguay Round* (Armonk, N.Y.: M. E. Sharpe, 1996), 52–55.
83. United States Trade Representative, *1998 Trade Policy Agenda and the 1997 Annual Report*, 244.
84. Ibid.
85. Destler, *American Trade Politics*, 132.
86. Krueger, *American Trade Policy*, 65–66.
87. Mastel, *American Trade Laws after the Uruguay Round*, 33–35, 51.
88. Krueger, *American Trade Policy*, 40.
89. Goldstein, *Ideas*, 217.
90. Krueger, *American Trade Policy*, 40.

91. United States Trade Representative, *1998 Trade Policy Agenda and 1997 Annual Report,* 238.
92. Ryan argues that 301 cases involving Japan, Korea, and Taiwan from 1974 to 1989 were initiated for at least one of two reasons: the commercial competitiveness of the industry and the GATT regime utility, i.e., whether the action was consistent with the GATT. See Ryan, *Playing by the Rules,* 46–47.
93. Destler, *American Trade Politics,* 133.
94. Destler, *American Trade Politics,* 237–38; 294; Krueger, *American Trade Policy,* 67.

7

Steel, Automobiles, and Semiconductors

Since the 1970s, American producers have not hesitated to seek government help to deal with foreign competition. Established manufacturing led the way, followed by high-technology industries. Steel, automobile, and semiconductor manufacturers have all taken this path. The origins and nature of their political activities differ, of course, but they share some important characteristics. Responding to the claims of all three industries, the U.S. government demonstrated its willingness to engage in decidedly illiberal trade policies. Trade restraint typically came in the form of a negotiated agreement with one or more foreign governments. These sectoral agreements constitute a policy adaptation to political realities. Although government officials may wish to pursue a policy of trade liberalization in the long term, they may, on occasion, find thinly disguised protectionist policies inescapable.

The series of voluntary restraint agreements (VRAs) on steel with various nations, the Japanese voluntary export restraint (VER) of its automobile exports to the United States, and the U.S.–Japan Semiconductor Trade Arrangement of 1986 (STA) and the subsequent agreement in 1991 illustrate this turn of events. They came about as a result of heavy political pressure conducted in a context in which government intervention to help an industry was acceptable. Together, they constitute a striking contrast in types of industry—products, production process, work force, capital, public visibility, and economic importance.

It should also come as no surprise that much of the focus of these agreements has been on Japan. Competition from Japanese firms has created problems for many American industries, from chips and autos to steel and consumer electronics. Alleged unfair trade practices by the Japanese—for example, government subsidies, dumping in foreign (mostly American) markets, and restricted access to the Japanese market for foreign-made products (again, mostly American)—have led business leaders, government officials, the media, and the American public in general to cast a wary eye toward Japan. Japan, Inc., however mythical or real, has served as an all-purpose justification for U.S. government intervention in trade between the two countries.

Steel, Cars, and Chips

The General Agreement on Tariffs and Trade (GATT) was intended to reduce tariffs globally, shrinking a major obstacle to free trade. Created largely because of American leadership, the multilateral agreement eschewed trade-limiting deals—mainly those involving quotas, either unvarnished or shrouded in free-trade rhetoric. It is ironic that in this environment, created in large part at America's behest, the United States aggressively negotiated trade-limiting deals with other countries for specific industries.

Steel, automobiles, and semiconductors illustrate the causes and consequences of major sectoral trade accords. These industries are strikingly different with respect to their industrial and political organization. Yet, at the same time, the policies that each industry worked so hard to achieve are generally similar. Steel is the figurative backbone of American manufacturing. Highly concentrated until the 1970s, the major integrated firms formed an oligopoly, cooperating on major management decisions. The automobile industry is the archetype of traditional heavy manufacturing in the United States. Unionized, bureaucratic manufacturing behemoths had dominated the industry for more than forty years, rolling out a machine that is the symbol of consumerism and the arrival of the middle class. Semiconductors, on the other hand, are emblematic of the new age of high technology. The guts of the computer, chips make modern electronic wizardry possible and hold the promise for future untold advances. As much as steel undergirds American manufacturing and the automobile embodies the twentieth-century American lifestyle, the semiconductor symbolizes technological magic. Dependent on highly educated specialists, the semiconductor industry is a decidedly white-collar industry with a much greater emphasis on knowledge than on heavy, blue-collar manufacturing.

The Steel Industry

By the 1950s, the American steel industry had become a bulwark of manufacturing. Imposing plants, unionized workers, and high-profile executives contributed to the image of manufacturing muscle and success. Yet, by this time, the industry was already beginning to feel the effects of problems that would plague it into the 1990s. Poor management decisions, excess capacity, imports, and the rise of the minimills undermined the economic position of the established steel firms. While experiencing problems as early as the late 1950s, from 1975 to 1985 the industry went into a tailspin, as demand plummeted, production and employment dropped, domestic market share shrank, and earnings were small or negative.[1] The industry responded to these problems with efforts to adjust firms' behavior to meet the demands of the new environment and with calls for help from the national government. The first category of actions was marked by some success but considerable failure. The second is a product of the relationship between business and government in the United States and the basic nature of the American political system, the outcome of which is open to some debate.

The steel industry shared some characteristics with the automobile industry. In the immediate postwar period, both were highly concentrated, though the automobile industry was more concentrated than steel and consequently was affected differently by protection. They both employed a high number of well-paid, unionized workers whose skills did not easily migrate to jobs in other industries. Both were also symbols of American economic might at the midpoint of the twentieth century. Their problems damaged the image of manufacturing in the United States, contributing to the wave of commentaries in the 1980s decrying the decline of America. The steel industry bears little resemblance to the semiconductor industry, of course, except perhaps in the distribution of large firms and small firms. At least insofar as its trade association was concerned, several large chip makers dominated the industry's political activities, while smaller, more specialized firms were not necessarily part of the political action. In a roughly similar way, eight large firms essentially dictated the political strategy of the steel industry.

Aside from the similarities and differences among these three industries, they all chose to use trade policy to address their economic problems. Each claimed that imports were largely responsible for their problems, and in most cases, these imports gained their competitive position as a result of unfair trade practices by the firms that made them or the governments of the countries in which they were manufactured.

Overview of the Steel Industry

Steel characterizes the American industrialized economy of the twentieth century more than any other. It is the basic component of any number of manufactured goods, ranging from automobiles to home appliances to bridges. The industry was highly concentrated until the 1980s, with a small number of large integrated firms (around ten) responsible for the bulk of production through the 1950s. These integrated firms controlled the entire production process, from processing iron ore to turning out the finished product. By the 1980s, the industry was no longer highly concentrated as minimills proliferated and large integrated firms declined, with many going out of business.[2]

Making Steel

There are two basic categories of steel mills: large integrated firms and minimills. The former were the mainstay of the steel industry until minimills came onto the scene in the 1970s and flourished in the 1980s.[3] The integrated plant starts the process with steel's basic raw ingredients, iron ore and coal. Using blast furnaces, these components are converted into pig iron ("hot metal"), which is then fed into a basic oxygen furnace (BOF), which replaced the less-efficient open hearth furnace in American plants in the 1960s, to create molten steel. Either of two processes then turns the molten steel into the basic shapes (billets, blooms, and slabs) that rolling mills finish into the final product. The older and less-efficient of these two processes involves two steps: first, making ingots using an ingot caster, and second, reheating the ingots in a primary mill to produce the basic shapes that go into the rolling mill. The newer and more efficient process uses continuous casting to create the basic shapes, avoiding the costly two-step process of the older method.[4]

Minimills have challenged integrated plants for market share. These firms are smaller than integrated firms, produce a more limited range of products, and use a truncated, more efficient production process. Minimills begin with scrap and directly reduced iron ore, skipping the first step employed by the integrated plants. Electric furnaces convert these materials into molten steel, which is then processed by the continuous casting method before being fed into the rolling mills. Minimills tend to be limited to producing billets, the smallest shape, for the rolling mills rather than all three basic shapes made by integrated plants, and the final products are limited, small structural shapes, rods, and bars.[5]

The First Problems

Until the 1960s, integrated firms relied on technology that was either obsolete or rapidly becoming so. Using open hearth furnaces, as most did almost exclusively, was an inefficient technique when others were available, and it added steps to the steel-making process. This was particularly problematic in the 1950s, when the demand for steel shot up. American steel manufacturers tried to meet this demand by investing in open hearth furnaces, in effect buying old technology to fit old plants using old techniques. The alternative was to invest in the new technology available at the time, basic oxygen furnaces, which operated much more efficiently than open hearth furnaces. Not doing so left American firms at a competitive disadvantage with respect to their Japanese and European counterparts, which had invested heavily in BOF.[6] By the second half of the 1950s, steel firms were suffering a declining rate of return, lower profits, and a worsening balance of trade position.[7]

American steel makers played a fierce game of technological catch-up in the 1960s, replacing the obsolete open hearth furnace with BOF at an impressive rate. But that was not enough to re-establish the industry's competitive edge sufficiently to stave off imports from Japan and Europe. The 1960s marks the first time the industry felt the effect of foreign competition, and it sought help from Washington.[8]

The steel industry turned to government for help. Working largely through the American Iron and Steel Institute (AISI), steel manufacturers formed a coalition with the United Steel Workers of America (USW), along with the oil and textile industries to lobby Congress successfully for quota legislation. President Lyndon Johnson threatened to veto the legislation, not wishing to undermine its commitment to freer trade. Senator Vance Hartke (D-IN), however, joined thirty-six cosponsors in introducing a new steel quota bill. Trying to avoid this turn of events, Japanese and European producers responded by working with the House Ways and Means Committee and the Senate Finance Committee to lay the groundwork for a voluntary restraint agreement. The result was a three-year VRA (1969–71) intended to give the American industry time to modernize and re-establish its competitive position.[9]

1970s: More Problems

American steel producers began the decade still suffering from the difficulties that the 1969 VRA was intended to correct. Foreign steel firms effectively circumvented the agreement by shifting production to higher-value products not covered by the VRA. The result was an increase of foreign imports to 17.9 percent of the U.S. market combined with a drop in the American steel industry's profits to less than one-half of the average of all U.S. manufacturers.[10] The steel industry, largely through the AISI, lobbied for more protection, and the Nixon administration came through with another VRA to extend from 1972 to 1974. The effects of this move, however, were virtually nonexistent, as the economy turned upward for a short period of time, causing increased demand for American steel accompanied by higher prices and a lower claim by imports on the American domestic market.[11]

Although this second round of VRAs turned out to be unnecessary, the American steel industry remained concerned with foreign imports. The AISI pressed the Nixon administration for additional guarantees of protection, this time in the form of beefed-up antidumping (AD) laws that were incorporated into the 1974 Trade Act. The 1974 bill gave the steel industry (and others) a formal legal way to challenge foreign producers that did not comply with U.S. antidumping laws.[12]

As the short-term boom faded in 1975 and 1976, the industry pursued still more protection through President Gerald Ford. Ford chose to impose a quota on specialty steel in 1976, helping to avoid antagonizing the European Economic Community (EEC) by erecting another VRA. The quota proved ineffective, and Ford continued to be resistant to industry pressure, as he refused to pursue its AD complaints, fearing that doing so would jeopardize trade relations with other nations.[13]

For the same reasons, President Jimmy Carter was equally disinclined to enforce steel industry AD claims. His administration responded to steel's economic problems and political pressure with the Solomon Plan, a multifaceted strategy intended to give the steel industry a chance to adjust to foreign competition. The trade component of the plan was the trigger price mechanism (TPM), which determined minimum prices for steel imports. The calculation was based on the costs of production and transport of Japanese steel to the U.S. market. Although intended to limit imports, its most immediate effect was to establish a floor price for steel in the United States, allowing producers to raise prices and therefore profits.[14]

In addition to this negative consequence, the TPM did not apply to imports from the EEC. When these began to mount, causing consternation among American steel manufacturers, the industry sought tougher AD and countervailing duty (CVD) provisions in the trade law, which they got in the Trade Agreements Act of 1979. The new law required the federal government to pursue AD and CVD claims and gave claimants the option of challenging government decisions by making United States International Trade Commission (USITC) decisions subject to judicial review.[15] Armed with this new legal tactic, the steel industry filed AD petitions against imports in 1980, including those from seven European countries. To avoid a foreign policy problem, the Carter administration canceled the TPM, and, among other actions, created a new TPM featuring a twelve percent increase in minimum prices.[16]

One problem that plagued the industry throughout the 1970s and into the 1980s was the low level of investment in new technologies. The problem, according to one analysis, was that American industry was not specialized; too many firms were trying to do too much. With all firms investing in a new technology, the result was excess capacity, which meant an insufficient return on the investment. Without specialization, then, the industry was trapped in an arrangement that made investment, which was otherwise necessary to compete, economically costly.[17]

In addition to the investment problem, American steel firms had a poor track record in labor–management relations. Although the USW found common ground with steel manufacturers when it came to pursuing import restraint, it was a demanding antagonist on wages, benefits, and work rules, exacting significant concessions from steel manufacturers until 1982. A particularly damaging agreement, from management's perspective, was the Experimental Negotiation Agreement of 1973, in which the USW pledged not to strike in exchange for a guarantee of a minimum 3 percent real-wage increase and cost of living adjustment in future contracts.[18] Steel executives agreed to the deal, since they believed that they stood to lose a great deal in the next several years of increased demand if workers went on strike. As it turned out, demand did not go up as the steel manufacturers had predicted.[19]

The 1980s

Past VRAs, TPMs, and unfair trade practice laws did not stem the tide of steel imports into the American market. The steel industry continued to address the problem presented by foreign competition by seeking various forms of protection—AD and CVD claims, an escape clause petition, and legislation intended to limit imports. In the end, however, it took a United States International Trade Commission decision to impose quotas on steel imports to force the hand of the Reagan administration. Like his predecessors, President Reagan sought to avoid quotas because of the threat they represented to stable trade relations. At the same time, Reagan had to deal with the USITC decision in 1984, an election year. Fearing that inaction would send important voters in key states into the camp of his opponent, Walter Mondale, Reagan negotiated still another set of VRAs (1985–89), this time establishing market share of imports at 18.5 percent. This set of VRAs included more precise definition of products and more exacting methods of enforcement.[20]

The late 1980s were better years for American steel manufacturers. Policies other than trade (e.g., tax investment credits) and economic growth contributed to a resurgence of the industry. Production costs dipped below those of the Japanese, imports dropped, capacity utilization increased, and several major integrated companies reported the highest profits in decades. Even with this success, the industry continued to pressure government for more protection in the form of legislation to extend import quotas and a wave of AD claims.[21] George Bush promised to renew the quotas during his presidential campaign, but once in office and therefore feeling the constraints of international politics along with a new domestic force of steel consumers opposed to protection, President Bush produced quotas for a duration of only two and one-half years, and increased import market share to 20.2 percent.[22]

Assessment

The American steel industry's response to decline was misplaced from a purely economic perspective. One could easily argue that the industry's problems lay with fundamental failures to innovate technologically and to make reasonably accurate assessments of demand. Steel executives did not switch to BOF from open hearth furnaces until they had paid a heavy economic price, nor did they correctly anticipate the downturns of demand in the 1970s. Bad decisions like these left them in poor competitive shape by the 1980s. Their choice to pursue trade policy as a means of helping their industry is hardly unusual; many industries did the same thing, and the steel industry capitalized on this as it joined forces with them in the 1970s to make a more effective appeal to the national government for trade protection.

Seeking trade remedies is appealing for several reasons. First, an industry can argue that protection is temporary, as the steel industry did in the 1960s. The industry simply needs some time to make the necessary adjustments to the new foreign competitive challenge. Second, if the industry does not adjust rapidly, it can go back to policy makers for more protection, claiming that it needs more time to adjust and, more importantly, foreign competitors have tilted the playing field in their favor by using unfair trade practices. Third, protection is appealing for its public relations value. Industry representatives can arouse nationalistic sentiments by claiming that foreigners are undermining an important aspect of the American social and economic fabric. Although such claims can slide into jingoism quite easily, they are nonetheless effective, at least as a public relations gambit. Fourth, the American political system is ideally set up to respond to pleas for protection, which tend to be narrow in nature. Members of Congress have a tough time turning away from the interests of major industries in their districts and states. Shrinking investment, disappearing capital, and lost jobs can cause the most free-trade–oriented legislator to find worth in protection. These simple points were not lost on steel industry executives.

Did Protection Work?

The American steel industry in the 1990s is certainly in much better shape than it was in the 1970s. The remaining integrated firms have cut costs dramatically and have become competitive with imports and with domestic minimills.[23] They have accomplished this remarkable turn-around by scrapping outdated technology and production processes, investing in new technology, and cutting hundreds of thousands of jobs. The result is an industry with lower capacity but with much higher rates of utilization and labor productivity. By 1994, the industry as a whole employed 238,000 workers, which is less than 40 percent of the number of workers employed twenty years earlier. Worse still, the number of employees of integrated firms dropped 75 percent over the same time period. Thus, regardless of the exact effect of protection, the steel industry made some dramatic adjustments to the new competitive environment.[24]

One can assess the consequences of protection for the steel industry from two vantage points: from the level of the firm and for the industry as a whole. In an evaluation of steel industry protection in the 1970s and early 1980s, Stefanie Lenway, Kathleen Rehbein, and Laura Starks found that firms benefited significantly from protection, but benefits were not distributed evenly across firms. This basic finding is true whether protection was in the form of quantity or price controls. Generally, firms that actively demanded relief benefited most, but the 1977 TPM did not necessarily help the big integrated firms, which have been the most politically active. Instead, small integrated firms seem to have benefited most from the trade measures. The results of a second TPM suggest that minimills benefited almost as much as the large integrated firms.[25]

A later study examined the differences between firms that lobbied for trade relief and those that did not. The findings indicate that less-competitive firms lobby more than others. These firms tend to be larger and less diversified than others in the industry, and their executives and workers get paid more than their counterparts in other firms. Because of their more entrenched position in the industry, these firms find it easier to exercise voice than exit; in other words, since their sole focus is steel, they have a difficult time leaving the industry. Spending resources on trade policy makes sense for firms in this strategic position. The study also finds that the restructuring that took place in the steel industry after protection saw more innovative firms leave the industry more than firms that lobby more, suggesting that protection decreased innovation in the industry rather than increasing it. In short, less-diversified firms with well-paid employees—that is, firms in comfortable positions—benefited from protection more than innovative firms.[26]

Robert W. Crandall's analysis indicates that protection of the steel industry had generally negative consequences. Trade restraint in the 1970s followed by the TPM increased industry profits, but had little effect on investment. Indeed, if protection had increased profits, the industry is likely to have been worse off, since the rate of return on costly investments would not have covered cost of capital. As Crandall argues, "(t)o the extent that protection stabilized or raised prices and contributed to the excessive optimism among steelmakers in the mid-1970s, it proved to be extremely counterproductive."[27] Compensation rose rapidly in the late 1970s, followed by a decline after 1982. The 1984 VRA's lack of effect on prices and profits contributed to the decline in wages, and the rise of minimills also put downward pressure on wages.[28] Finally, Crandall found an increase in productivity, but does not attribute it to trade protection.[29]

These analyses do not give one much reason to have confidence in the capacity of protection to allow an industry to adjust to a new competitive environment. An alternative view suggests quite opposite conclusions, however. Robert E. Scott and Thea M. Lee argue that steel VRAs played a pivotal role in the industry's adjustment to the new competitive environment. They contend "that the combination of competitive pressure from low-cost electric furnace producers (the minimills), and some imports, along with the stability provided by the VRAs, worked to foster higher levels of investment and the resulting productivity growth."[30] Scott and Lee conclude that, while the VRAs were not the best way to restrain trade,[31] their effect was to improve wages and productivity, saving American jobs and helping the steel industry recover its competitiveness.[32] A study conducted by the Economic Strategy Institute (ESI) endorsed this conclusion, arguing that the VRAs in the 1980s were crucial in allowing the steel industry to undergo the restructuring necessary to meet the new competitive challenge. This study points to heavy expenditures in the 1980s on new equipment, coupled with new agreements with the USW, as the major sources of a significant turnaround in the industry's fortunes. Under the VRAs in the 1980s, import penetration of the domestic market fell from their peak of 26 percent in 1984 to 18 percent in 1989. The Steel Import Stabilization Act, under the auspices of which President Reagan negotiated the VRAs, moreover, required steel makers to use revenues generated by the VRAs for capital investment and worker retraining. According to the ESI study, this resulted in $7.8 billion in investments that aided the industry's rebound.[33]

Thus, there is some disagreement on the effects of protection for the steel industry. The conventional view has been that the various forms of trade restraint imposed by the national government since the late 1960s have done little to cause the industry to adjust, and are very likely to have done some damage, particularly to the consumer. The dissenting view suggests the opposite. I cannot settle the dispute here, of course, but this sketch of the assessments of trade policy with respect to a single industry suggests the unsurprising but nonetheless important point that there is no perfect agreement on protection for the steel industry, and because of that, policy becomes subject to high-stakes politics.

The Politics

The steel industry enjoyed some political advantages that likely helped it obtain trade restraint. In the 1960s and 1970s, when the industry began lobbying for protection in earnest, steel was concentrated among a handful of large, integrated firms. The concentration probably permitted coordinated political pressure, because there were fewer players to organize and the benefits of pursuing trade policy were clear.[34] Concentration of firms and workers in congressional districts and states also enhances the industry's political clout. Members of Congress are likely to pay attention to special pleas from firms and workers in their districts. Indeed, the Congressional Steel Caucus, a bipartisan group of representatives and senators, formed in 1977 to allow members to do just that.[35] Congress is especially receptive to narrow interests, and the industry evidently capitalized on that.

The steel industry enjoyed one additional advantage that deserves some discussion. The USW was a powerful, well-heeled union, with ample political experience and success. Its joining forces with firms (with few exceptions) to obtain import restraint most certainly added to the effectiveness of the political effort. When it comes to trade policy in the United States, class politics, assuming that it exists at all, takes a back seat to shared economic interest.

The political advantages enjoyed by the steel industry do not explain its strategy. The industry chose tactics that took advantage of various access points to policy makers. The industry used numerous AD and CVD complaints to pressure the executive into action. Realizing that successful resolution of these complaints results in trade sanctions, which could undermine U.S. relations with other countries, several presidents opted to negotiate VRAs or to impose import quotas rather than risking the consequences of sanctions aimed at unfair trade practices. This became an especially effective tactic for the industry after the 1979 trade bill toughened AD and CVD procedures, making it more likely that a president would have to act on positive USITC findings. In addition to taking the regulatory route to protection, the industry directly pressured Congress to enact quota legislation, again with the effect of putting pressure on the executive to act to avoid outcomes that could harm U.S. foreign relations.

Conclusion

The steel industry case illustrates a typical pattern of the creation of protectionist policies. The industry, and in this case the major union, took advantage of the multiple access points to policy making in American government. While executive action was the outcome in most cases, the path to moving the executive ran through Congress some of the time, and through the administrative regulatory system at others. The industry succeeded politically, whether or not the economic effects could be called successful, because of its concentrated nature, the help it received from the USW, and the claims it could make to vague notions of the worth of American values embedded in this traditional manufacturing industry. The steel industry is similar to the automobile industry in these ways, but remarkably dissimilar to the semiconductor industry.

The Automobile Industry

The automobile industry has been a mainstay of the American economy for most of the twentieth century. It is one of the remaining major heavy manufacturing industries in the United States, employing 971,000 people throughout the country in 1997.[36] The industry's manufacturing work force consists of blue-collar employees, most of whom are members of the United Automobile Workers (UAW).

Until the 1970s, American automobile manufacturers dominated the American market. After years of sifting out smaller companies, the 1970s began with only four major American car companies remaining: General Motors Corporation (GM), Ford Motor Company, Chrysler Corporation, and American Motors Corporation (AMC). The number quickly shrank to the Big Three when Chrysler swallowed up AMC. But the unchallenged position of American car companies in their own market came to an end as foreign car companies began to make inroads into the American market. In the 1950s and 60s, Volkswagen (VW) demonstrated that Americans would buy a small, fuel-efficient economy car with the storied success of the Beetle. Japanese car companies followed VW into the American market. First, Toyota found some willing customers with its Corona and Corolla. Nissan came along shortly after Toyota, selling several models initially under its Datsun nameplate.[37] Several other Japanese car companies saw the potential in the American market and quickly tested their luck there as well. Mazda, Subaru, and Mitsubishi (initially as a captured import sold by Chrysler) gained a small, but steady, share of the market. Their efforts were dwarfed, however, by Honda's entry into the United States. Americans had already become familiar with the Honda name through sales of its small engines and, especially, motorcycles. The arrival of a Honda car took some adjustment on the part of the consumer, but Americans took to the new import quickly.

American car companies were caught off guard by the rapid success of foreign-made cars, mainly those from Japan. The explanation for their failure to compete effectively with Japanese-made cars has been evaluated numerous times. The general consensus for why Japanese car makers were able to strike such an effective blow against their American counterparts turns on a few key points. First, American automobile executives failed to anticipate the Japanese companies' ability to sell cars in the United States. This was probably a matter of ignorance rather than miscalculation, as American firms paid little attention to what was going on in Japan. Second, company officials did not recognize the shift in consumer tastes in the United States. With the oil crises of the 1970s serving as the catalyst, Americans were eager to buy smaller, more fuel-efficient cars than Detroit had been producing. While huge, gas-guzzling land vessels lumbered off American assembly lines, the Japanese cranked out small, nimble cars with relatively petite fuel appetites. Third, American consumers came to the conclusion that Japanese-manufactured automobiles were better-made than American ones. Detroit got, and earned, the reputation for poor design, engineering, and workmanship. Owners of Fords, Chevys, and Chryslers could count on higher repair bills and more frequent visits to the garage than Toyota and Datsun drivers. The image matched the record, as Japanese cars surpassed their American competitors in design, quality, and reliability. Finally, recognizing that when given a choice the consumer would choose higher quality over lower, in the 1980s American executives sought to improve dramatically the quality of their cars to match that of Toyota, Nissan, and other Japanese imports. Their efforts have proved somewhat successful—the quality of American-made cars has improved into the 1990s—but foreign-made automobiles still occupy most of the top ten slots in car quality.[38]

The American automobile industry's problems have been well publicized. Indeed, the car has become the symbol of American manufacturing decline. The car companies' woes began as early as the 1960s when GM suffered major blows to its credibility in its effort to muzzle its chief critic, Ralph Nader, who made clear to the consumer that American cars could be unsafe.[39] Even with the car companies' integrity in question, the public paid for the bailout of Chrysler in the later 1970s.[40] Finally, as foreign-made cars became a growing presence on American roads, the public could not help but notice the not-so-gradual replacement of familiar American makes with foreign ones.

The final development that signaled trouble for American car companies to the benefit of their foreign competitors is the latter's establishment of factories in the United States. Faced with obstacles to exporting cars to the United States, several Japanese companies and two German ones built, or plan to build, assembly plants in the U.S. By 1989, Nissan, Honda, Toyota, and others were making cars in the U.S.,[41] and Mercedes-Benz planned to make cars in Alabama, while BMW built cars in South Carolina.

The central point here is that the automobile is a visible consumer product. Americans are familiar with the car, which is the symbol of various lifestyles. The decline of American car companies, then, easily becomes a symbol for bad times for American manufacturing in general. The public, presumably, will be responsive, or at least attuned, to the Big Three's complaints about foreign competition and their efforts to enlist government support to protect them from it.

Political Organization of the American Automobile Industry

General Motors, Ford, and Chrysler maintain major political operations in Washington. Like many large companies, they have their own lobbying capability, along with an array of lobbyists on retainer and political consultants of various types. In addition, the Big Three belong to their major trade association, the American Automobile Manufacturers Association, in addition to the National Association of Manufacturers (NAM), the United States Chamber of Commerce, the Business Roundtable, and other major business organizations.

American car companies have a major political ally in the United Automobile Workers insofar as trade policy is concerned. The UAW is the natural enemy of car companies, their most outspoken antagonist on contract negotiations and labor legislation and regulation. However, the UAW and the Big Three have found common ground on trade. Lost revenues to the manufacturers mean lost jobs, lower wages, and reduced benefits. Thus, the UAW led the way in the early 1980s in the political campaign to get domestic content legislation enacted[42] and joined Chrysler and Ford in their efforts to obtain protection from Japanese imports. It is noteworthy here that GM did not support the drive for protection. For example, GM opposed domestic content legislation because it would prohibit American car makers from using foreign suppliers, which could easily be the cheapest source of parts, and import restrictions could lead to the spread of protectionism, which could hurt American auto exports.[43]

The structure of the American automobile industry gives it tremendous potential political clout. Distributed fairly widely across the country, the industry is set up well for influencing a significant number of members of Congress. Add to this a willing cadre of UAW members available for grassroots work. Finally, the visibility of the industry, coupled with the symbolic value of the car, give it access to considerable media coverage.

The industry's political strategies flow naturally from its sectoral characteristics. It has successfully pressured Congress for concessions on a variety of issues, not least of which is trade. This is hardly surprising given congressional susceptability to constituent pressure, especially if the constituent employs a large number of the legislator's supporters and makes a significant contribution to the economy in the area the legislator represents. United Automobile Workers pressure, coordinated with that of the major companies, makes an even more effective political force. With congressional receptivity to industry demands, both from the companies themselves and from the UAW, it makes sense that both are major sources of campaign funds through their political action committees (PACs). Campaign contributions may not buy votes, but they certainly buy access to the member of Congress, a necessary component of political influence.

The automobile industry has also been successful in applying political pressure at the other end of Pennsylvania Avenue. The distribution of the industry and its partnership with the UAW on trade matters play as well in the White House as they do on Capitol Hill. The sheer size of the industry adds to these political advantages. With its contribution to the American economy both in terms of gross domestic product and employment, the automobile industry is difficult to ignore. Besides which, no White House incumbent wants to preside over the decimation of one of America's industrial symbols. Thus, the president and the executive in general, nominally free-trade–oriented, will be swayed by the automobile industry's impressive political clout.

To sum up, the characteristics of the American automobile industry lead to certain political advantages. Visible, big, widely distributed, and the symbol of American lifestyles, the industry can exert enormous political pressure on both Congress and the executive. The political organization, strategies, and effectiveness are all evident in the automobile industry's successful campaign for protection from Japanese competition in the domestic market.

The Voluntary Export Restraint on Automobiles

In April 1981 the Japanese government agreed to limit the number of cars Japanese manufacturers exported to the United States. The quota was the result of a VER agreement with the United States, which had been negotiated by the Reagan administration. The VER represented a dramatic departure from the free-trade ideology espoused by the administration—in effect, a protectionist agreement made necessary by political pressure. The roots of the political pressure can be traced to a decade of decline in the U.S. automobile industry and the political pressure it produced.

By 1980, American car companies had become accustomed to requesting assistance of various kinds from the federal government. In the face of resurgent consumer demand for small cars, which the Big Three were not making, Detroit sought help from Washington. Although chastised by government officials for their lack of business acumen (and common sense, for that matter), the automobile industry requested four government measures:

> Delays in programs involving auto emissions and fuel efficiency standards. Tax credits for Americans who buy small, fuel efficient U.S.-built cars and small business loans for car dealers. "Content" legislation requiring inclusion of a certain percentage of U.S. parts in each imported car sold in the United States. A joint resolution asking the administration to press forward with negotiations with the Japanese for a voluntary import restraint program until the U.S. industry can convert production to more small cars.[44]

At this point, the American automobile industry was hardly unified on the trade issue. The UAW and Ford enthusiastically advocated government action to assist the automobile industry. Opposed to protectionist policies, the Carter administration offered other policies designed to help the industry. Finding these measures unsatisfactory and remaining convinced that trade actions were necessary, in August 1980, the UAW and Ford petitioned the United States International

Trade Commission for administrative relief under provisions of the escape clause.[45] General Motors opposed trade restraint, at least in part because it could "lead to protectionism that would hurt U.S. auto sales abroad,"[46] and because it had planned to meet the foreign competition by importing small cars under its nameplate from Japan. Having recently won a controversial federal government bail-out, Chrysler found it difficult to request further government assistance in the form of protection.[47]

Members of Congress had been considering limiting imports—mainly from Japan—for several months. Charles A. Vanik (D-OH), Chairman of the House Ways and Means Trade Subcommittee, had presided over hearings on limits to foreign imports. Vanik, who criticized American car makers for their current predicament, nonetheless warned the Japanese that, unless they limited exports to the United States, the Congress would act to set formal quotas. The central issue for many legislators was jobs. They were concerned not only for auto workers, but for workers in other industries that depended on the success of car makers—for example, the rubber, steel, and aluminum industries.[48] Most focused on the issue, of course, were members who represented these industries, especially those from Michigan. Their efforts resulted in the introduction of two quota bills in the spring of 1980. HR 6718 would reduce all foreign car imports by 35 percent and would require all cars sold in the United States to have 75 percent American content by 1985. Somewhat less draconian, HR 6645 would keep the number of imported cars coming into the United States to 10 percent market share.[49]

While congressional concern for the American automobile industry caused serious consideration of import restrictions in 1980, it was not until Ronald Reagan assumed the presidency that the threat of the passage of such legislation seemed credible. In office for only a few months, President Reagan had been a committed devotee of supply-side economics and the virtues of the free market. It seems odd, then, that this president adopted a blatant protectionist measure less than five months into his term of office. In spite of his ideology, Reagan found it necessary to negotiate the VER on autos with Japan to forestall more drastic congressional action.

In 1981, Congress resumed its deliberations over the problems caused by Japanese automobile imports for the American car industry. The fundamental issue remained constant: Japanese cars displaced

American cars, costing car companies revenue and workers their jobs. To address these problems, the Senate was considering S 396, which would impose a quota of 1.6 million Japanese-made autos exported to the United States in each of three successive years. The House was considering a similar bill, HR 1823.

Douglas R. Nelson argues that three factors contributed to congressional willingness to use trade policy to address the problems plaguing the American automobile industry. First, the issue was defined in terms of unfair trade. The decline of the Big Three, in the public's view, was attributable to illicit trade practices by foreign competitors—mainly from Japan. While the USITC failed to find that foreign competition was the cause of the American car manufacturers' problems, the public perception carried the day. Second, American automobile industry interests had "standing" before Congress. Car companies were the injured party and therefore had a right to take their complaints to Congress. American dealers of Japanese cars had no such standing, since they were perceived to be doing well. Because it is difficult to organize consumers into an effective interest group, they were left out of pleadings before Congress as well. Third, the American automobile industry controlled the terms of debate, selecting the type of administrative relief that the government ought to implement as well as when it should do so.[50] Taken together, these factors influenced congressional deliberation, so that the question was not whether protection would be used, but only when and what kind.

The Reagan administration took little time to seek a protectionist deal with Japan. Concerned with broader foreign policy considerations, like defeating communism, and bowing to intense political pressure from business, a natural Republican constituency, the otherwise free-trade administration was remarkably quick to conclude a decidedly anti–free-market deal with one of American's principal trading partners. Congressional pressure abated once the deal was struck; Senators John C. Danforth (R-MO) and Lloyd Bentsen (D-TX), along with Representative Bob Traxler (D-MI), agreed to shelve their respective quota bills when the Reagan administration had successfully concluded a VER with Japan.[51]

The VER was a three-year agreement. In the first year, Japan agreed to limit auto exports to the United States to 1.68 million cars. In the second, the limit was set at 1.68 million cars plus a 16.5 percent increase in the projected American auto market. The Japanese government would decide whether it needed to limit exports to the United States in the third year.[52]

In its effort to force the administration to act, Congress was responding to intense pressure from American car companies and the UAW. For these interests, Congress was the most receptive part of government to their claims. The traditionally free-trade executive was currently occupied by a free-market zealot, and the USITC, in response to a Section 201 petition filed by Ford Motor Company and the UAW, determined that the industry's problems were not attributable to Japanese imports. The UAW and the industry used the right approach; following the 10 November 1980 USITC decision, on 2 December 1980, a lame-duck Congress authorized the president to negotiate an orderly marketing agreement limiting auto imports.[53]

Reagan negotiated with the Japanese on auto imports because of this constant, credible congressional pressure. Failing to come up with a consensus on the issue with Congress, the administration was convinced that Congress would pass legislation imposing quotas on Japanese car imports. Reagan did not want to sign such a bill, nor did he want to be put in the politically vulnerable position of having to veto it. A negotiated VER with the Japanese government seemed a good way out of a situation that had no good exits.[54]

As promised, the VER limited Japanese exports to the United States. The quota was not an issue during the first two years of the agreement because the depressed American economy generated insufficient demand to cause it to go into effect. In 1983 and 1984, higher consumer demand made the limit on Japanese exports significant, causing prices to go up on cars sold in the United States. The election year politics of 1984 resulted in the Reagan administration's continuing the VER through 1985 with the quota expanded to 1.85 million vehicles. At this point, the administration was willing to allow the VER to lapse, but the Japanese government announced its willingness to continue the policy, largely because of the additional profits Japanese car manufacturers garnered resulting from the ability to restrict production and charge higher prices for their cars.[55] The quota had reached 2.3 million cars by 1993, at which time the Japanese government volunteered to continue the trade restraint at the level of 1.65 million cars. The move apparently was intended to preempt the incoming Clinton administration, which might have called for a lower ceiling.[56]

The VER arguably caused several changes in the American automobile industry as well. In addition to reducing the number of cars Americans seemed to want in the 1980s, Japanese executives devised new strategies to cope with American protectionism. Perhaps the most significant of these were stepped-up efforts by Japanese firms to locate manufacturing plants in the United States. It is not difficult now to buy a Honda, Toyota, or a Nissan made in America.

Explaining the Automobile VER with Japan

The automobile VER with Japan demonstrates the vulnerability of a free-trade presidency to political pressure. The events that culminated in the VER do not fit easily into the three-step domestic policy process. But they do reflect the power of business, allied in this case with labor, in American politics.

The Policy Process

The VER was a product of domestic and international political necessity. On the domestic side, the Reagan administration found it impossible to ignore the automobile industry's political pressure. Internationally, both the Japanese government and the administration sought a low-profile way to avoid quotas. Imposing quotas would run counter to the Reagan administration's commitment to free trade; such blatant protectionism was unacceptable to the president. A VER, while in effect a quota, allowed the president to claim that the Japanese government had taken action to remedy a business problem. Recognizing the strong likelihood that Congress would impose quotas on imports, the Japanese government agreed to the VER, preferring to deal with the administration rather than the Congress.

The events that led up to the VER involved implementation and legislation, but not in the typical order. The USITC's decision that foreign competition was not the cause of the American automobile industry's woes was a matter of implementation. The commission's determination gave Reagan an excuse not to take action to help the automobile industry; without a finding that foreign competition was damaging an American industry, the president was under no obligation to do anything. In spite of this political cover, the administration found the political pressure sufficiently intense to force it to act nonetheless. Reagan's negotiation of the VER with Japan, then, did not grow out of implementation. Quite the opposite occurred; had the administration chosen to adhere to the implementation of U.S. trade law closely, it could have done nothing at all.

Congress was central to the creation of the VER. Finding the implementation path to protection closed, and forced to deal with a free-trade president, interests connected to the automobile industry turned to Congress, the institution most susceptible to pressure from particular interests. Congress played its part predictably. Behind bipartisan leadership, it successfully forced the administration to find a way to provide relief to the American automobile industry. Congress did not legislate as such, but its threat to do so, however, was enough to push Reagan into negotiating the VER with Japan.

The executive's actions in this episode of U.S. trade policy illustrate the vulnerability of the institution most resilient to protectionism even when occupied by a president who was adamantly free-trade–oriented. Reagan would not have responded to direct industry pressure alone. Having enlisted congressional support, however, the car companies along with the UAW were too much for the president. Political pressure funneled through the institutional arrangement peculiar to American government created a fissure in the institutional liberalism that usually characterizes the executive on trade policy.

Business–Government Relations

The effectiveness of the automobile industry's political efforts is part of the larger picture of business–government relations in the United States. As is true for the semiconductor industry, the sectoral characteristics of the automobile industry helped to determine its political organization, strategy, and effectiveness. The industry's political strength lay in its geographic distribution and its connection to other industries. While originating in Detroit, American car makers maintain plants across the United States, from New Jersey to California. Thus, many members of Congress have an interest in maintaining the health of the industry. This, of course, gives the industry and the UAW considerable potential political clout. In addition to its geographic disbursement, the health of the automobile industry is important to a number of others that are the chief suppliers to car makers: steel, aluminum, and rubber, to name the major ones. Members of Congress who represent constituencies containing these industries, therefore, also have a strong interest in seeing to the economic well-being of the American automobile industry.

The Big Three and the UAW suspended their usually adversarial relationship to work together on the problem of Japanese imports. This temporary alliance enhanced the political effectiveness of the automobile sector. The traditional connections between congressional Democrats and the UAW, combined with the friendly relationship between business and the Republican Party, made for a remarkably broad political front.

In sum, the automobile VER with Japan demonstrated the vulnerability of American governmental institutions to intense political pressure. A free-trade president succumbed to protectionist pressure mainly because of the domestic political consequences of not doing so. Interests, processed through Congress, overcame the institutional trade liberalism of postwar U.S. trade policy. It is not the only such incident, and at the same time, it is hardly the norm. The episode does illustrate, however, the political clout of business, especially when labor agrees, with respect to public policy.

From Imports to Exports

In the 1990s, the American automobile industry added to its trade concerns access to foreign markets—especially Japan's. American car companies have found the Japanese market to be nearly impossible to penetrate. Japanese vehicle standards and certification procedures have served as a major nontariff barrier to the Japanese market. Such requirements as additional taxes, inspections, handling costs, required alterations, and a controlled distribution system have made the going difficult for American companies in Japan. Modifying American cars to meet Japanese environmental and safety standards can, at times, be costly. Moreover, the automobile dealer system in Japan is difficult to accommodate to American cars. The practice of exclusive dealerships for an automobile company makes "piggybacking" on an established dealer network impossible. In addition, real estate prices in Japan are exorbitant. And American car companies are not accustomed to the Japanese practice of selling cars door-to-door.[57]

As the VER stabilized the sales of Japanese cars in the United States, President George Bush made an initial effort to sell American products, including cars, in the Japanese market. On one celebrated trip to Japan, Bush brought along top corporate executives to demonstrate the U.S. commitment to expanding into Japanese markets. In the case of automobiles, however, the effort was somewhat embarrassing, as commentators noted that American manufacturers tried to sell cars that had not been adapted to driving on the left side of the road.[58]

The Clinton administration has pursued opening the Japanese automobile market to imports more aggressively than its predecessors. Under its leadership, on 23 August 1995, the United States signed an agreement with Japan concerning automobiles and auto parts. The general goal of the deal is to expand access to the Japanese market for American manufacturers. Among the key provisions are Japanese commitments to improve foreign access to Japanese auto dealerships, provide financial and other support to increase auto and auto imports into Japan, increase purchases from non-*keiretsu* parts suppliers in Japan, examine auto performance and technical standards, provide vehicle registration data for use in market research, and deregulate barriers to selling replacement parts in Japan.[59] Although American exports have done better in Japan than in the past, total market share remains small. For example, Big Three sales in Japan improved from 0.9 percent market share in 1995 to 1.1 percent in 1996.[60]

The effort to open the Japanese market to American cars and parts grew out of domestic political pressure. First, and somewhat clumsily, the Bush administration turned a state visit into a traveling sales show for a variety of America products, including automobiles. The administration was attempting to demonstrate its commitment to American producers and to increased exports in general. The Clinton administration refined this effort considerably, making this sort of bilateral negotiation a major feature of its trade policy. Still, it reflects the political sensitivity of the administration to powerful domestic political interests.

The Semiconductor Industry

Semiconductors are the key component of computers. Invented in the United States in the 1950s, the chip has spawned a huge, high-technology industry containing some of America's leading firms—for example, Intel and IBM. The semiconductor is emblematic of American technological prowess and dominance, fostering to some extent a certain patriotic zeal about which country is most prominent in the industry.

By the 1970s, the American semiconductor industry had earned the reputation of being a leading-edge, high-technology industry run by brilliant, risk-taking entrepreneurs. The industry was created in the 1950s based on the invention of the transistor, which replaced the vacuum tube as the principal component of electronic products. The transistor was a fraction of the size of the vacuum tube, ran at lower temperatures than its predecessor, and was more reliable. The transistor was followed by the invention of the integrated circuit, which placed a transistor on a single silicon wafer. Subsequent developments allowed an increasing number of transistors to be placed on wafers, greatly enhancing the power of the chips. This invention launched the semiconductor industry into prominence in electronics for civilian and defense use.[61]

With the spectacular achievements and possibilities of the semiconductor industry as a backdrop, two characteristics of semiconductors make the industry a candidate for special treatment in trade policy. First, semiconductors are the main component of electronic products and an incredible range of other manufactured goods. Semiconductors are the technological basis for virtually all consumer electronics products—televisions, stereo systems, compact disk players, video cassette recorder/players, camcorders, telephones, and so on. A host of other products also use semiconductors, from automobiles and clothes dryers to aircraft navigation systems and medical diagnostic equipment. In addition to these products, semiconductors, of course, are the principal component of computers; advances in computers depend upon advances in semiconductors. These uses of semiconductors highlight the centrality of the industry to other industries and therefore to the economy as a whole. The critical position of semiconductors is reason to give them special consideration in trade policy, special enough to warrant managed-trade policies by committed free traders.

In addition to the importance of semiconductors in the civilian economy, chips are critical in military hardware. Advanced, highly sophisticated weapons rely on a dependable supply of increasingly sophisticated semiconductors. Without an American industry, one could imagine a worst-case scenario in which American weapons makers could not get needed chips, because foreign producers were unwilling to supply them and no American firms were able to do so. A national security argument emerges for government intervention to maintain an American semiconductor industry.[62]

Based in northern California's Silicon Valley, American semiconductor firms grew rapidly in number and size, leading the world in the development of new, increasingly sophisticated products. Industry leaders eschewed government intervention in their business; they were able to conquer foreign markets without meddlesome government assistance. But by the later 1970s, the American semiconductor industry was experiencing its first major problems caused by competition from Japanese semiconductor firms. Owing to the 1975–76 global recession in the semiconductor market, American manufacturers of dynamic random access memory chips (DRAMs), the main product of the time, did not expand production capacity. Japanese firms, spurred on by government guidance and deep pockets, expanded capacity and were therefore in position to take advantage of the upturn in demand for DRAMs. This development cost the American industry considerable market share globally, and caused the industry to turn to government for the first time to address its problems.[63]

Working independently and through its new trade association, the Semiconductor Industry Association (SIA), U.S. semiconductor firms began to pressure federal government officials to stop alleged Japanese unfair trade practices in semiconductors. This effort, begun in the late 1970s, was the beginning of government action that led to the STA.

U.S. Government Response

Accusing Japanese electronics firms of unfair trade practices was nothing new, even in the late 1970s. The U.S. government had been involved in negotiating the opening of Japanese markets to U.S.-manufactured electronics products since the early 1960s.[64] Addressing such issues with respect to semiconductors, however, was new.

The U.S. government initially was not sympathetic to the semiconductor industry problems, nor was it terribly enthusiastic about pressuring the Japanese government to address trade issues. Government officials suggested that the complaints coming from Silicon Valley were unwarranted, more the response of inefficient, poorly managed companies, than of an industry with legitimate problems.[65] Moreover, government officials disagreed about the need for trade deals at all. While Commerce Department officials and their counterparts in the Office of the United States Trade Representative (USTR) were generally sympathetic to the semiconductor industry's complaints, officials in the State Department and National Security Council in particular, were disinclined to address them through trade negotiations, believing that maintaining sound diplomatic relations with Japan was more important than trade.[66]

Nevertheless, the United States negotiated several agreements with Japan on trade in semiconductors. The issues did not involve formal, legal changes in Japan that would open its markets to foreign semiconductor manufacturers; Japan had already eliminated most of such barriers. But the legal restrictions were quickly replaced by informal practices that effectively closed the Japanese semiconductor market to anyone but Japanese firms. Thus, between 1973 and 1975, Japan was compelled by U.S. pressure "to eliminate its formal import and investment restrictions."[67] But Japan immediately took "liberalization countermeasures" to undermine the legal elimination of these restrictions, including, for example, "MITI (Ministry of International Trade and Industry) subsidies to encourage product specialization among the producers and proposals to cooperate in research, product development, production, and sales."[68]

The 1980s

The U.S.–Japan negotiations in the early 1980s were aimed at the dumping of Japanese-produced semiconductors in the American market and opening the Japanese market to foreign-made chips. The first agreement provided for the Japanese to coordinate chip prices. While potentially effective, the U.S. Justice Department quashed it by threatening anti-trust action against Japanese firms.[69] A 1983 agreement attempted to create long-term relationships between U.S. chip makers and Japanese users—in this case, electronics firms. This too appeared to work at the outset, but when demand for semiconductors skyrocketed, the long-term relationships ended within a year.[70] Meanwhile, the two countries were involved in ongoing talks under the auspices of the U.S.–Japan Work Group on High Technology. Although the group met regularly throughout 1982 and 1983, the meetings had little effect on opening the Japanese semiconductor market or on other unfair trade practices attributed to Japanese firms.[71]

In sum, the U.S. government had been dealing with the Japanese government to address issues connected to trade in semiconductors for a number of years prior to the STA. Though marked by legal accomplishments and occasional signs of progress, these efforts were not enough to forestall the problems confronted by the U.S. semiconductor industry resulting from competition from Japanese producers.

The Semiconductor Trade Arrangement of 1986

The U.S.–Japan Semiconductor Trade Arrangement of 1986 was the result of years of disputes and negotiations between the United States and Japan over trade in semiconductors. The STA did two things: (1) It set restrictions on alleged dumping of chips by Japanese firms in the U.S. market, and (2) it established a schedule and targets for opening the Japanese semiconductor market to foreign manufacturers. This episode in U.S. trade policy history has been well documented, applauded, and criticized.[72] The American semiconductor industry had experienced serious decline in various products since the late 1970s, and by the mid 1980s, it looked to many industry observers as though the days of American dominance of the global semiconductor industry were numbered. The STA reflected an unusual U.S. government effort to address the competitiveness problems of a key industry, going beyond the straightforward protection employed in other troubled industries such as steel, textiles, and automobiles.[73]

Events Leading to the STA

The STA was concluded in 1986 after several hectic months of activity by the SIA, individual American semiconductor firms, and by the U.S. government itself. By 1985, the plight of the American semiconductor industry was becoming clear and difficult to ignore. Skidding sales and market share coupled with layoffs called attention to a once highly-touted industry now in trouble. Several firms filed antidumping petitions against Japanese semiconductor firms, joined by the Commerce Department's own petition, an unprecedented action.[74] In addition, the SIA charged Japan with unfair trade practices under Section 301 of the Trade Act of 1974. This action eventually culminated in the conclusion of the U.S.–Japan Semiconductor Arrangement.[75] The STA was a negotiated settlement of the dispute raised in the SIA petition. It "had formal legal status as an agreement concluded pursuant to Section 301(d)(2) of the Trade Act of 1974, and the President indicated that any failure by the Japanese government to adhere to the Arrangement would itself constitute a violation of Section 301,"[76] which would result in U.S. action.

The STA addresses two major trade problems with Japan: dumping and market access. With respect to dumping, the STA provided that Japanese firms would stop dumping chips in the U.S. market at below fair market value.[77] The fair price was to be determined on a company basis by the U.S. Department of Commerce with information supplied by Japanese firms. When in 1987 the United States determined that the Japanese had, in fact, violated the STA, President Reagan took retaliatory action, which apparently impressed the Japanese sufficiently to bring them into compliance.[78]

The second major issue addressed by the STA is access to Japanese semiconductor markets. This provision of the STA was stated in a so-called secret side letter to the U.S. negotiating team, which indicated that the Japanese government accepted a target of 20 percent of the Japanese market for foreign-manufactured semiconductors by 1991 and that the Japanese government would encourage Japanese users to buy more foreign-manufactured chips.[79] This provision has also been the center of controversy. Chips manufactured by foreign-based firms did not account for 20 percent of the Japanese market by 1991, the expiration date of the STA. This shorfall caused considerable consternation among American semiconductor manufacturers, and as a result, the 20 percent target was made formal in the successor to the STA, the New Semiconductor Trade Agreement of 1991.

Several factors led the United States to pursue the STA in 1986. First, an otherwise unenthusiastic administration faced unprecedented trade deficits—over $150 billion globally, and over $50 billion with Japan. The sheer size of these imbalances caused the administration to look for possible ways to reduce them. Second, Congress continued to support action against the Japanese quite vocally. Although Congress did not formally enact the STA, it supported the administration's doing so. Third, key government officials in the Commerce Department and the USTR continued to press for government action to address trade problems with Japan. Experienced in trade negotiations with Japan, these individuals energetically pursued an agreement between the United States and Japan on semiconductors. Fourth, the Defense Department began to be concerned about the availability of semiconductors for use in weapons. For national security reasons, a strong domestic semiconductor industry now seemed important.[80] Combined, these factors allowed this unusual agreement to be concluded.

Explaining the STA

Executive branch officials were interested in dealing with the problem of trade with Japan in semiconductors. Top political appointees in the Commerce Department, along with officials from the USTR, sought to open the Japanese semiconductor market to American firms and to curtail unfair trade practices—mainly dumping—by Japanese semiconductor firms in the U.S. market. Lionel Olmer and Clyde Prestowitz of the Commerce Department participated in the years of negotiations with the Japanese that led to the STA. These officials were motivated by the goals of achieving an agreement with Japan that addressed the two principal problems in trade in semiconductors.[81]

In addition to the direct participation by motivated negotiators in the Commerce Department and USTR, the Reagan administration tried to induce the Japanese government to modify the trade practices of Japanese semiconductor firms. For example, the Commerce Department took the unprecedented step (for a federal government agency) of filing an antidumping petition against Japanese semiconductor firms. This action, along with similar complaints filed by some American semiconductor firms and the SIA, caused the Japanese government to come to the negotiating table, eventually agreeing to the STA.[82]

Congressional Concern

The semiconductor industry does not employ great numbers of people, nor is it geographically distributed so that it would have a noticeable presence in a significant number of states and congressional districts.

Nonetheless, its success became a subject of congressional concern in the early to mid 1980s. Perhaps owing to its importance in the American civilian economy and national security, Congress held hearings to publicize the trade problems with Japan the industry had been experiencing. Although not resulting in a specific law, these hearings served notice to the Japanese that there was significant official government concern about semiconductor trade with Japan. Bearing in mind Congress's reputation for being willing to impose trade sanctions on foreign countries, these hearings helped to set a serious tone on the part of the U.S. government for dealing with Japan on the issue.[83]

Interest-group Influence

The SIA, the major trade association representing American semiconductor manufacturers, does not maintain a political action committee, nor does it keep a formal office in Washington, D.C.[84] Because the industry employs relatively few people and because of its geographic distribution, the industry is denied widespread, constituent-based access to members of Congress. Yet the American semiconductor industry, largely through the SIA, has managed to play a significant part in trade policy, particularly in relation to Japan.[85]

The SIA's success is attributable to several factors. First, the SIA concentrated its policy efforts at the federal level on several key issues: intellectual property protection, dumping by foreign firms in the U.S. semiconductor market, and access to foreign markets, mainly Japan's. Keeping a narrow focus, the association was able to maintain its members' support and avoid costly disputes among them while also concentrating its efforts on a few, select, winnable targets. Second, capitalizing on the industry's high-technology, can-do image, the SIA brought top company executives to Washington to lobby members of Congress directly. Their technical and business reputations preceding them, these executives frequently impressed legislators and their staffs, which certainly contributed to their influence over policy making. Third, the association has been tenacious in its pursuit of certain objectives, especially those relating to trade policy. Association staff members have been with the group for many years during which they have established long-term working relationships with government officials. These relationships allow for constant interaction between industry representatives and government, arguably creating consensus in support of policies, and certainly increasing the input of industry in policy making.[86]

The American Electronics Association (AEA) worked with the SIA on the STA, endorsing its position on semiconductor trade issues with Japan. Individual companies supported the position as well, adding to the coalition pressuring U.S. government officials to do something about semiconductor trade with Japan.

The SIA's considerable involvement in the development of U.S. trade policy with Japan is consistent with the long-acknowledged influence of interest groups over trade policy. Concentrating on a relatively narrow set of issues and working closely with government officials—particularly in the executive branch—an interest group was able to exert considerable influence over trade policy.

Balancing Free Trade with Market Access

The STA included two major provisions: (1) stop Japanese firms from engaging in unfair trade practices in the American market (dumping); and (2) open Japan's semiconductor market to foreign—almost entirely American—manufacturers. A free-trade–oriented administration, as the Reagan administration most certainly was, would have a difficult time accepting the antidumping provisions of the STA if this were all that the agreement included. While dumping is legitimately considered to be an unfair trade practice, taking action to prevent it might be interpreted as protectionist, or at least a step that would likely lead to more protectionist policies. Measures to stop dumping, however, can be made more politically acceptable if they are accompanied by actions that are intended to increase trade. The STA provisions intended to open the Japanese market for foreign-made semiconductors fall into this category. A policy that increases trade balances a trade that constricts it, making the whole package more acceptable.[87]

Free-trade Administration

Since the 1930s, Congress has been delegating trade policy authority to the executive branch. Taking a broader national interest, the executive is more able to resist protectionist pressures from domestic industries in favor of free-trade policies that benefit the nation as a whole.[88] The Reagan administration was no exception to this trend, and added to the structural relationship its ideological preference for free-trade policies.

The Reagan administration nevertheless supported policies that could be considered nothing but protectionist with respect to the automobile industry.[89] The reason lies in the fact that, although the presidency is more insulated from pressure from special pleaders, it is not completely isolated. Presidents must stand for reelection, and persistent, powerful interests located in key electoral states can get the administration's attention and favor. Moreover, understanding the need to deal with the problems of politically potent industries like automobiles, the administration may choose to accept some relatively small measure of protectionism in order to avoid more protectionism in policies produced by Congress. This is arguably the rationale behind the Reagan administration's policies on trade in automobiles and textiles.

Similarly, one could extend the argument to semiconductors. Fearing increasing hostility in Congress on trade with Japan, the administration chose not only to accept a partially protectionist policy on semiconductors, but to pursue one. This might have been motivated in part by the dramatic increase in the trade deficit with Japan. Thus, the willingness—indeed, some might say the enthusiastic support—of the Reagan administration for the STA lay in the historical relationship between Congress and the presidency on trade policy. While being able to resist protectionist pressures more than Congress, the presidency is unable to prevent such policies altogether, requiring it to accommodate interests with some protection in order to avoid even more if it did not do so.

Summary and Observations

Several factors explain the pursuit and conclusion of the STA. The balanced nature of the agreement and the critical position of semiconductors in the American economy, combined with the special case of Japan, permitted normatively free-trade executive branch officials to find one justification for pursuing a policy consistent with managed trade. The administration could find another justification for coming dangerously close to endorsing a protectionist policy in arguing that doing so effectively preempted the generation of more dramatic protectionist policies in Congress. Interest-group pressure played a role. In this case, interest groups did not weigh in with overwhelming political clout. Rather, through a deliberate strategy of keeping goals focused and priorities clear, the SIA developed a close working relationship with government officials, allowing it to have considerable input in the development of the STA. Meanwhile, Congress helped set the tone for the STA, articulating a clear concern for the problem in semiconductor trade with Japan.

In the STA episode, the Commerce Department and the USTR played their roles as expected. The former helped to precipitate the negotiations leading to the agreement by filing an antidumping petition against Japanese semiconductor firms. Commerce Department officials, moreover, were heavily involved in U.S.–Japan negotiations on trade in electronics in the early 1980s. At least part of the initiative to direct the United States to a tougher stand on trade with Japan (not limited to semiconductors) was channeled through Commerce Secretary Malcolm Baldridge, who enjoyed a close relationship with President Reagan. The USTR took the lead role in negotiating the arrangement in keeping with its function as the chief trade agency in the executive branch.

The Commerce Department and the USTR behaved in ways their institutional characters predict. The Commerce Department's close connection with business helps to define its mission as American business's protector. The USTR's role as the top trade agency in the executive branch put it in a position to carrying out the policy of negotiating a bilateral, sectoral trade agreement with Japan.

Subsequent Agreements

The 1986 STA expired in 1991, at which time the Japanese and U.S. governments negotiated a new semiconductor deal. Both sides made clear that this agreement was not formally an extension of the 1986 STA. Instead, it was ostensibly a new arrangement based on the experience of the prior one. The 1991 Semiconductor Trade Agreement changed the dumping provisions of its predecessor. The Commerce Department ended its practice of calculating floor prices, while MITI assumed responsibility for a new antidumping procedure that "required Japanese companies to continue to collect the data previously given to the Commerce Department" to be used in any new antidumping case.[90] The relaxation of the U.S. position on dumping came at least in part as a result of the efforts of major American chip consumers who feared the loss of reliable sources of comparatively cheap semiconductors resulting from excessive antidumping provisions.[91] The 1991 accord formalized the Japanese commitment to allocate 20 percent of its domestic semiconductor market to foreign producers, a target that had been set originally in the secret side letter that accompanied the 1986 STA.

The two major provisions of the 1991 pact reflect the negotiations between the principal trade associations representing the semiconductor industry and the computer industry, the major chip consumer in the United States. The Computer Systems Policy Project (CSPP), consisting of large computer manufacturers, took a strong position on the antidumping provisions of the 1986 deal. For this group, renewal of this part of the pact was unacceptable. For its part, the SIA was fully aware of the controversy surrounding the fair market value provision of the 1986 STA and was willing to negotiate on the issue. However, access to Japanese markets remained a central goal for the chip association. The CSPP and the SIA came to a natural compromise. The computer manufacturers won changes in the antidumping provisions of the agreement, while semiconductor manufacturers got a formal Japanese commitment on market share going to foreign producers.[92]

One of the most striking aspects of the process leading to the 1991 pact was the influence private associations had over the negotiations. While responsible for the formal negotiations, of course, U.S. government agencies did the bidding of private industry. With government approval, the CSPP and the SIA worked out the two major provisions of the agreement.[93]

The Japanese and U.S. governments were at the negotiating table again in 1996. With the 1991 agreement close to expiration, negotiators sought a new pact that reduced direct government intervention while increasing the importance of private industry.[94] Negotiated in Vancouver, B.C., Canada, the 1996 accord transfers some governmental responsibilities to a private council consisting of industry representatives from Japan and the United States, with the possible addition of other countries later. The council's general task is to gather data on trade flows and market conditions in Japan and elsewhere.[95]

The dramatically reduced level of government intervention in this trade accord reflects changes in the global semiconductor industry that have mitigated U.S. concerns originally expressed in the 1986 STA. American companies are no longer concerned with the prospect of Japanese firms controlling major technologies. The American semiconductor industry is spending as much or more on research and development as the Japanese and are seeing appreciably better results from their efforts. In addition, foreign manufacturers now claim a 31 percent share of the Japanese semiconductor market; American firms alone hold a 20 percent market share in Japan. That fact goes a long way toward negating U.S. concerns prominent in 1986 about opening the Japanese market to foreign-made chips. Finally, American and Japanese firms no longer dominate the global semiconductor industry. Korean, Taiwanese, and some Chinese firms have established themselves in the industry, commanding the attention of U.S. and Japanese negotiators in Vancouver. For this reason, the 1996 accord remains open to the inclusion of new countries in a global semiconductor pact.[96]

Economic factors—in Japan, the United States, and globally—changed the nature of the 1996 agreement. The diffusion of the industry warrants admission of additional countries to the negotiating table. As a domestic political issue, the Clinton administration needed to conclude a semiconductor deal with Japan to demonstrate the president's success in trade policy. With his political support in Silicon Valley considerably weaker than it was in 1992, the president wanted to claim victory—although a modest one—to shore up whatever high-technology support he could get for his 1996 reelection bid.[97]

Conclusion

Sectoral agreements serve the critical purpose of providing an escape route from the path to free trade. Mounting political pressure, generated by industries adversely affected by foreign competition, is sometimes irresistible, and government officials find no recourse but to appease them. In the semiconductor case, the industry and the Commerce Department had begun the process of seeking administrative relief. Based on alleged dumping and restrictive access to the Japanese market, the industry and its government ally petitioned for antidumping and Section 301 remedies. The United States and the Japanese negotiated the STA to avoid full enforcement of these remedies. The automobile VER is an instance where U.S. trade law did not respond very well to an industry with dubious claims about the causes of its problems. The USITC, for example, determined that, while the American automobile industry was suffering losses to Japanese car makers, the fault lay with executives in Detroit, not with foreign competition. In spite of the absence of a legitimate justification for government action, the political heat applied by American car companies and the UAW forced the government to act. Steel illustrates the persistence of an industry in placing demands on the government for trade restraint. Over the course of twenty-five years, steel makers effectively used avenues to policy makers to obtain VRAs.

Substantively, the steel VRAs and the automobile VER were the more clear cases of protection, although the latter did a better job of cutting off imports than the former.[98] The STA was less blatantly protectionist, though it served the purpose of shielding American semiconductor manufacturers from foreign competition. The STA was set apart from the voluntary agreements in steel and automobiles by the market-opening provision added to it by the side letter in which the Japanese indicated that foreign chips would take 20 percent of the Japanese market by 1991. Because of this provision, proponents of the deal could argue that the STA would lead to more trade, thus a plausible step in the direction of trade liberalization.

The sectoral characteristics and political organization of the two industries had a great deal to do with the eventual trade deals. Because of these distinctions, the industries' political claims were attended to by different governmental institutions. In all three cases, industry pressure caused an institutional response. The executive responded to direct pressure from the steel industry and indirect pressure routed through Congress and the system of administrative relief. Congress was at the center of the automobile deal, while the executive—by means of the administrative relief process—was the principal focus of the chip pact. In all cases, the executive closed the deal with foreign governments. To sum up, the automobile VER was old-fashioned protectionism; the executive negotiated a limit on exports in the face of the strong likelihood that Congress would pass a bill that would establish quotas. The STA was more complicated, reflecting the importance of Section 301 and antidumping provisions of the U.S. trade law. It had the effect of protecting American producers by means of antidumping provisions.

At the same time, it captured the goal of export-oriented American firms wishing to sell more goods overseas. The steel industry also used AD and to a lesser extent CVD provisions in the law to pressure the executive into action, the outcome of which was protection.

Sectoral agreements are the result of successful business efforts to get government to help it with respect to international trade. They demonstrate how a determined industry can take advantage of this connection to achieve policy objectives that are antithetical to the general thrust of U.S. trade policy. This dynamic is wholly consistent with the pluralist model of American politics, as determined minorities foist their will upon a resistant government. The success, however, does not mean a complete reversal of public policy. It is instead a compromise made by public officials, a concession to the private sector made necessary by the porous character of American government, but one that can be successfully undertaken without losing sight of the central goal of trade liberalization.

Endnotes

1. Michael L. Dertouzos, Richard K. Lester, and Robert M. Solow, *Made in America: Regaining the Productive Edge* (New York: HarperPerennial, 1990), 278.
2. Donald F. Barnett and Robert W. Crandall, *Up From the Ashes: The Rise of the Steel Minimill in the United States* (Washington, D.C.: Brookings Institutions, 1986), 1–2.
3. Ibid., chap. 2.
4. Barnett and Crandall, *Up from the Ashes*, 2–5. For a readable description of these processes in some detail, see Christopher G. L. Hall, *Steel Phoenix: The Fall and Rise of the U.S. Steel Industry* (New York: St. Martin's, 1997), chap. 1.
5. Barnett and Crandall, *Up from the Ashes*, 5.
6. Donald F. Barnett and Louis Schorsch, *Steel: Upheaval in a Basic Industry* (Cambridge, Mass.: Ballinger, 1983), 51—52.
7. Harland Prechel, "Steel and the State: Industry Politics and Business Policy Formation, 1940–1989," *American Sociological Review* 55 (1990): 648.
8. Barnett and Schorsch, *Steel*, 52–54.
9. Prechel, 656.
10. Ibid.
11. Ibid.

12. Ibid., 658.
13. Ibid.
14. Ibid., 659.
15. Ibid.
16. Ibid.
17. Barnett and Schorsch, *Steel*, 54.
18. Dertouzos, Lester, and Solow, *Made in America*, 285.
19. Hall, *Steel Phoenix*, 68–72.
20. Prechel, 661.
21. Ibid., 662.
22. Ibid.
23. Hall, *Steel Phoenix*, 267–73.
24. Roger S. Ahlbrandt, Richard J. Fruehan, and Frank Giarratani, *The Renaissance of American Steel: Lessons for Managers in Competitive Industries* (New York: Oxford Univ. Press, 1996), 24–27.
25. Stefanie Lenway, Kathleen Rehbein, and Laura Starks, "The Impact of Protectionism on Firm Wealth: the Experience of the Steel Industry," *Southern Economic Journal* 56 (April 1990): 1079–93.
26. Stefanie Lenway, Randall Morck, and Bernard Young, "Rent Seeking, Protectionism, and Innovation in the American Steel Industry," *The Economic Journal* 106 (March 1996): 410–21.
27. Robert W. Crandall, "The Effects of U.S. Trade Protection for Autos and Steel," *Brookings Papers on Economic Activity* 1 (1987): 280.
28. Ibid., 281.
29. Ibid., 283.
30. Robert E. Scott and Thea M. Lee, "The Costs of Trade Protection Reconsidered: U.S. Steel, Textiles, and Apparel," in Robert A. Blecker, ed., *U.S. Trade Policy and Global Growth* (Armonk, N.Y.: M. E. Sharpe, 1996), 114.
31. A VRA allows foreign firms to keep prices higher than they would have been otherwise, thus benefiting from the trade policy. Protection by other means, say a tariff, would send those extra dollars to the federal government instead.
32. Scott and Lee, "The Costs of Trade Protection Reconsidered," 113–17.
33. Lawrence Chimerine, Alan Tonelson, Karl von Schriltz, and Gregory Stanko, *Can the Phoenix Survive? The Fall and Rise of the American Steel Industry* (Washington, D.C.: Economic Strategy Institute, 1994), 64–66.
34. See Mancur Olson, *The Logic of Collective Action: Public Goods and the Theory of Groups* (Cambridge, Mass.: Harvard Univ. Press, 1971), 53–57.
35. Hall, *Steel Phoenix*, 124–25.
36. American Automobile Manufacturers Association, "Employment in the Motor Vehicle and Equipment Manufacturing Industry," <http:// www.aama. com/data/table14.html> 1998 (18 August 1998). This figure includes the following employment categories: SIC 3711, Motor Vehicles and Car Bodies;

SIC 3714, Parts and Accessories; SIC 3713, Truck and Bus Bodies; SIC 3715, Truck Trailers; and SIC 3716, Motor Homes.

37. Nissan dropped the Datsun nameplate in the early 1980s, selling its cars under the Nissan name. For an excellent narrative of Nissan's development and eventual entrance into the American market, see David Halberstam, *The Reckoning* (New York: Avon, 1986).

38. The annual automobile ratings in *Consumer Reports* for 1995, 1996, and 1997 consistently demonstrate the quality of foreign-made vehicles (mostly Japanese and German) in the American market, although they are far from dominant. Foreign products do well in small, medium, sports, and wagon categories, while American nameplates do well in large, minivan, sport-utility, and compact pickup categories. See *Consumer Reports,* April 1995, 255–57; *Consumer Reports,* April 1996, 48–49; *Consumer Reports,* April 1997, 54–55.

39. Ralph Nader, *Unsafe at Any Speed: The Designed-in Dangers of the American Automobile* (New York: Grossman, 1965).

40. Chrysler repaid the loans in full, although CEO Lee Iacocca argued that an additional charge in the form of warrants on Chrysler's stock held by the federal government should not have to be born by the company. Iacocca turned out to be unpersuasive, and Chrysler eventually bought the warrants from the government in an auction. Robert B. Reich and John D. Donahue, *New Deals: The Chrysler Revival and the American System* (New York: Times Books, 1985), 254–57.

41. James P. Womack, Daniel T. Jones, and Daniel Roos, *The Machine That Changed the World* (New York: Rawson, 1990), 201–02.

42. Domestic content legislation would have required foreign auto makers to build their cars using an increasing percentage of American-made parts. The goal, according to one plan, was 90 percent American parts in imported vehicles. The legislation did not pass in any form. See Philip A. Mundo, *Interest Groups: Cases and Characteristics* (Chicago, Ill.: Nelson Hall, 1992), 136n.

43. Dale Tate, "Sagging U.S. Auto Industry Pleads for Federal Help," *Congressional Quarterly Weekly Report,* 10 May 1980, 1264; Ikuo Kabashima and Hidea Sato, "Local Content and Congressional Politics: Interest-group Theory and Foreign-policy Implications," *International Studies Quarterly,* 30 (1986): 298.

44. Dale Tate, "Import Restraints Urged: Sagging U.S. Auto Industry Pleads for Federal Help," *Congressional Quarterly Weekly Report,* 10 May 1980, 1262.

45. Douglas R. Nelson, "The Political Economy of U.S. Automobile Protection," in Anne O. Krueger, ed., *The Political Economy of American Trade Policy* (Chicago, Ill.: Univ. of Chicago Press, 1996), 138. See chapter 6 for a discussion of the escape clause.

46. Tate, "Import Restraints Urged," 1264.
47. Nelson, "The Political Economy of U.S. Automobile Protection," 138.
48. Tate, "Import Restraints Urged," 1265.
49. Ibid., 1266.
50. Nelson, "The Political Economy of U.S. Automobile Protection," 139–43.
51. Judy Sarasohn, "Legislation on Hold: Auto Import Curbs Shelved As Japan Agrees on Limits," *Congressional Quarterly Weekly Report*, 9 May 1981, 798.
52. Ibid., 798.
53. Tate, "To Help U.S. Automakers: Congress Prepared to Slow Influx of Japanese Autos If Negotiations Founder," *Congressional Quarterly Weekly Report*, 28 March 1981, 551.
54. Sarasohn, "Legislation on Hold," 798; Tate, "To Help U.S. Automakers," 551.
55. Nelson, "The Political Economy of U.S. Automobile Protection," 144–45.
56. Jerome B. McKinney, *Risking a Nation: U.S.–Japanese Trade Failure and the Need for Political, Social, and Economic Reformation* (Lanham, Md.: Univ. Press of America, 1995), 203.
57. Ibid., 202.
58. Low, *Trading Free*, 117.
59. United States Trade Representative, *1997 Trade Policy Agenda and 1996 Annual Report of the President of the United States on the Trade Agreements Program* (Washington, D.C.: U.S. Government Printing Office, 1997), 170.
60. Ibid., 171.
61. Clyde V. Prestowitz, Jr., *Trading Places: How We Allowed Japan to Take the Lead* (New York: Basic Books, 1988), 29–32.
62. The U.S. semiconductor industry benefited from the willingness of the federal government, through the Defense Department and the National Aeronautics and Space Administration, to underwrite research and development. See Prestowitz, 32; and Thomas R. Howell, Brent L. Bartlett, and Warren Davis, *Creating Advantage: Semiconductors and Government Industrial Policy in the 1990s* (San Jose, Calif. and Washington, D.C.: Semiconductor Industry Association and Dewey Ballantine, 1992), 134–35.
63. Mundo, *Interest Groups*, chap. 3.
64. Howell, Bartlett, and Davis, *Creating Advantage*, 25–133.
65. Prestowitz, *Trading Places*, 48–49, 56.
66. Ibid., 52, 56.
67. Howell, Bartlett, and Davis, *Creating Advantage*, 77.
68. Ibid., 77–78.
69. Prestowitz, *Trading Places*, 49.
70. Ibid., 53–54.
71. Ibid., 50–53.

72. For an account of the process leading to the 1986 agreement, see Prestowitz, *Trading Places,* chap. 2. For a balanced assessment of the agreement, see Kenneth Flamm, *Mismanaged Trade? Strategic Policy and the Semiconductor Industry* (Washington, D.C.: Brookings Institution, 1996), chaps. 4 and 5; and Tyson, *Who's Bashing Whom?,* chap. 4. For a defense of the agreement, see Howell, Bartlett, and Davis, *Creating Advantage,* 49–133.

73. Low, *Trading Free,* chap. 5.

74. Tyson, *Who's Bashing Whom?,* 107–08.

75. Howell, Bartlett, and Davis, *Creating Advantage,* 80.

76. Ibid.

77. Fair market value is usually considered to be the price at which a product is sold in the producer's home market or in a third market. U.S. law also allows fair market value to be determined based on estimations of production costs of the product. See I. M. Destler, *American Trade Politics,* 3rd ed. (Washington, D.C.: Institute for International Economics, 1995), 311.

78. The STA's antidumping provisions were controversial from the moment the Arrangement was signed. Critics contend that these provisions induced the Japanese government to form a semiconductor cartel supported by a floor price, which limited supply of chips to U.S. consumers and kept their prices artificially high. Supporters argue that the STA did not cause an increase in chip prices in the United States and that Japanese cartel behavior was not related to the STA. Tyson provides a balanced view, suggesting that while the STA did not cause the Japanese to form a semiconductor cartel with its attendant consequences for price and supply, but that it gave them an excuse to do so. See Tyson, *Who's Bashing Whom?,* 111–30. See also Flamm, *Mismanaged Trade?,* chaps. 4 and 5.

79. According to Howell, Bartlett, and Davis, the more complete statement is as follows: (1) The Government of Japan recognizes the U.S. semiconductor industry's expectations that semiconductor sales in Japan of foreign capital-affiliated companies will grow to at least slightly above 20 percent of the Japanese market in five years. The Government of Japan considers that this can be realized and welcomes its realization. The attainment of such an expectation depends on competitive factors, the sales efforts of foreign capital-affiliated companies, the purchasing efforts of the semiconductor users in Japan and the efforts of both Governments. (2) The Government of Japan will encourage Japanese users to purchase more foreign-based semiconductors and to provide further support for expanded sales by foreign capital-affiliated semiconductor companies in Japan through the establishment of an organization to provide sales assistance for foreign capital-affiliated semiconductor companies and through promotion of long-term relationships between Japanese semiconductor purchasers and foreign capital-affiliated semiconductor companies. See Howell, Bartlett, and Davis, *Creating Advantage,* 80.

80. Tyson, *Who's Bashing Whom?*, 106–09; and Prestowitz, *Trading Places*, 105–09, 146–78.
81. Prestowitz, *Trading Places*, chaps. 2 and 3.
82. Tyson, *Who's Bashing Whom?*, 106–07.
83. Congress held numerous hearings on the topic of trade—specifically, the trade balance with Japan. See, for example, Joint Economic Committee, Subcommittee on Economic Goals and Intergovernmental Policy, *Impact on the U.S. Economy of Imbalanced and Unfair Trade Relations—the Case of Japan*, 99th Congress, 1st sess., 22 August 1985.
84. Mundo, *Interest Groups*, chap. 3.
85. Ibid.; David B. Yoffie, "How an Industry Creates Political Advantage," *Harvard Business Review* 66 (May–June 1988): 82–89.
86. Mundo, *Interest Groups*, chap. 3; Yoffie "How an Industry Creates Political Advantage."
87. The NSTA, which replaced the STA in 1991, dropped most of the antidumping measures of its predecessor, focusing almost exclusively on opening up the Japanese market to semiconductors manufactured by U.S. companies. Tyson, *Who's Bashing Whom?*, 130–32.
88. Destler, *American Trade Politics*, chap. 2.
89. Low, *Trading Free*, 111–18.
90. Flamm, *Mismanaged Trade?*, 224–25.
91. The Computer Systems Policy Project (CSPP) and the SIA quietly negotiated this sensitive part of the agreement in preparation for U.S. negotiations with Japan.
92. Douglas A. Irwin, "Trade Politics and the Semiconductor Industry," in Anne O. Krueger, ed., *The Political Economy of American Trade Policy* (Chicago, Ill.: Univ. of Chicago Press, 1996), 56–58.
93. Ibid., 58.
94. David E. Sanger, "U.S. and Japan in Last-Minute Effort to Reach Accord," *New York Times*, 1 August 1996, D1, D4.
95. Andrew Pollack, "A U.S.–Japan Chip Industry Council (Or, Is It a Cartel?)," *New York Times*, 6 August 1996, D3.
96. David E. Sanger, "For U.S.–Japan Trade Pact, Less at Stake," *New York Times*, 3 August 1996, D1, D2.
97. Ibid.
98. Crandall, "The Effects of U.S. Trade Protection for Autos and Steel," 272–77.

8

Conclusion

The U.S. government has been dealing with trade issues since the founding of the republic. From the outset, officials linked trade policy to domestic economic concerns. Tariffs protected infant American industries against mature foreign producers, and they provided a reliable source of revenue to the federal government. In this and other ways, politics and economics were joined from the beginning of the country. Throughout trade policy's history in the United States, government constantly adjusted to new challenges coming from within and beyond the nation's borders. Economics may have driven politics, but it is certainly true in international trade that policy affected economics as well.

Pointing out that politics and economics are related is hardly novel, but trade policy is peculiar; it straddles the line between domestic policy and foreign policy. This makes it a useful tool for understanding a broader trend in politics, which is the increasing penetration of domestic politics by international issues. Communications technology, access to information through the Internet, cable news, the traditional print and electronic media, and relatively easy travel worldwide have shrunk the globe, connecting developments outside the United States to domestic policy issues. The connection between international and domestic issues puts new stress on political institutions.

International trade captures these developments in particularly clear ways. Raising or lowering tariffs is not purely a domestic matter, of course. Any country that does so must consider the internationally agreed-upon rules embedded in the General Agreement on Tariffs and

Trade (GATT) and in the World Trade Organization (WTO). The new reality does not necessarily mean that governments, including the United States, will not act in what they view to be their best national interests, but it does mean that they must take account of ever tighter constraints and must devise clever ways to deal with them. In short, the response of American political institutions to the pressure of international and, to some extent domestic, economic changes appears in U.S. trade policy.

Since many nations face problems similar to those confronted by the United States, examining the response of American political institutions to economic changes embodied in trade issues provides the extra benefit of considering American exceptionalism. Is the American political system fundamentally different from other developed representative democracies? Certainly the basic arrangement of government institutions is unique; no other country exactly copies the separation of powers and federalist structure of the United States. Examining U.S. trade policy is a way to keep an eye turned toward the possibility that the American political response to new pressure is different than others or perhaps even unique.

The Domestic Foundations of Trade Policy

I have argued in this book that most, but not all, U.S. trade policy is rooted in domestic politics. How trade policies directly affected Americans has been a major concern of policy makers for most trade policy decisions; this means that domestic political institutions and processes create trade policy. Whether the causes for changes in policy come from economic changes within the United States or from developments outside it—the much ballyhooed globalization of the economy—trade policy makes its way through the domestic policy process.

The domestic policy process involves two major analytic concerns. The first is the nature of the process itself. One can conceptualize it as a three-stage process: agenda setting, program adoption, and implementation. For analytic purposes, it is convenient to imagine each phase as isolated from the other two and that the three proceed in a logical, linear sequence. Applying the basic model to reality quickly results in complexity and compromise of neat categories. One phase typically merges into the next, and information is constantly in motion, moving among the three phases of the process. So, for example, experience with implementing a particular program frequently leads to new elements getting on the agenda and eventually becoming part of a new program. Program adoption, which usually involves Congress, can attract numerous agenda items from all sorts of policy areas, resulting in legislation that combines a remarkable number and variety of issues. The point is that in the real world the policy process is messy and riven with loose ends, compromises, and imperfection.

The second analytic concern has to do with the factors that largely determine policy outcomes: ideas, interests, and institutions. Identifying and assessing the interaction of these factors is useful in any aspect of politics, including the development of trade policy. Ideas, interests, and institutions play some role in each of the three phases of the policy process. The goal of this book has been to determine the importance of each at different points in the policy process and to conclude what, if any, difference that makes.

Trade Policy and the Political Response to Economic Change

The other half of a systemic perspective on political economy is government. Keeping in mind that U.S. trade policy is mostly a matter of the domestic policy process, the central point here is that American political institutions involved with trade policy have dealt with these economic changes in a uniquely American way. If this means that the United States is different than other countries in dealing with internal and external economic stress, then it is safe to conclude that American exceptionalism is alive and well.

Ideas

An observer of U.S. trade policy at the end of the twentieth century would have to conclude that trade liberalization is clearly the norm. The idea that free trade is in the national interest in the long run has come to dominate the trade debate. Not everyone agrees that free trade is a good thing, nor is there uniform opinion about how to effectuate trade liberalization. The fact that free trade is the starting point of discourse on the topic, however, means that it sets the parameters of the debate.

Adopting the idea was a functional adaptation of the American political system to emerging economic realities. Recognizing the costs trade liberalization would impose on some segments of American society, yet convinced of its long-term benefits, political leaders—especially the president—moved toward the goal of free trade, at different rates but without exception. The State Department was in the logical position to steer U.S. trade policy. Congress, however, created the United States Trade Representative (USTR), in part because the State Department considered trade a secondary issue. By the 1980s, the USTR became the voice of U.S. trade policy. Attuned to domestic political interests, the USTR nonetheless continued on the path of trade liberalization, following the predictable preferences of the White House.

Even Congress could not resist the logic of trade liberalization. More susceptible to particular interests than the executive, Congress has had a more difficult time balancing the need to be responsive to American producers with the willingness to pursue free-trade policies. Congress, however, has done just that. Sometimes moving in fits and starts, Congress has devised remarkably creative ways to attend to the interests of American industry while allowing trade liberalization to stay on track.

Interests

Producer interests have dominated trade policy battles for most of this century. The most striking example of their influence was the passage of the Smoot–Hawley Tariff in 1930. The enactment of the law became a feeding frenzy for protectionist groups, all seeking higher tariffs.[1] Since the 1930s, producer groups have continued to dominate the interest-group landscape focused on trade policy.

Although this continues to be the case, interest groups in favor of trade liberalization began to appear on the political scene in the 1960s and 1970s, and they have won some significant victories. Ideological or single-issue groups support free trade for analytic or normative reasons. Free trade is a good thing; opposing it is simply the act of parochial interests out to save their own businesses. Consumer groups occasionally weigh in on the side of trade liberalization, but the liberal tilt of such groups as Nader's Raiders leaves them suspicious of free trade: note, for example, Ralph Nader's opposition to the North American Free Trade Agreement (NAFTA). There is a growing number of businesses, however, in favor of free trade, not for normative reasons, but because it is in their interests. The Computer Systems Policy Project (CSPP) effectively articulated the position of major American computer companies that limiting the import of Japanese semiconductors—as the Semiconductor Trade Arrangement of 1986 did—damaged them. Thus, the CSPP was able to insert significant changes in the 1991 follow-up accord, making Japanese and other foreign-manufactured chips more easily available to American computer makers. As industries become more flexible in where they obtain inputs, they are likely to favor trade liberalization.

Institutions

American political institutions have absorbed the idea of free trade and devised ways to fend off protectionist interests. They have done so in ways quintessentially American. Congress has deflected protectionist pressure to the executive, the institution most able to take a broader national view and in a political position that allows it to offend the sensibilities of certain industries and their trade associations. Regardless of who has occupied the White House, interestingly enough, the chief executive has used the institutional powers available to him to adhere to trade liberalization.

The American bureaucracy provides an excellent institutional home for a contradictory trade policy. The Commerce Department has responded to its clientele—American business. But the insulation of the United States International Trade Commission (USITC) has allowed it to provide a buffer against automatic findings of unfair trade practices and injury due to imports. This has occurred in part because of the USITC's standing as an independent regulatory commission—a nineteenth-century invention intended to keep some key economic decisions out of politics. Although not completely immune to political pressure, the USITC can act without having to deal with powerful interest groups at the door.

Finally, the USTR provides the conduit through which parties with an interest in trade policy can reach the top levels of decision making.

Shielding the president somewhat from tough decisions, focusing the nation's policy goals, and providing a tough voice abroad, the USTR is ideally suited to accomplishing the dual task of placating protectionist pressure while pursuing trade liberalization.

All of these institutions must operate in a framework of domestic politics. Although concerned with international issues, of course, they must produce policy in accordance with the domestic policy process. In this sense, they provide a unique bridge between domestic and foreign policy in the U.S. government structure.

The Main Elements

The core of U.S. trade policy lies in the statutes enacted by Congress throughout American history. Although the law in some ways dates back to the nineteenth century, the Reciprocal Trade Agreements Act of 1934 (RTAA) is the usual starting point for contemporary U.S. trade law. The RTAA has been the statutory base that Congress has amended in major pieces of trade legislation.

The politics of these episodes has been characterized by questions of presidential and congressional authority, heavy interest-group involvement, increasing competitive pressure from foreign producers, and the need to factor into U.S. law the constraints embodied in the GATT. Enactment of these major pieces of legislation—such as the Omnibus Trade and Competitiveness Act of 1988—typically involved allocation of trade policy authority between Congress and the president. Presidents brought to the debate initiatives on international trade, usually in the spirit of trade liberalization through expansion of the GATT. To accomplish this, Congress had to grant the president authority to negotiate the new multinational agreement; and to give the executive credibility in these negotiations, Congress gave it fast-track authority. It is difficult to overestimate the importance of such a delegation of congressional authority—constitutionally, the branch of government responsible for commerce and revenue—to the president. So, as one would expect, the high stakes were reflected in the intensity and caution of the debate.

At issue here was the basic relationship between two major government institutions. The delegation of authority changed that relationship, with positive and negative consequences for both branches.

Congress gave up a measure of discretion over trade policy, but also benefited from not having to make the tough decisions that would deny American producers protection in order to further the cause of trade liberalization. The president won power over trade policy along with credibility in the international arena, but also took on greater accountability when he chose to deny American producers protection. Assuming the long-term objective of trade liberalization remained constant, the institutional relationship was functional. From the politician's perspective, it was an agreeable exchange of power and accountability. From a systemic perspective, the American political system adjusted in its own peculiar way to accommodate a long-term policy in the context of international and domestic political constraints.

Interest groups fought it out over the major trade bills. Realizing that much was at stake in these pieces of legislation, American producers sought ways to maintain access to some sort of trade relief, which as it turned out was in the form of administrative procedure. This development illustrates the politics of major trade legislation quite well. Members of Congress found it necessary to respond to particular interests; they did so by channeling their concerns to the executive branch in the form of administrative relief. This was a move induced by a domestic political process conducted in the context of an ongoing trend toward free trade. It demonstrates how an American political institution responded to international pressure—the generally agreed-to goal of trade liberalization—and to domestic pressure in the form of interest groups representing American producers.

Sectoral agreements constitute backsliding on the long road of free trade. They are the result of successful political pressure brought to bear on government officials by American producers and their interest groups. Negotiated limits, such as those placed on steel, automobiles, and semiconductors, dampen trade and have an effect that goes in the opposite direction from trade liberalization. If one assumes that policies that keep the United States on the path toward freer trade are successful, then sectoral agreements are failures.

United States policy makers negotiate bilateral agreements such as these when they do not have the political will or cover to resist protectionist political pressure. In this sense, the institutional adjustment to deflect protectionist pressure breaks down. These trade-restraining agreements have resulted from petitions for administrative relief under the unfair trade provisions of the U.S. trade law filed by American producers. Using these administrative methods as political leverage, all three industries succeeded in getting presidents to negotiate what amounted to protectionist deals with foreign governments. Perhaps for electoral reasons or possibly for policy reasons, in these cases, the president chose not to pursue trade liberalization in the face of intense protectionist pressure, but at the same time sought to avoid damaging U.S. foreign relations by imposing trade sanctions.

Interest groups representing American producers were the clear winners in sectoral deals. For those who criticize American politics because the national government is too responsive to interest groups, these policies are grist for the mill. For critics who make their claims based on the idea that business has undo influence over policy makers, the conclusion is more cloudy. In cases where organized labor had a stake—steel and automobiles—unions joined forces with corporations for protection. Jobs, as well as profits, were at stake.

Another type of bilateral agreement does not deal with a specific industry, but instead addresses a category of trade problems. U.S. efforts to improve intellectual property protection in China and to reduce nontariff barriers (NTBs) in Japan have resulted in bilateral agreements with more breadth than sectoral deals; these also tend to be rules-oriented pacts, avoiding import or export quotas, which are antithetical to trade liberalization.

The North American Free Trade Agreement

Trade policy rarely captures the drama of a showdown between Congress and the president the way NAFTA did. Linking Canada, Mexico, and the United States, the trade agreement promised to increase trade among the three countries, with everyone better off in the long run. Opposition to NAFTA grew out of a concern for American jobs; the main problem was that cheaper labor could very well attract American industry south of the border, throwing thousands of Americans out of manufacturing jobs. Possible degrading of the environment and a worsening of working conditions in Mexico also caused consternation among NAFTA's opponents. Supporters claimed that the trade pact would do none of these things, and even if it were not enacted, a freer flow of goods and services among the three countries would take place anyway.

The battle lines were drawn, and Congress and the president struggled to a conclusion in a classic no-holds-barred American political donnybrook. The odd thing about the conflict was that a Democratic president was forced to ally himself with congressional Republicans against members of his own party. The president and his Republican allies prevailed, sending one part of the Democratic Party, at least, down to defeat.

At stake in the NAFTA battle were domestic economic issues. Trade policy as such did not concern unions and environmental groups as much as jobs and pollution. The agreement raised the economic fears of Americans at the low end of the economic ladder, making them particularly responsive to the populist claims of Patrick Buchanan and Ross Perot. The battle over NAFTA was the political manifestation of the uncertainty raised by economic change in the United States. More than any other aspect of trade policy considered in this book, NAFTA illustrates how changes in the global and domestic economies find their way into high-stakes politics.

Administering Trade

Administrative relief has proved to be the ultimate safety valve for American producers seeking protection from foreign competitors. Set in quasi-judicial administrative procedures, U.S. trade law provisions identifying unfair trade practices as reason to give government help to American industry have been a favorite of American companies in trouble since the 1980s. Administrative relief is largely a matter of implementation and regulation. The politics connected to it therefore are essentially bureaucratic; to understand how and why administrative relief is used to deal with changes in the global and domestic economies, one needs to understand the role and position of bureaucracy in the American political system.

Administrative relief is an ingenious political accommodation to new circumstances created by economic change. At the individual politician's level, delegating tough decisions to the bureaucracy allows one to avoid blame for either betraying trade liberalization or for selling out a constituent to the vague specter of economic globalization. A member of Congress can stand for free trade, at the same time providing a useful way for industries to get some trade relief. At the system level, administrative relief allows the president to stay on the path of trade liberalization using trade sanctions based on unfair trade practices as a way to relieve the pressure against free trade.

The Persistence of the Idea of Free Trade

U.S. trade policy, at least since 1934, has been guided by the sometimes distant goal of free trade. Finding the definitive explanation for this goes beyond this book, certainly, but two general possibilities come to mind. Judith Goldstein has presented a convincing case that the idea of trade liberalization, finding its way into U.S. trade policy through Cordell Hull, became embedded in government institutions.[2] Ideas do not exist in vacuums, however, and it is impossible to separate this idea from economic developments that seem to have a certain inevitability. Changes in technology have made new products available at an increasingly rapid pace, and great leaps forward in communications and transportation have made the world a more accessible place. Combined, these forces produce a powerful logic that demands the elimination of trade barriers. Economic change and recognition by key political leaders of the benefits it can bring have led to a political push for trade liberalization. While the movement toward this objective is hardly smooth, and it is by no means guaranteed to succeed, outright opponents are left on the political extremes. Mainstream liberals like Representative Richard Gephardt (D-MO) may oppose some programs, but would not reject trade liberalization in principle. That ground is left to the extreme left and extreme right.

The free-trade idea persists and infuses U.S. trade policy. American political institutions have dealt with the dominance of free trade in ways specific to each organization. Perhaps falling somewhat short of allowing trade liberalization to become embedded in agencies responsible for U.S. trade policy, they have embraced the idea nonetheless. Congress, the bureaucracy, and the president have found remarkably effective ways to pursue free trade while placating home-grown protectionist interests. The dynamics of this development are best characterized in terms of the domestic policy process; indeed, the response of American political institutions to trade issues has been to deal with them in terms of their domestic political consequences. The interests involved in this process are based on economic concerns; the stakes are close to home and profoundly affect the economic well-being of American industry and labor. Their fight has to do with domestic matters, regardless of whether or not they emanate originally from beyond the nation's borders.

Trade Policy as an Instrument of Foreign Policy

The previous section summarizes the main points of this book. Even the casual observer of international trade is unlikely not to notice that there are several issues missing from this account. These trade-related issues involve the use of trade policy to accomplish foreign policy objectives. In the next few pages, I discuss some of these matters, where they fit in U.S. trade policy, and how they are related to the central themes of the book.

Trade Sanctions

The United States has used economic force against countries to change their behavior in numerous cases. In the 1990s, the United States has limited trade to such nations as Iraq, Libya, Iran, Yugoslavia, and Cuba because of American disapproval of the political regimes in those countries.[3] For many years prior to the end of apartheid, the United States joined other nations in using trade sanctions against South Africa in the hopes that the economic hardship they caused would force the end of the racist political system. Employing economic sanctions is using trade policy for political ends—trade policy becomes an instrument of foreign policy. Domestic political factors in the United States have nothing to do with most decisions to use sanctions and, for that reason, they are not analyzed in depth in this book. The exceptions to this generalization are U.S. economic sanctions against Cuba and annually-threatened sanctions against China. Even in these instances, however, the domestic political conflict involved in large part foreign affairs and not home-grown issues.

Cuba

Fidel Castro's government in Cuba has been a constant source of discomfort to American politicians since its inception in 1959. Every president since John F. Kennedy has had some unpleasant dealings with the Cuban leader and all, to one degree or another, would have been happier without him than with him. The political heat increased as Cuban emigres migrated to the United States, settling mainly in South Florida. The new Cuban Americans quickly established themselves as a political force, and politicians recognized that they could not be ignored.

The political power of the Cuban community in the United States, coupled with the longstanding stridently anti-Castro U.S. policy, set the stage for a dramatic U.S. response to Cuban war planes' shooting down civilian American aircraft flying in international air space near Cuba. Judged as a hostile act beyond the limits of widely recognized standards of international behavior, this action caused a massive outcry in the United States among Cuban Americans and strongly anti-Castro politicians alike. The result was quick congressional passage of the Helms–Burton Act, which went beyond the usual economic sanctions in place on Cuba. Signed by a reluctant, but politically cornered president concerned about getting reelected, the law contains several main provisions, all of which are controversial. Helms–Burton (also known as the Cuban Liberty and Democratic Solidarity Act) codified U.S. embargo restrictions against Cuba and barred American private investment in Cuba's domestic telephone system. Two additional provisions of the law attracted considerable criticism, especially from American allies: First, Helms–Burton created a right for U.S. citizens, who lost property in Cuba through government confiscation, to sue the Cuban government and foreign investors who use or profit from these properties in U.S. court. Second, the law permits the United States to deny American visas to executives and their families of foreign-based companies involved in U.S.-claimed properties in Cuba.[4] So, for example, the executives of a Canadian firm that conducted business in Cuba could be denied American visas.

This unilateral action generated an uproar of protest from foreign governments, all of which are close allies of the United States. Claiming that Helms–Burton was illegal according to international law, and that enforcing it would damage relations between the United States and its closest political and economic partners, foreign leaders registered protest after protest with the United States and with international organizations. The Clinton administration sought an accommodation by delaying the implementation of Helms–Burton, but not by trying to repeal it. In effect, with the election behind him, President Clinton used administrative discretion to deflect the most objectionable parts of the law.

The politics of Helms–Burton had little to do with domestic economic issues. The debate was about foreign policy; domestic political forces influenced the deliberations, certainly, but they had little to do with economics as such.

China

Far more complex is the U.S. position with respect to China, a potentially huge market for American exports and an increasingly powerful country both militarily and politically. It is difficult for American officials to treat Sino–U.S. relations lightly. The recurring policy question regarding China is whether the United States should grant the Asian giant most-favored-nation (MFN) status.[5] Should the United States continue to offer the same low-tariff levels to China as it does to all other diplomatically acceptable nations?

According to the 1974 trade act, the United States may give other nations MFN status depending on the acceptability of their domestic and foreign policies. In the case of China, the United States has chosen not to grant permanent MFN status, but instead to consider whether to do so every year. The main reason for the continuation of this practice is U.S. disapproval of China's human rights record, in addition to its negligent intellectual property protection and willingness to sell arms to rogue nations. Use of child labor, imprisonment and persecution of political opponents, and the absence of dependable rule of law more than anything else have raised the ire of many Americans. Politicians and citizens alike express outrage at these practices within China and contend that one of the only ways the United States can cause the Chinese government to stop doing these things is to use economic sanctions. One convenient sanction is the denial of MFN status, making it very difficult for Chinese exports to reach the American market.

The argument against denying MFN is based on the value of engagement. Proponents of this position contend that economic sanctions will not induce Chinese political leaders to stop violations of human rights. The better way to influence these leaders' behavior is to continue to engage China economically as well as politically. Maintaining MFN status for China will likely increase trade between it and the United States, giving the United States an economic inroad into domestic Chinese affairs. In addition, canceling MFN status will harm the United States in the long term by denying American consumers access to Chinese imports and by placing an obstacle in the way of selling U.S. exports in China, because Chinese leaders would most likely retaliate against denial of MFN status by closing their market to American products. As the Chinese economy grows rapidly, and given the huge population of nearly 1.2 billion, American industrial leaders salivate at the opportunity to exploit this gigantic emerging market.[6]

The debate over MFN status to China, then, is partly about non-economic issues—human rights, arms sales to rogue countries—and partly about domestic economic well-being—mainly opening a potentially huge market to American producers and creating an economic bonanza for at least some components of the American economy. Thus, the politics of MFN status for China is considerably more complex than it is for issuing trade sanctions against Cuba.

In sum, the China–MFN status debate lies partly in the domain of foreign policy; trade sanctions become an instrument of foreign policy. The issue also lies partly in trade policy, with the major political discourse involving interest groups and the congressional response to them. In the end, the president has always chosen to extend MFN status to China for another year, reflecting the chief executive's broader political view and concerns.

Thinking about Trade Policy

Understanding trade policy can lead to different analytic contexts and concerns. I have focused on trade policy as a function of the domestic policy process. Thinking about trade policy in these terms sheds some light, perhaps, on other related issues. How trade policy is made in the United States tells us something about the American political economy—the relationship between politics and economics in the United States. It also gives us an indication of how American political institutions adapt to new pressures from both within and outside the United States.

Political Economy

Analyses of trade policy are frequently categorized as a matter of political economy. This is reasonable enough, but doing so begs the frequently begged question of what exactly political economy means and what insights it offers into a policy area. Political economy has to do with the relationship between politics and economics in a society. This characterization opens the door to additional, more specific possible meanings of political economy. It can focus, for example, on the calculations individuals make in deciding how best to pursue their interests in society. The activities of elected officials, political appointees, bureaucrats, interest groups, and ordinary citizens can be considered in terms of how they carry out this rational calculus. Political economy can also refer to the relationship between the economic system and political system in a society. The character of the economic system (the extent to which it depends on market mechanism for distribution of resources) and the basic design of the political system (presidential system in a representative democracy) are related somehow. The nature of that relationship is the focus of this variant of political economy.[7]

U.S. trade policy provides a wealth of examples of individuals attempting to see to their own interests. Certainly interest groups do this; trade associations representing American producers constantly lobby Congress and petition the executive for trade policies that benefit them in the American and foreign markets. One can also argue that rational, self-seeking activities also exist in the bureaucracy. Commerce Department officials, for example, seem to be biased in favor of American producers in their analyses of antidumping and countervailing duty petitions. This makes sense; the Commerce Department is linked to American business, and working in its favor may generate political support.

Members of Congress engage in rational behavior in ingenious ways. Wishing to avoid blame either for denying protection to an industry on which they rely for political support or for giving into protectionism when the dominant idea is that trade liberalization is in the nation's interest, legislators devised a mechanism of administrative relief that allows them to do both of these things while avoiding blame for either. Administrative relief provides protection for American producers in a quasi-judicial manner without daily congressional involvement—a perfect solution for rational, self-seeking legislators.

U.S. trade policy sheds considerably more light on American political economy conceptualized as the relationship between the economic and political systems. The central concerns here are how and to what extent these two systems affect each other. More specifically, how do economic changes affect the political system, and how do political actors affect economics? Examining trade policy from this perspective offers some additional insights into two central themes of this book: the consequences of unavoidable economic change for politics and the use of government to manage those changes.

In the last two decades of the twentieth century, the American economy has undergone sweeping changes affecting economic growth, the distribution of wealth, employment, and organization. The American economy entered the post-industrial era as services supplanted manufacturing to some extent in economic importance. Although much has been said about the arrival of the service economy, two important points should be kept in mind: First, although the service sector has grown in recent years, manufacturing remains crucial to the health of the American economy. Second, service industries are a mixed bag; some provide good jobs for well-trained professionals in growing high-technology fields, while others are dead ends for employees, requiring little education and paying the minimum wage or close to it.[8]

As services have become more important in the American economy, the organization of production has undergone dramatic change. The 1980s and 1990s have been the era of downsizing in corporate America. Seeking to become ever more efficient and responsive to customer preferences, large firms have fired thousands of workers—mostly mid-level administrators—and restructured themselves to be able to respond more quickly to shifts in the market. Restructuring has typically taken two forms. In most cases, companies have decentralized, distributing decision-making authority, responsibility, and accountability throughout the organizations. For example, IBM was subdivided into several organizations responsible for specific product lines. In addition to decentralization, restructuring has meant a sharp increase in outsourcing of a range of functions once performed by company employees. Basic maintenance and technical support of information systems, for example, are performed by outside firms or individuals under contract to the corporation. This is an efficiency move; outsourcing such tasks gives the firm more flexibility (no permanent workers to deal with) and costs less (the firm does not pay for benefits).

White-collar workers have felt the squeeze of downsizing in recent years, but blue-collar workers have suffered the effects of economic changes for many more years. Beginning as early as the 1960s and picking up steam in the 1970s and early 1980s, large American manufacturers laid off countless blue-collar workers. Employment in such American manufacturing stalwarts as steel and automobiles has dropped by as much as half in some places. These workers' skills are limited to the specific jobs they held in manufacturing. Retraining efforts have not met with much success, as the former assembly line workers—many of whom belonged to unions—find work in low-end service jobs, which pay considerably less and offer much stingier benefits, it they provide any at all.[9]

The effects of the increasing importance of services, the decline of some manufacturing industries, and the organizational restructuring that has swept corporate America have had major consequences for the economy. Whether working with a service or manufacturing industry, a person needs to be able to deal with information. That requires literacy and basic competence in mathematics, both of which are sometimes hard to find in segments of the American population. Service jobs can be good and bad. At the high end, financial experts, lawyers, physicians, and so on reap the benefits of an increasingly information-based service economy. At the low end, people with poor educations end up in low-wage jobs with little hope for improvement. This raises problems for those concerned with social equity. The new economy is ruthless with respect to people with few or no skills. It is no longer possible to graduate from high school with minimum achievement and find a union job in manufacturing that promises a decent wage, generous benefits, and access to the American middle-class dream.

Countless analyses of these changes, their causes, and consequences have come from academic economists, political pundits, corporate consultants, think tanks, advocacy groups, and the media. One of the dominant themes emerging from them is that the changes in the American economy are mostly attributable to international economic changes. Globalization of the economy, according to this way of thinking, has put the American economy under stress. Increased international trade, foreign competition, and outsourcing to foreign countries where the labor is cheaper have all helped to induce major changes in the United States. The exact consequences of all this remain unclear. There is considerable reason to believe, however, that growing inequities, especially as measured by wages, can be connected to globalization, and this presents enormous social and political difficulties.[10]

Having said all this, the significance of U.S. trade policy should be kept in perspective. It is certainly important; after all, trade has increased, benefiting and sometimes injuring American producers and consumers. It is likely to increase; even if globalization has been overstated in analyses of the American economy, developments beyond American borders are likely to have an increasing effect on it. Thus, trade policy is important, but it is only one of several policy areas in which the U.S. government can respond to economic change.

The American economy has become a leaner, meaner place. Public policy has endorsed a shift in faith from government regulation to the market. The market allocates resources more efficiently than government and insures greater economic growth. By the 1990s, this had become accepted doctrine by both Republicans and Democrats in top leadership positions. Workers can lose their jobs, companies can suddenly disappear in mergers, firms come and go. The uncertainty bred by this dynamic economic environment creates social and political problems. At the same time, there is an element of inevitability about the onset of a more ruthless, and more productive, capitalist economy. Whether a result of international or domestic forces, developed economies around the world are struggling with the same sort of changes, both in the private sector and in public policy. The problems boil down to a central trade-off: economic growth versus a more equitable distribution of wealth. The American economy has become the leader in economic growth. At the June 1997 Summit of the Eight in Denver, Colorado, President Clinton was able to stand tall among other world leaders, having earned economic bragging rights based on a remarkable history of growth. At the same time, however, the gap between the richest and the poorest people in the United States has grown. Even if the poorest are better off than they would have been without economic growth, they are farther behind the better-off in American society.[11] Whether this is a good state of affairs or an acceptable one is a political question. Conservatives contend that this is the right path; everyone, after all, is better off. Liberals acknowledge the benefits of the new economy, but worry about laid-off workers, low-skilled young people, and the more dramatic economic stratification of American society.

How the United States resolves the questions raised by these developments will not necessarily be copied in other developed countries. As European nations struggle to transform their economies, critics warn against emulating the United States. Cutting generous social welfare programs in order to reduce budget deficits and to invigorate the private sector has not gone over uniformly well with European electorates. Note, for example, the difficulties German Chancellor Hemlut Kohl has faced and the May 1997 electoral repudiation of such policies by French voters. Nonetheless, the fact that these nations are confronting these problems suggests a certain irresistibility of economic change.

American Exceptionalism

The U.S. movement toward a market economy domestically and trade liberalization internationally reflects a culture that is suspicious of government intervention. This is no libertarian utopia; Americans have come to depend on and expect benefits from government. But moving away from them has been easier in the United States than in other developed countries. For those who wish to maintain social programs and shrink the gap between rich and poor, and who are generally more concerned with the distribution of wealth than achieving maximum growth, recent trends in the American political economy have proven discomforting.[12]

The American political response to economic change both domestically and abroad has been classically American. The institutional structure of the American political system has processed the pressures of changing economic realities differently from the way other countries have. Trade policy is part of this overall pattern. It has captured the idea of trade liberalization while simultaneously satisfying domestic interests to the point that they have not derailed movement toward trade liberalization. Taken together, the elements of U.S. trade policy are sloppy, inconsistent, at times contradictory, potentially extremely slow, and yet in the end, well-suited to reaching a generally accepted goal. I can think of no better description of American public policy.

Endnotes

1. E. E. Schattschneider, *Politics, Pressure, and the Tariff* (New York: Prentice Hall, 1935).
2. Judith Goldstein, *Ideas, Interests, and American Trade Policy* (Ithaca, N.Y.: Cornell Univ. Press, 1993).
3. United States International Trade Commission, *The Year in Trade 1996* (Washington, D.C.: U.S. International Trade Commission, 1997), 157–63.
4. United States International Trade Commission, *The Year in Trade 1996*, 160.
5. Most-favored-nation status is something of a misnomer. Granting a country MFN status does not give it special privilege; rather, it means that the United States will treat imports from that country in the same way it treat imports from other nations with which the United States has acceptable diplomatic relations.
6. R. Morris Barett, AllPolitics, "House Approves Normal Trade Status For China," <http://www.allpolitics.com/1997/06/24/china.vote/>25 June 1997 (25 June 1997).
7. See James A. Caporaso and David P. Levine, *Theories of Political Economy*, (New York: Cambridge Univ. Press, 1992), chap. 1.
8. Robert B. Reich, *The Work of Nations: Preparing Ourselves for 21st Century Capitalism* (New York: Knopf, 1991). For a comprehensive study of service industries, see U.S. Congress, Office of Technology Assessment, *International Competition in Services*, OTA-ITE-328 (Washington, D.C.: U.S. Government Printing Office, 1987).
9. Federal government statistics indicate the general trend. See United States Bureau of the Census, *Statistical Abstract of the United States*, 116th ed. (Washington, D.C.: U.S. Government Printing Office, 1996), 409.
10. See Dani Rodrik, *Has Globalization Gone Too Far?* (Washington, D.C.: Institute for International Economics, 1997); and Gary Burtless, Robert Z. Lawrence, Robert E. Litan, and Robert J. Shapiro, *Globaphobia: Confronting Fears about Open Trade* (Washington, D.C: Brookings Institution and Progressive Policy Institute; New York: The Twentieth Century Fund, 1998), chap. 7.
11. For a recent discussion, see Jon Neill, ed., *Poverty and Inequality: The Political Economy of Redistribution* (Kalamazoo, Mich.: W. E. Upjohn Institute for Employment Research, 1997).
12. See, for example, Robert Kuttner, *Everything for Sale: The Virtues and Limits of Markets* (New York: Knopf, 1997).

Index

General Accounting Office, 208
General Agreement on Tariffs and Trade,
12, 21, 23–24, 26, 53, 55, 57, 59, 61,
63, 67n.55, 78, 91, 97, 109, 120, 157,
191, 232, 275–76, 280; and antidumping, 218; and countervailing duty, 218;
development of, 22, 48, 50, 110–11,
117; and free trade, 118; and ideas, 141;
and intellectual property protection,
119; Kennedy Round of negotiations,
116; and service industries, 119, 131;
Uruguay Round of negotiations, 131,
134–35, 159, 164; Uruguay Round of
negotiations and Congress, 136–40,
142–43; and Section 301, 219–23; and
Section 201, 205; Tokyo Round of ne-
gotiations, 112–13
General Motors Corporation, 29n.20,
30n.32, 112, 244–46, 249
General System of Preferences, 25
Gephardt amendment, 122, 125
Gephardt, Richard, 75, 122–23, 126, 128,
130, 138, 167, 284
Gillespie, Charles, 169
Gingrich, Newt, 169, 184
Globalization, x, 1, 56, 225, 276, 283,
291–92
Goals, 83–85, 88, 160, 278
Goldstein, Judith, 208, 219, 284
Gore, Albert, Jr., 170–71
Gourevitch, Peter Alexis, 42
Grayson, George W., 154, 165
Great Society, 24, 54
Greenpeace, 187n.49
GSP. See General System of Preferences

Hamilton, Alexander, 35–37, 71; on active
government, 36; on the tariff, 36
Harrison, Benjamin, 40
Hartke, Vance, 236
Heath, Edward, 113
Heclo, Hugh, 100
Helms-Burton Act, 286–87
Helms, Jesse, 139, 148n.84
Heritage Foundation, 78, 141, 186n.16
High-technology industries, 60–62, 80–82,
119–20, 132, 174, 198, 231, 255–56;

and electronics manufacturers, 105n.39,
171
Hills, Carla, 158, 162–65, 178, 222
Hollings, Ernest, 136, 138–39, 142–43,
188n.63
Honda, 244, 246, 252
Hoover, Herbert, 43–44
Hull, Cordell, 45–46, 66n.49, 78
Human rights, 28n.9, 197, 287

Iacocca, Lee, 271n.40
IBM, 256, 290
Ideas, 18–19, 70, 100–01, 277–78, 289;
and administrative relief, 192; and competitiveness policy, 132; economic, 78;
of free trade, 118, 284; and the GATT,
110, 140; and NAFTA, 152, 156–57,
160, 184; and the news media, 83; in
the 1988 trade bill, 132
Ideology, 181, 182
IMF. See International Monetary Fund
Implementation, 16, 19–21, 69, 81, 90,
95, 102, 252–53, 276–77; of administrative relief, 191–92, 197–98, 200,
223–25, 283; agencies involved in, 96;
of antidumping, 218; Commerce Department, role in, 202–03; congressional committees, role of, 91;
congressional delegation of authority in,
195; congressional monitoring of, 97;
discretion in, 195–96; and NAFTA,
152, 156–57, 182–84; of Section 337,
218; of Super 301, 221–22; of TAA,
207; USITC, role in, 203–04; USTR,
role in, 201–02; of VER, 253
India, 222
Industrial policy, 71, 82, 121, 132
Infant industry, 37, 71–72, 275
Information, 182, 276, 291
Information Technology Association of
America. See ADAPSO
Inglis, Bob, 174
Ingot caster, 234
Ingots, 234–35
Institutional trade liberalism, 253–54
Institutions, 18–20, 100–01, 195, 254,
275–77, 279–80, 288; adaptation of,